MW00559307

The Verbal System of Biblical Aramaic

Studies in Biblical Literature

Hemchand Gossai
General Editor

Vol. 116

PETER LANG
New York • Washington, D.C./Baltimore • Bern
Frankfurt am Main • Berlin • Brussels • Vienna • Oxford

Michael B. Shepherd

The Verbal System of Biblical Aramaic

A Distributional Approach

PETER LANG
New York • Washington, D.C./Baltimore • Bern
Frankfurt am Main • Berlin • Brussels • Vienna • Oxford

Library of Congress Cataloging-in-Publication Data

Shepherd, Michael B.
The verbal system of biblical Aramaic: a distributional approach /
Michael B. Shepherd.
p. cm. — (Studies in biblical literature; v. 116)
Includes bibliographical references and index.
1. Aramaic language—Verb. I. Title.
PJ5214.S54 492'.29—dc22 2007040371
ISBN 978-1-4331-0201-1
ISSN 1089-0645

Bibliographic information published by **Die Deutsche Bibliothek**.
Die Deutsche Bibliothek lists this publication in the "Deutsche Nationalbibliografie"; detailed bibliographic data is available on the Internet at http://dnb.ddb.de/.

The paper in this book meets the guidelines for permanence and durability of the Committee on Production Guidelines for Book Longevity of the Council of Library Resources.

29 Broadway, 18th floor, New York, NY 10006
www.peterlang.com

Printed in Germany

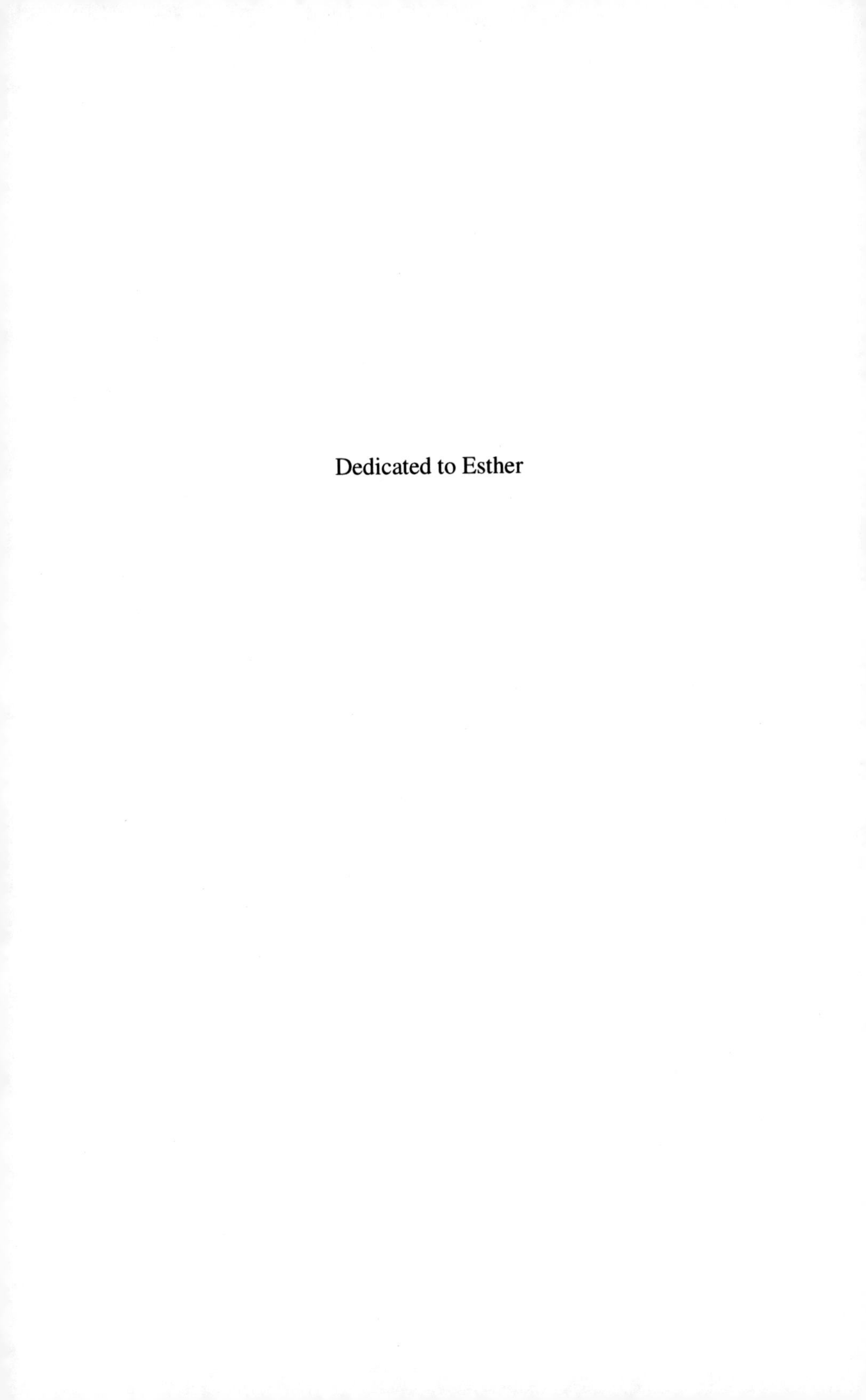

Dedicated to Esther

Table of Contents

Tables

Editor's Preface

More than ever the horizons in biblical literature are being expanded beyond that which is immediately imagined; important new methodological, theological, and hermeneutical directions are being explored, often resulting in significant contributions to the world of biblical scholarship. It is an exciting time for the academy as engagement in biblical studies continues to be heightened.

This series seeks to make available to scholars and institutions, scholarship of a high order, and which will make a significant contribution to the ongoing biblical discourse. This series includes established and innovative directions, covering general and particular areas in biblical study. For every volume considered for this series, we explore the question as to whether the study will push the horizons of biblical scholarship. The answer must be yes for inclusion.

In this volume Michael Shepherd examines the verbal system of Biblical Aramaic with a three-fold emphasis: identifying the fundamental relationship between *qtl* and *yqtl*; presupposing that Biblical Aramaic is a dead language and thus scholars who work in this are not in a position to attest to its stature otherwise; employing a proper textlinguistics. In this latter regard, the author observes that modern linguists focus almost exclusively on spoken language and thus by definition Biblical Aramaic is left unattended. After a thorough overview and critique of the established and standard grammars, the author argues that the essential way of discerning the relationship between *qtl* and *yqtl* is oppositional, and merely translating the Aramaic verb is insufficient. An acknowledgment of an oppositional relationship points to the tension between narration and discourse. I believe that this study will take its place alongside long established grammars, and grammarians will find in this volume arguments and trajectories that must be reckoned with for future study.

The horizon has been expanded.
Hemchand Gossai
Series Editor

Preface

Behind the façade of agreement on a "perfect" and an "imperfect" is a general uneasiness about the adequacy of the traditional view of the Semitic verb. For Biblical Aramaic, the standard grammars by Emil Kautzsch, Hans Bauer and Pontus Leander, and Stanislav Segert have served scholarship well. But this does not mean that development in the study of the language is forever arrested. On the contrary, current research is in a position to stand on the shoulders of these predecessors.

Traditional grammarians have focused on three categories: tense or time (past, present, and future), aspect (how the action is viewed), and *Aktionsart* (the kind of action). Because these grammarians have started with foreign, function-oriented categories, they have acted as living informants. But Biblical Aramaic is a dead language for which there are no living informants. Rather than a function-oriented approach, what is needed is an analysis of formal distribution.

The thesis here is that Biblical Aramaic has a primary verbal form for narration (*qtl*) and a primary verbal form for discourse (*yqtl*). The first chapter reviews the standard grammars along with the alternative proposal offered by H. B. Rosén. The second chapter discusses textlinguistics, modern linguistics, and the study of dead language. The third chapter outlines the database approach to distributional analysis and presents the results of this analysis along with extra-biblical parallels. The fourth chapter is a grammatical commentary on the relevant texts. And the final chapter provides an overall conclusion.

Chapter One

The Modern History of Research

The modern history of research in Biblical Aramaic refers to the scholarship of the last two centuries.[1] During this time, there have been many advances in grammar, philology, and linguistics. Over one hundred years passed between the publication of Emil Kautzsch's Biblical Aramaic grammar in 1884 and the third edition of Stanislav Segert's grammar of Ancient Aramaic in 1986. Even in the last twenty years, computer-assisted analysis has considerably changed the face of grammatical research.

The Standard Grammars

Standard grammars for Biblical Aramaic have been produced by Emil Kautzsch and by Hans Bauer and Pontus Leander.[2] Stanislav Segert's grammar for Ancient Aramaic includes Biblical Aramaic.[3] In addition to these major German works are the introductory English grammars such as those by Franz Rosenthal and Alger Johns.[4] Several comparative grammars, journal articles, and monographs have also contributed to the treatment of Biblical Aramaic.[5]

Review of E. F. Kautzsch

Kautzsch explains the *qtl* form or suffixed conjugation as follows: "The perfect serves for the expression of *completed* actions, events, or states-of-being…the respective actions or states-of-being can fall in the time sphere of the past, present, or future" (author's translation).[6] Thus, the *qtl* can be a pure perfect, a historical tense (aorist), a past perfect, a *modus rei repetitae*, or a representation of future action.[7]

For the *yqtl* form or prefixed conjugation, Kautzsch explains, "As in the other Semitic dialects the imperfect serves for the expression of *incomplete* actions or states-of-being...in the past, present, or future..." (author's translation).[8] The *yqtl* can represent the pure future; it can be used in conditional clauses, indirect questions, and temporal clauses; it can be used as a jussive, an optative, and as a cohortative; it can be used in circumstantial clauses; it can be employed as a narrative tense; and it can represent the present.[9]

Many grammarians view the participle as a verbal predicate in Biblical Aramaic. According to Kautzsch, "The participle expresses in general, corresponding to its nominal character, a state, without a reference to whether it is to be thought of as past, present, or future" (author's translation).[10] The participle can serve as the predicate of a nominal clause or as a complement to the verb of being in a verbal clause; the passive participle can refer to completed action.[11] Although the participle is a nominal form (i.e., a verbal adjective), the grammars tend to stress its verbal characteristics to the exclusion of its nominal characteristics. Even Kautzsch, who makes reference to its nominal character, treats the form somewhat like a stative verb.

It is not difficult to see the influence of H. Ewald, Wilhelm Gesenius, and S. R. Driver in this description of the verb.[12] It is appropriate to ask at this point what sets the forms (*qtl*, *yqtl*, and participle) apart from one another. According to Kautzsch's presentation, the forms appear to be interchangeable.

Review of Hans Bauer and Pontus Leander

Bauer and Leander describe the verbal forms in Biblical Aramaic in terms of their understanding of proto-Semitic. Thus, the *qtl* is not a "perfect," but a "nominal"; the *yqtl* is not an "imperfect," but an "aorist."[13] For the "nominal," Bauer and Leander have two main categories: the present or resultative perfect and the historical perfect.[14] It is noteworthy that their examples of the resultative perfect are all instances in which a character recounts or narrates an event—often an event from a previous part of the narrative. The historical perfect is the usual tense of narration. A narrative often consists of a series of "nominal" forms.

But Bauer and Leander do not distinguish the "nominal" from the "aorist" by means of form ("aorist" is not a formal description) or by means of perfective aspect. According to Bauer and Leander, the *qtl* form ("nominal") does not always designate completed action. With certain verbs, the form itself can express a kind of durative action: "The fact that the nominal in no way always designates a completed action, but frequently designates simply an event belonging to the past, has the result that with verbs of a durative kind of action (such as to sit, to stand, to be) it expresses a duration in the past (= he was sitting, he was standing, he was being)" (author's translation).[15] This explanation is a mixture of grammatical, lexical, and contextual factors. The grammatical form (*qtl*) does not always designate a completed event. It frequently designates a simple event belonging to the past. This feature allows the form to express duration in the past with lexically durative verbs. Although the terminology is different, it appears that what Bauer and Leander mean by "duration" is similar to Kautzsch's *modus rei repetitae*.

Biblical Aramaic preserves from proto-Semitic the full aorist and the short aorist.[16] The uses of the full aorist in Bauer and Leander correspond to the participle. The few uses of the short aorist express the desire that something would or would not happen. The discussion of the "aorist" in Bauer and Leander is primarily a discussion of the full aorist.

The *yqtl* or so-called "aorist" can function in the past, present, and future.[17] According to Bauer and Leander, the imperfect function of the "aorist" resembles the circumstantial clause in Arabic.[18] The imperfect "aorist" does not represent a major moment of the narrative; rather, it represents a minor moment that is subordinated logically and psychologically to the major moment represented by the "nominal."

As in Kautzsch's presentation, the *yqtl* or "aorist" can serve as the volitional form in Bauer and Leander: jussive, optative, and cohortative.[19] Unlike Kautzsch, however, Bauer and Leander do not speak of the "aorist" as a narrative tense. But they do refer to the *yqtl* as an "aorist" on the analogy of the Akkadian preterite.[20] Their comments on the use of the "aorist" in the past are interesting in light of their view of the durative "nominal":

> [The aorist is used] for the expression of simultaneous action in the past, as a rule in dependence upon a nominal, which functions as a historical tense and places the whole in the preterital sphere. According to the kind of action of the verb, the expression of (continuous) duration or repetition (= discontinuous duration) results.

> The dependence on an actual expressed or imagined preterite is essential for the aorist in this function (author's translation).[21]

Thus, both the "nominal" and the "aorist" are capable of expressing duration in the past. Furthermore, the description of the "aorist" in Bauer and Leander is vulnerable at least to the logical conclusion that the *yqtl* form can be an undefined past tense employed for narration.

The close relationship between the "aorist" and the participle in Bauer and Leander can be seen in their description of the participle:

> The participle contains, viewed as a nominal form, no reference to a definite time, but where its verbal character makes itself felt, the active participle naturally designates as a rule the present sphere, the passive participle the perfective sphere. The semantic domain of the active participle corresponds consequently on the whole to the aorist, and it has taken over in part the function of the latter. Here as there it results only out of the context whether the present, future, or imperfect is meant (author's translation).[22]

The participle is not a purely verbal form. It contains both nominal and verbal characteristics. Because the participle has no reference to a definite time, it can function in the past, present, or future.[23] The participle can also express either imperfective or perfective aspect, depending on whether it is active or passive.

The participle is used in two other ways in Biblical Aramaic. The first is its use in periphrastic construction with verbs of being.[24] The second is its use for the advancement of the narrative. There are cases in Daniel in which a participle stands where a *qtl* is expected. For instance, when the three friends come out of the fiery furnace in Dan 3:26, the action is narrated with a participle. Bauer and Leander call this a peculiar use of the participle in the book of Daniel.[25]

Not only is the treatment of the details of the Biblical Aramaic verb in Bauer and Leander strikingly similar to that of Kautzsch, but also the same general problem arises for both. How are these forms to be distinguished from one another? Is there any fundamental opposition between the *qtl* and the *yqtl*? The lack of distinction and the apparent interchangeability of the forms in their explanation do not seem to cause concern for Bauer and Leander.

Review of Stanislav Segert

According to Segert, the origin and use of the so-called "perfect" and "imperfect" represent perhaps the most difficult problem in every Semitic language.[26] In Old Aramaic, the *qtl* and *yqtl* became suitable means of expression for the perfection and imperfection of the action.[27] For Segert, these are aspectual functions that depend on the subjective choice of speakers.

Segert describes a basic shift that took place early in the development of the Aramaic language in which the "perfect" began to be used as a past tense and the "imperfect" as a future tense.[28] Also very early the participle began to be used as a verbal predicate that often expressed states and actions in the present.[29] Thus, Segert, more so than Kautzsch or Bauer and Leander, views tense or time as much more of a distinguishing factor.

The Aramaic verbal forms were employed in a variety of texts before, during, and after the general time period of the Biblical Aramaic corpus. It is thus noteworthy when Segert observes that the richest development of the expressive capabilities of the "perfect," "imperfect," and predicate participle can be found in the complex web of narratives and visions in the Aramaic of Daniel.[30] He also recognizes the originality of the documents in Ezra and their validity as examples of the official Persian language.[31] The Aramaic texts connected to the documents in Ezra are examples of Aramaic historical narrative.[32]

Although Segert explains the "perfect" primarily as a past tense, the "imperfect" primarily as a future tense, and the participle primarily as a present tense, he also speaks of the resultative and future "perfect," the past and present "imperfect," and the past and future participle.[33] Of course, many of the other categories from the earlier grammars are found in Segert as well.

By now the standard treatment of the verb in Biblical Aramaic has become somewhat predictable. Whatever is true for one of the forms is apparently true for all of the forms. It seems inexplicable why more than one form ever developed in the language. It is easy to see why the verb is one of the most difficult problems in Semitic studies.

Synthesis and Evaluation

The standard grammars work from the outset not with formal distribution, but with three function-oriented categories borrowed from Greek and Latin: tense or time (past, present, and future), aspect (how the action is viewed: aoristic, perfective, and imperfective), and *Aktionsart* (the kind of action). Although they do have a category for a narrative tense, it is by no means the primary description of any one of the forms. There is no category for a discourse tense.

What is remarkable about these grammars is not how much they differ—and they do differ—but how much they are alike. The treatment of the verb in Biblical Aramaic has changed very little over the years. Is this because each subsequent generation has been able to confirm independently the findings of preceding generations, or is it because the traditional view has been left unchallenged? Traditional views should be examined critically, particularly when they address something of the magnitude of a biblical language's verbal system. If the tradition is found to be acceptable, then so be it. But if it is not, then it must be replaced.

According to Kautzsch, the *qtl*, *yqtl*, and participle can all represent the past, present, and future. That is, there is no distinction among the forms on the basis of tense. On the surface, Kautzsch distinguishes among the forms in the following way: the *qtl* expresses completed action, the *yqtl* expresses incomplete action, and the participle expresses a state. This is primarily a distinction according to aspect. But Kautzsch also gives examples of the *qtl* as a *modus rei repetitae*, the *yqtl* as a narrative tense, and the passive participle as completed action. Even if the *qtl* is viewed as a completed whole, the *modus rei repetitae* is incomplete action within the whole. The use of the *yqtl* as a narrative tense is a non-use as an expression of incomplete action. The use of the passive participle to express completed action is clearly not the expression of a state. Not only does Kautzsch lack distinction according to tense, but also his categories of aspect and *Aktionsart* overlap considerably among the forms.

Bauer and Leander also see the ability of the *qtl*, *yqtl*, and participle to function in the past, present, and future. They primarily describe the *qtl* in terms of a "perfect," but they also make it very clear that the *qtl* does not always designate completed action. The *yqtl* in the present and future has very little aspectual definition in Bauer and Leander. The past *yqtl*, however, expresses imperfective and circumstantial action. It must also be kept in mind that for Bauer and Leander the *yqtl* is an "aorist" on the analogy of the Akkadian preterite. As for the participle, it can express either imperfective or perfective aspect, depending on whether it is active or passive. Once again, all of the labels are applied to all of the forms. Although the label "completed action" is never explicitly applied to the *yqtl*, the term "aorist" allows the label "undefined" over against "incomplete action." Regardless, Bauer and Leander never state that "incomplete action" is the distinguishing trait of the *yqtl*.

The overlap among the verbal forms in Segert is mostly with regard to tense. It is ironic then that he categorizes the forms not according to aspect, but according to tense. Segert, as well as the other grammarians, does point out some non-shared uses. For example, no forms other than the *yqtl* and the imperative can be volitional forms. No forms other than the participle can be in a periphrastic construction with a verb of being. But these considerations are very much beside the point. The non-shared uses are not the primary uses. They do not define the uses of the forms in a comprehensive way.

The rules of the standard grammars are so outweighed by exceptions that the rules cease to be meaningful. This situation has been created by a neglect to explain the verbal system in terms of the dead language of Biblical Aramaic. What has taken place instead is an explanation of how the Biblical Aramaic verb translates into German. Modern German requires translation into tense, aspect, and *Aktionsart*. Thus, the traditional grammarians have acted as living informants on how to translate the Biblical Aramaic verb into their own language.

The Biblical Aramaic verb in translation does not provide much insight into the Biblical Aramaic verb in Biblical Aramaic. There are no living informants for Biblical Aramaic; therefore, the grammarian is left to describe the written texts in terms of the patterns that emerge from analysis of formal distribution. It will not suffice to say that speakers of a language with a limited number of verbal forms use the available forms interchangeably. "In such a linguistic environment, the result would theoretically be either an inability to discern communication or a survival of only one of the forms, a form that would bear all."[34] The authors of the Biblical Aramaic texts, however, seem to assume that distinctions among the forms can be understood. Since the fundamental oppositions of the verbal system of Biblical Aramaic are not associated with tense, aspect, and *Aktionsart*, it is time to look elsewhere.

H. B. Rosén

H. B. Rosén has introduced a massive paradigm shift to the study of the verb in Biblical Aramaic, particularly the Aramaic of Daniel. He works with some of the same categories as the standard grammars, but he has completely reassigned the labels. According to Rosén, "The use of a preformative tense form for the expression of non-past is firmly established (Bauer-Leander, p. 278), yet a tense possessing identical morphological characteristics (whether or not originally identical with the former) is, not unlike the Akkadian preterite, more widely used as a narrative tense than is usually admitted, and was usually understood as such by the translators."[35] By "translators," Rosén means the Septuagint and Theodotion.[36] Rosén does not note that the vast majority of his examples of this phenomenon are not narration, but narration within discourse.[37] These examples are scattered over chapters 4–7 of Daniel. Unlike the *qtl*, however, a significant string of *yqtl* forms in narration is nowhere to be found.

Rosén expresses his disagreement with the view of Bauer and Leander that the *yqtl* is often circumstantial. He argues that the verbal forms preceding the *yqtl* forms should bear this label instead.[38] At the same time, Rosén concedes that "it may very often be a matter of interpretation to decide which of the actions or facts referred to in any sentence is to be regarded as 'main' and which as 'accompanying.'"[39] Indeed, a great deal of Rosén's intuitive theory of the verb in the Aramaic of Daniel is "a matter of interpretation."

Rosén also argues that the participle is used as a narrative tense: "Much wider use as a narrative tense is made of the 'participle' (Bauer-Leander, p. 292), a phenomenon occasionally met with in Akkadian (cf. von Soden, *Grundriß der akkadischen Grammatik*, p. 111)."[40] His first set of examples consists of periphrastic constructions with a preterite copula. In these instances, however, the *qtl* of the verb of being is most likely the narrative tense.[41] His second set of examples corresponds to the statement of Bauer and Leander about the use of the participle for the advancement of the narrative: "A peculiar use of the participle as a kind of independent tense for the introduction of single events is found in the book of Daniel" (author's translation).[42] But Rosén's number of examples of this usage far exceeds that of Bauer and Leander. Certainly the many occurrences of the two participles in the expression "he answered and said" cannot be admitted as genuine instances of narration. Such an introductory formula is little more than a fixed preparation for discourse.[43]

In contrast to the *yqtl* and participle, the *qtl* is not used as a narrative tense in Rosén's view. He states that "it does not seem to be the fact that the Biblical-Aramaic tense variously called 'perfect,' 'nominal,' etc., which we shall here for obvious reasons term 'stative,' serves as a narrative tense, as it does in other types of Aramaic and Semitic."[44] This "stative" tense suitably implies logical subordination and expresses anterior circumstances, whether preceded by a hypotactic marker or not.[45] Such a designation for the *qtl* has not been so obvious to other grammarians. According to Bauer and Leander, the *qtl* is "das gewöhnliche Tempus der Erzählung und darum ungemein häufig."[46] Carl Brockelmann comments that the use of the *qtl* as a narrative tense is so regular in all Aramaic dialects that it requires no example.[47]

Could it be that Biblical Aramaic alone, among all the "other types of Aramaic and Semitic," does not employ the *qtl* as a narrative tense? The sheer frequency of the *qtl* in Biblical Aramaic narrative presents an insurmountable difficulty for an affirmative answer to this question. "Out of 643 main clauses in Biblical Aramaic, 220 are narration, excluding discourse, narration within discourse, and reported speech. Of these 220 clauses, 132 have *qtl* as the primary verbal form."[48] Once again, Rosén appeals to Akkadian.[49] But this is not Akkadian; it is Aramaic. The fact that Rosén's subordinate, stative *qtl* is not exemplified in other Aramaic texts should be a clue to its basic incorrectness. Even more so than his views of the *yqtl* and the participle, Rosén's theory for the *qtl* in Biblical Aramaic comes across as a case of special pleading.

Rosén concludes that there are two groups of verbs in the Aramaic of Daniel: (1) point aspect verbs "whose narrative tense is the participle, whose future-volitive is preformative and whose subordinative is a simple stative" and (2) linear aspect verbs "whose participle denotes a present, whose preformative tense is narrative, and which supply the rest of their forms (subordinative and future-volitive) by means of compound tenses containing the copula in the corresponding tense forms."[50] No less a scholar than E. Y. Kutscher has declared Rosén's presentation a "brilliant revolutionary article" that "[n]o Semitist in general and no Aramaist in particular can disregard."[51] Nevertheless, Kutscher does have some misgivings about Rosén's construction. For example, Rosén's analysis requires the root *khl* ("to be able") to be considered a "point class" verb.[52]

Rosén is to be commended for his creativity, but his work could use a greater measure of objectivity—the kind of objectivity afforded by distributional analysis. Although Rosén's theory can be called "brilliant," it also comes close to being idiosyncratic. Would the Biblical Aramaic texts have yielded such a result to any other scholar? It is difficult to speculate, but the objective data of distributional analysis would have eliminated this question of repeatability in the academic community. Rosén's aspectual classification may be considered a comprehensive account of the data, but it does not meet the criterion of simplicity. A good hypothesis is one that gives a simple and comprehensive account of complex details.

Excursus: Why Is There Aramaic in the Bible?

The Aramaic of the Bible never constitutes an entire biblical book; the Aramaic texts are always coupled with Hebrew texts.[53] Biblical Aramaic is widely recognized as Imperial Aramaic, but is it composed Aramaic or translation Aramaic? This question has important implications for the study of the language of Biblical Aramaic. The target language of translations, particularly literal translations, is often forced out of its own idiom in order to match certain formal features of the source language. This situation requires a different set of sensitivities than composed Aramaic.

In order to have a clearer picture of the object of study in Biblical Aramaic research, it is imperative to address the question of Aramaic in the Bible. This is ultimately a question of biblical composition. One blanket theory does not cover all of the involved compositions. Each composition must be examined on a case-by-case basis.

The bilingualism of Daniel has given rise to a plethora of theories regarding the book's composition. Some have suggested that the entire work was originally written in either Hebrew or Aramaic.[54] Others have argued that the author was a bilingual author who wrote for a bilingual audience.[55] Still others have maintained that the book was a composite work brought together from a multiplicity of authors.[56] More recently it has been en vogue to posit various "literary" motivations for the book's bilingualism.[57]

What appears to be lacking in each of the proposals is an adequate text theory for the book of Daniel. The assumption has been that biblical authorship is virtually the same as that of a modern novel. Those who have recognized that this is not the case have abandoned the notion of an author in favor of an editor. But biblical unity does not mean uniformity. The biblical authors have skillfully stitched the "pieces" of their compositions together into unified wholes.

The author of Daniel worked with two pieces of material—one in Aramaic (Dan 2:4b–7:28) and one in Hebrew (Dan 8–12). The author employed the Hebrew material as a commentary on the Aramaic material. The model for this comes not from Ezra, but from Jeremiah (i.e., Jer 10:11–12), a book of major importance for the author of Daniel (Dan 9:2). After a brief survey of some of the suggested approaches to the composition of Daniel, an outline of what may be called an "inner-textual" approach to the book's composition will be proposed here.

In an article published in 1898, George Barton followed in a line of impressive scholars who had argued that the book of Daniel was composite.[58] Barton explained the book's bilingualism in the following way:

> On the whole, the best explanation of the presence of the two languages is that now accepted by several scholars who hold that it was written in Hebrew, and that then the author, or some friend of his, issued an Aramaic edition. Later, when a part of the Hebrew was in time of persecution lost, its deficiency was supplied from the Aramaic version, hence the present bi-lingual form of the book.[59]

The immediate difficulty with this view is that there is no extant evidence for a Hebrew original. Beyond this, the neatness with which the Aramaic section begins and ends would have been a remarkable coincidence for material lost in the midst of persecution.

Barton posited three writers for the book of Daniel: (1) a Babylonian writer composed chapters 2, 4, 5, 7, and 8, (2) a Jewish writer composed chapters 6 and 9, and (3) a Persian writer composed chapters 10–12.[60] According to Barton, a final editor put these writings together, prefixed chapter 1, and added various other redactional features.

Barton's editor is not far from the actual author. Nevertheless, Barton's division of the material goes beyond the evidence; and his focus on the authors of the sources causes him to miss the intention of the final author. Barton rightly identifies chapter 1 as an introduction, but his understanding of chapters 2–7 is too fragmented. He concedes that chapters 3 and 6 have much in common,[61] but he does not allow these chapters as integral parts of the Aramaic section. In this Barton has not only underestimated the relationship between chapters 3 and 6, but also he has overlooked the close relationship between chapters 6 and 7. N. T. Wright comments:

> Here [Dan 6], as there [Dan 7], the human figure is surrounded by threatening 'beasts'; as we saw, the first beast in 7:4 is like a lion, making the connection with the previous chapter about as explicit as it could be. Here, as there, the king comes in his authority: Darius in chapter 6 acts the part that will be taken by the Ancient of Days in chapter 7. In both, the human figure (Daniel in chapter 6; the 'son of man' in chapter 7) is vindicated and exalted, lifted up out of the reach of the beasts. In both, the one true god is glorified, and the enemies of his people subjugated. Both end with a celebration of the kingdom/kingship of the one true god. Dramatically, poetically the sequence is identical.[62]

Barton does, however, see the links between chapters 7 and 8, so much so that he attributes the two chapters to the same hand. But what he fails to see is that chapter 7 as it now stands is programmatic not only for chapter 8, but also for chapters 9–12.

In his excellent commentary on Daniel, James Montgomery followed Gustaf Dalman in saying that chapters 1–6 were originally Aramaic and that chapters 7–12 were originally Hebrew; chapters 1 and 7 were then translated into Hebrew and Aramaic respectively in order to unify the composition.[63] This was an attempt to account for the overlap between the book's division according to content (stories [Dan 1–6] and visions [Dan 7–12]) and its division according to language (Hebrew [Dan 1–2:4a; 8–12] and Aramaic [Dan 2:4b–7:28]). But why would the author have chosen to unify the book in such a disjointed way? Why was the entire book not cast into one language? It is surely untenable to say that the introduction was translated into Hebrew for the sake of canonicity. It is equally implausible to say that the Chaldeans' speech determined the use of Aramaic, as if their discourse were sustained through Dan 7:28. The inability to answer such objections renders this view unacceptable as a satisfactory explanation of the book's bilingualism.

H. H. Rowley sought to defend the unity of Daniel in a new way:

> ...Daniel was a legendary hero concerning whom popular stories were current in the post-exilic period...a Maccabean author worked up some of these stories and issued them separately in Aramaic for the encouragement of his fellows. Chapters 2–6 were thus issued. Later, chapter 7 was similarly issued in Aramaic. The author had now passed over, however, to a different type of literature, which was less suitable for popular circulation. This he recognized by writing subsequent eschatological visions of this type in Hebrew. When he collected his stories and visions into a book, he wanted a fuller and more formal introduction than he had used for the first story when it was issued separately.[64]

Rowley, like Barton, correctly identified chapter 1 as an introduction. He also saw the unity of chapters 2–6, but he felt compelled to speak of chapter 7 as a separate transition. Rowley ran into difficulty, however, when he insisted on a continuous writing hand through the Aramaic and into the Hebrew. He was then forced to contrive an explanation for the Hebrew. Was it necessary for eschatological visions to be written in Hebrew? Was Aramaic only for popular consumption? Why was chapter 7 not written in Hebrew? Rowley's theory must be abandoned at this point.

It is evident that the book of Daniel requires a theory that accounts for the author's skillful use of "pieces" in the formation of the whole composition. In Jer 10:11–12 is found a kind of microcosm of the inner-textual relationship between the Aramaic and Hebrew in Daniel. Scholars have often turned to Ezra as a model, but the use of Aramaic in Ezra is driven more by concerns to preserve original documents. The text of Jer 10:11–12 reads as follows:

> כדנה תאמרון להום אלהיא די שמיא וארקא לא עבדו יאבדו מארעא ומן תחות שמיא אלה
> עשה ארץ בכחו מכין תבל בחכמתו ובתבונתו נטה שמים
> "Thus you will say to them, 'The gods who did not make the sky and the land, may they perish from the land and from under these heavens.'" He is the one who makes land by his strength, who establishes a world by his wisdom, and who stretches out sky by his understanding (author's translation).

Jeremiah 10:11 functions as a hinge between the preceding section on idolatry (Jer 10:1–10) and the new unit that extends from verse 12 through verse 16.[65] The verbal links between verses 11 and 12 are apparent enough. "The gods who did not make the sky and the land" are contrasted with the "one who makes land by his strength, who establishes a world by his wisdom, and who stretches out sky by his understanding." "The gods who did not make the sky and the land" will perish from the very creation of the true maker. Thus, the Hebrew text of verse 12 interprets the gods of the Aramaic verse 11 as false gods (i.e., idols) because they did not make the world.

The main Hebrew text of Daniel (Dan 8–12) also functions as an interpretation in relation to Aramaic material (Dan 2:4b–7:28). It interprets the four kingdoms and the eternal kingdom of the Aramaic stories (Dan 2 and 7) in terms of four world empires and a future messianic kingdom (Dan 8–11). The hope in time of distress found in chapters 3 and 6 of Daniel is interpreted in Daniel 12 as hope in the resurrection (cf., 2 Macc 7).

It is possible that the Aramaic section is a linguistically set apart, eschatological interpretation or midrash of the Hebrew Scripture in chapter 8, but this would not account well for its relationship to chapters 9–12 as a whole. Rather, what appears to be the case is that the author begins and ends the book with Hebrew for a bilingual, though primarily Hebrew-speaking audience for whom an interpretation in Hebrew would be apropos.

The unity of most, if not all, of the Aramaic material has been demonstrated from a variety of angles.[66] But the most obvious expression of its interwoven nature is the chiastic structuring of the chapters: the kingdoms of chapter 2 are parallel to the kingdoms of chapter 7; the fiery furnace of chapter 3 is parallel to the lions' den of chapter 6; and the humbled king (Nebuchadnezzar) of chapter 4 is parallel to the humbled king (Belshazzar) of chapter 5.[67] Chapters 2 and 7 can hardly be understood apart from one another. Daniel 2:28 puts the entire sequence of kingdoms in the context of "the end of the days"; and Dan 7:13 identifies the ruler of the eternal kingdom as one "like a son of man."[68]

As for the unity of chapters 8–12, Rowley states, "It is generally agreed that chapters viii–xii come from a single hand."[69] Daniel's prayer in chapter 9 is perhaps the one exception to this, but it has been adapted (see the headings at Dan 2:1; 7:1; 8:1; 9:1; 10:1; 11:1).[70] Thus, it seems that the author has essentially worked with two pieces: a unified Aramaic section (Dan 2:4b–7:28) and a unified Hebrew section (Dan 8–12). The author has also provided an appropriate introduction (Dan 1) that sets the stage with the main characters: Nebuchadnezzar, Daniel, and the three friends.[71] It is possible that Dan 2:1–4a is a translation of an Aramaic original, but there is no textual evidence for the omission of ארמית in Dan 2:4a.[72]

In a discussion of the appropriate location of Daniel within the Tanak, John Sailhamer highlights the central role of Daniel in the two pre-Christian shapes of the canon.[73] Of particular importance is the mention of the time "from the issuing of a word to restore and build Jerusalem until Messiah Ruler" (Dan 9:25). The arrangement of books in Codex B19a places Daniel and Ezra-Nehemiah as the last two books of the canon. The decree of Cyrus to rebuild the temple comes at the outset of Ezra-Nehemiah in Ezra 1:2–4. Sailhamer comments, "In that position, the edict of Cyrus identifies the historical return under Ezra and Nehemiah as the fulfillment of Jeremiah's vision of seventy years."[74] The arrangement in *Baba Bathra* 14b, however, has Chronicles at the end, which concludes with the decree of Cyrus (2 Chr 36:23). Sailhamer notes:

> In this arrangement, the edict of Cyrus has been shortened from that in Ezra/Nehemiah (Ezra 1:2–4), so that it concludes with the clause "Let him go up" (2 Chron 36:23). In the book of Chronicles, the subject of that clause is identified as he "whose God is with him." For the Chronicler this is possibly also a messianic image (cf. 1 Chron 17:12).[75]

This latter shape of the Tanak looks beyond the return from exile and "fits well with what appears to be the Hebrew text (*Vorlage*) of the Septuagint of Jeremiah and the reading of these texts by the NT."[76] Either way, the book of Daniel plays a central role in the formation of the Hebrew canon.[77] But the Tanak that concludes with Chronicles seems to be truer to the composition of Daniel itself. Like the Septuagint of Jeremiah, the messianism of Daniel looks to a future fulfillment beyond the historical fulfillment of Ezra-Nehemiah.

It is no accident that the text that plays such an important role on the canonical level, Dan 9:25, is found within the interpretive Hebrew material of Daniel (Dan 8–12). The author of Daniel has linked this material to the equally messianic Aramaic section (Dan 2:4b–7:28), which is also not without its own inter-textual connections. In Dan 2:28, the Hebraism באחרית יומיא ("at the end of the days") sets the stage for the eschatology of the book.[78] This phrase in Hebrew is used strategically in the composition of the Pentateuch (Gen 49:1; Num 24:14; Deut 4:30; 31:29). Sailhamer has demonstrated that three of the occurrences of the phrase within the Pentateuch (Gen 49:1; Num 24:14; Deut 31:29) stand at the beginning of prominent poetic seams in which a major character from the preceding narrative proclaims a coming king from Judah to appear "at the end of the days."[79] The present author has further noted:

> The phrase falls into disuse in the Former Prophets. Although the hope of a Messiah (1 Sam 2:10; 2 Sam 22:51; 23:1) and an everlasting kingdom (2 Sam 7:12–13) is expressed, the fulfillment is not. Each successive king is marked by failure to some degree. The phrase then reemerges (Isa 2:2; Jer 23:20; 30:24; 48:47; 49:39; Ezek 38:16; Hos 3:5; Mic 4:1). Once again, the hope is a future king (Hos 3:5). The two final occurrences of the phrase come in Daniel; thus, it has an important function in each division of the Tanak.
>
> The use of "at the end of the days" in Daniel links the eschatology of the book to that of the rest of the canon. Therefore, the coming king from Judah is the most likely candidate for the head of the everlasting kingdom in Daniel (Dan 2:44; 3:33; 4:31; 6:27; 7:14, 18, 27). God is the ruler of his kingdom, and he gives it to

> whomever he pleases (Dan 4:14, 22, 29). His choice is the coming king from Judah—the one "like a son of man" in Dan 7:13.[80]

Thus, the eschatological "messianism" of the Pentateuch and the Prophets is taken up by the author of Daniel in the Aramaic section. This is then interpreted in the Hebrew section (Dan 9:2, 25) in relation to the issuing of a decree to restore and rebuild Jerusalem (Jer 25:11, 12; 29:10; 2 Chr 36:23).

Although several of the previous approaches to the bilingualism of Daniel have been insightful in many ways, none provides an adequate text model for the composition of the book itself. The notion of biblical authorship must include the act of working with "pieces." This is not redaction. The manner in which an author puts his pieces together is just as much an act of authorship as any other. In the case of Daniel, the author has framed and interpreted his Aramaic material for a bilingual, though primarily Hebrew-speaking audience. The Aramaic of Daniel stands not as translation Aramaic, but as composed Aramaic.

Jeremiah 10:11–12 makes for a good analogy, but ultimately the evidence within the book of Daniel must speak for itself. The internal unity of the two pieces of material, the messianic inner-textuality, and the eschatological inter-textuality of the composition both give rise to and validate the text theory proposed herein.

The book of Daniel has received by far the most attention in discussions of the presence of Aramaic in the Bible, but the situation in Ezra is no less intriguing. Nineteenth-century scholarship treated the official documents in Ezra as forgeries (Ezra 4:11–16, 17–22; 5:7–17; 6:2–5, 6–12; 7:12–26).[81] But according to Franz Rosenthal, three scholars brought significant clarification to the matter in the year 1896: E. Meyer, A. Klostermann, and C. C. Torrey.[82] For example, E. Meyer concluded that the texts in question did not violate the historical facts, that they could only be viewed as genuine official documents from the time of the Persian Empire, and that no doubt about their full authenticity is allowed.[83] More recently Segert has announced that the documents in Ezra are now generally considered as basically original.[84] This new consensus brings the Aramaic of these documents into a new light.

The Edict of Cyrus in Ezra 6:2–5 makes for an interesting case study. This edict has been preserved in four forms: the Cyrus Cylinder, Ezra 1:2–4, Ezra 6:2–5, and 2 Chr 36:23. Rolf Rendtorff summarizes the relationship of these documents in terms of their reliability:

> Most exegetes see Ezra 6.3-5 as a reliable historical source which may even have preserved the original wording of the 'Cyrus edict' of 538 (thus already Meyer, 46ff.: de Vaux, etc.). This is indicated e.g. by the use of Aramaic, since Aramaic was introduced by the Persians as an official language. (This form of Aramaic is therefore designated 'imperial Aramaic'.) In contrast, Ezra 1:1ff. is usually seen as a free formulation by the author of Ezra. (Cf. Galling, 61ff.; Bickerman differs, regarding both documents as authentic: he says that 6.3-5 was intended for the royal administration and 1.2-4 for the Hebrew-speaking Jewish exiles.)[85]

All of the biblical versions mention the building of the house of God. This is in accord with the Cyrus Cylinder in which the restoration of sanctuaries is reported. The return of the exiles is another matter, but Rendtorff suggests that the Cyrus Cylinder may also mention the return of former inhabitants to other regions.[86]

When the biblical versions are compared and contrasted in synoptic fashion, Ezra 1:1–4 and 2 Chr 36:22–23 share the most material. The 2 Chronicles passage is basically a truncated version of the Ezra passage. Both passages speak of the edict as a fulfillment of "the word of the LORD by the mouth of Jeremiah." Cyrus narrates his appointment to build the house of God in Jerusalem with *qtl* forms, as if the text were a translation of an Aramaic original; yet the Aramaic version in Ezra 6:2–5 does not contain this narration. The Aramaic version appears to expand two portions of the version in Ezra 1:2–4. The call to build the house of God is expanded to include the dimensions of the house; and the support of silver and gold mentioned in Ezra 1:4 is interpreted in Ezra 6:5 as the return of the gold and silver that Nebuchadnezzar took from the temple (Ezra 5:14; cf., 1 Esd 2:1–15).

Now that the authenticity of the official Aramaic documents in Ezra has been generally accepted, it remains to be explained why there are also intervening Aramaic narratives in Ezra (Ezra 4:8–11, 17, 23–24; 5:1–7; 6:1–2, 13–18). Daniel Snell has suggested that these narratives are somehow attracted to the Aramaic of the official documents.[87] On the other hand, B. T. Arnold has argued that the use of Aramaic in Ezra is due to a shift from an internal point of view to an external point of view:

> In 4:6, the narrator is in an externalized viewpoint, as he describes the events of the reign of Ahasuerus and the accusation against "the inhabitants of Judah and Jerusalem". Rather than the internal intimacy of 1:1-4:5, the narrator's point of view has shifted at 4:6-6:18. Recognition of this new point of view helps with understanding the use of Aramaic in 5:1-2. Since the narrator's viewpoint was to

> continue through 6:18, he continued to externalize himself for the introduction of the prophets Haggai and Zechariah.[88]

The proposals of Snell and Arnold are difficult to evaluate. What does it mean that a text is attracted to the language of another text? How convincing is the notion of external viewpoint for the whole of Ezra's Aramaic? The viewpoint of Ezra 5:1–5 and Ezra 6:13–18 does not seem to be as "externalized" as the other portions, even though Arnold has presented some evidence that it is.

Some of the Aramaic narrative in Ezra (Ezra 4:8–11, 17; 5:6–7; 6:1–2) is simply introductory for the Aramaic documents. At least one of the narratives (Ezra 4:23–24) can be described as an epilogue to the preceding Aramaic document. Ezra 5:1–5 is a separate piece of Aramaic narrative that has been positioned as a continuation of Ezra 4:24. Ezra 6:13–18 is then a continuation of the narrative in Ezra 5:1–5, but it is not immediately clear why Ezra 6:19 switches to Hebrew.

The major conclusions of this excursus for the purposes of the proposed thesis may be summarized as follows: (1) the Aramaic of Daniel is not translation Aramaic, but composed Aramaic and (2) the official Aramaic documents in Ezra are authentic. However the lesser details about the presence of Aramaic in the Bible are resolved, the fact remains that analysis of the language can proceed with full confidence that the texts are examples of genuine Imperial Aramaic.

Notes

[1]The corpus of Biblical Aramaic includes: Gen 31:47; Jer 10:11; Dan 2:4b–7:28; Ezra 4:8–6:18; 7:12–26. It may be asked whether or not this constitutes enough material for grammatical analysis. According to Hans Bauer and Pontus Leander, "Eine Grammatik des Biblisch-Aramäischen muß darum naturgemäß Stückwerk bleiben, und die wissenschaftliche Aufgabe einer solchen wird vor allem darin liegen, die entsprechenden Erscheinungen aus dem sonstigen westaramäischen Sprachmaterial nach Möglichkeit zu beleuchtet" (Hans Bauer and Pontus Leander, *Grammatik des Biblisch-Aramäischen* [Halle: Niemeyer, 1927; 4th unrev. reprint, Hildesheim: Georg Olms, 1995], 9).

[2]E. F. Kautzsch, *Grammatik des Biblischen-Aramäischen* (Leipzig: Vogel, 1884); Bauer and Leander, *Grammatik.*

[3]Stanislav Segert, *Altaramäische Grammatik*, 3d ed. (Leipzig: Enzyklopädie, 1986).

[4]Franz Rosenthal, *A Grammar of Biblical Aramaic* (Wiesbaden: Harrassowitz, 1961); Alger F. Johns, *A Short Grammar of Biblical Aramaic*, rev. ed. (Berrien Springs, Mich.: Andrews University Press, 1972).

[5]E.g., Carl Brockelmann, *Grundriß der vergleichenden Grammatik der semitischen Sprachen*, vol. 2, *Syntax* (Berlin: Reuther & Reichard, 1913; 4th reprint, Hildesheim: Georg Olms, 1999); H. B. Rosén, "On the Use of the Tenses in the Aramaic of Daniel," *JSS* 6 (1961): 183–203; Takamitsu Muraoka, "Notes on the Syntax of Biblical Aramaic," *JSS* 11 (1966): 151–67; E. Y. Kutscher, "Aramaic" (1971), in *Hebrew and Aramaic Studies*, ed. Zeev Ben-Hayyim, Aharon Dotan, and Gad Sarfatti (Jerusalem: Magnes, 1977), 347–404.

[6]"Das Perfektum dient zum Ausdruck *vollendeter* Handlungen, Ereignisse oder Zustände, mag nun die Vollendung eine thatsächliche oder eine bloss vorgestellte sein und mögen die betreffenden Handlungen oder Zustände in die Zeitsphäre der Vergangenheit, Gegenwart oder Zukunft fallen" (Kautzsch, *Grammatik*, 132); cf., Brockelmann, *Grundriß*, 2:153; Rosenthal, *A Grammar*, 42; Johns, *A Short Grammar*, 21.

[7]Kautzsch, *Grammatik*, 132–34.

[8]"Wie in den übrigen semitischen Dialekten dient das Imperfekt zum Ausdruck von noch *unvollendeten*, kürzere oder längere Zeit andauernden Handlungen oder Zuständen, mögen dieselben nun in die Vergangenheit, Gegenwart oder Zukunft fallen; im letzteren Falle können sie ebensowohl als gewiß bevorstehend, wie als nur eventuell eintretend gedacht sein" (ibid., 135); cf., Brockelmann, *Grundriß*, 2:152–53; Rosenthal, *A Grammar*, 42; Johns, *A Short Grammar*, 23.

[9]Kautzsch, *Grammatik*, 135–37; Kautzsch suggests that the use of the *yqtl* (with a prefixed *waw*) as a narrative tense in the place of the *qtl* is due to the influence of the Hebrew *waw* consecutive (ibid., 136).

[10]"Das Participium drückt im Allgemeinen, entsprechend seinem nominalen Charakter, eine Zuständlichkeit aus, ohne einen Hinweis darauf, ob dieselbe als eine vergangene, gegenwärtige oder künftige zu denken ist." (ibid., 138); cf., Brockelmann, *Grundriß*, 2:163; Rosenthal, *A Grammar*, 55; Johns, *A Short Grammar*, 25.

[11]Kautzsch, *Grammatik*, 139–42; the participle can also be combined with the particle *itai*.

[12]E.g., E. F. Kautzsch, ed., *Gesenius' Hebrew Grammar*, trans. A. E. Cowley, 2d ed. (Oxford: Clarendon, 1910), 309–19.

[13]Bauer and Leander, *Grammatik*, 96, 100.

[14]Ibid., 284–87; Bauer and Leander also mention the use of the "nominal" as a past perfect (ibid., 287–88).

[15]"Der Umstand, daß der Nominal keineswegs immer einen vollendeten, sondern häufig einfach den der Vergangenheit angehörigen Vorgang bezeichnet, hat zur Folge, daß er bei Verben von durativer Aktionsart (wie sitzen, stehen, sein) geradezu eine Dauer in der Vergangenheit ausdrückt (= sedebat, stabat, erat)" (ibid., 289).

[16]Ibid., 88–89; the imperative is built on the analogy of the *yqtl* (ibid., 99–100).

[17]Ibid., 278–83.

[18]Ibid., 281.

[19]Ibid., 283–84.

[20]Ibid., 278.

[21]"Zum Ausdruck der Gleichzeitigkeit in der Vergangenheit, in der Regel in Anlehnung an einen Nominal, der als tempus historicum fungiert und das Ganze in die präteritale Sphäre versetzt. Je nach der Aktionsart des Verbums ergibt sich hierbei der Ausdruck der (kontinuierlichen) Dauer oder der Wiederholung (= diskontinuierliche Dauer). Die Anlehnung an ein wirklich ausgedrücktes oder vorschwebendes Präteritum ist für den Aorist in dieser Funktion wesentlich" (ibid., 280).

[22]"Das Partizip enthält, als Nomen betrachtet, keinen Hinweis auf eine bestimmte Zeit, wo aber sein verbaler Charakter sich geltend macht, bezeichnet naturgemäß das aktive Partizip in der Regel die präsentische Sphäre, das passive Partizip die perfektische Sphäre. Der Bedeutungsbereich des aktiven Partizips entspricht demnach im ganzen und großen dem des Aorist, und es hat zum Teil die Funktionen des letzteren übernommen. Hier wie dort ergibt sich nur aus dem Zusammenhang, ob das Präsens, das Futur oder das Imperfekt gemeint ist" (ibid., 290).

[23]Ibid., 290–94

[24]Ibid., 293–94.

[25]Ibid., 294–95; the same use of the participle appears to be at work in 11QtgJob 38:4 (= Job 42:11).

[26]Segert, *Altaramäische Grammatik*, 369–70; see also Brockelmann, *Grundriß*, 144.

[27]Segert, *Altaramäische Grammatik*, 370; Segert also mentions the constative perfect, which represents the action completed as a whole.

[28]Ibid.

[29]Ibid., 370–71.

[30]Ibid., 373.

[31]Ibid., 444.

[32]Ibid.

[33]Ibid., 376–87.

[34]Michael B. Shepherd, "The Distribution of Verbal Forms in Biblical Aramaic," *JSS* 52 (2007): 231.

[35]Rosén, "On the Use of the Tenses," 183.

[36]It is highly questionable whether or not the Greek translations bring anything definitive to this discussion. The Greek language has a larger number of available verbal forms, and these forms do not provide one-to-one correspondence with the verbal forms in Biblical Aramaic. The Greek translations can be characterized generally as "literal," but the issue of *Vorlage* always requires caution, especially for chapters 4–6 of Daniel. It is not necessarily clear how well the translators knew Aramaic, but it is fairly clear that they knew what they wanted to do with the Aramaic. This is manifest in their relative consistency in translation. An analysis of the Septuagint of Dan 2:4b–28 indicates the following: the aorist indicative (the default tense of Greek narrative) is preferred for the *qtl*, the future indicative is preferred for the *yqtl* (except when a nuance requires an aorist subjunctive), and both the participle and the present indicative are preferred to translate the Aramaic participle.

[37]The category of discourse is never addressed in Rosén's article.

[38]Rosén, "On the Use of the Tenses," 183–84.

[39]Ibid., 184.

[40]Ibid.

[41]See Muraoka, "Syntax of Biblical Aramaic," 157; although Muraoka is primarily speaking about the verb of being as the primary indicator of time in periphrastic constructions, the same may be said about indication of narration.

[42]"Eine eigenartige Verwendung des Partizips als einer Art selbständigen Tempus zur Einführung einmaliger Ereignisse findet sich im Buche Daniel" (Bauer and Leander, *Grammatik*, 294); Rosén, "On the Use of the Tenses," 185.

[43]By "fixed" it is not meant that participles are always used for this formula; when in plural, or when one of the words ("answered" or "said") stands alone, the *qtl* form is often used (Bauer and Leander, *Grammatik*, 295).

[44]Rosén, "On the Use of the Tenses," 185.

[45]Ibid., 186–91.

[46]Bauer and Leander, *Grammatik*, 286.

[47]Brockelmann, *Grundriß*, 2:153.

[48]Shepherd, "The Distribution of Verbal Forms," 233, n. 36.

[49]Rosén, "On the Use of the Tenses," 187.

[50]Ibid., 192.

[51]Kutscher, "Aramaic," 379.

[52]Ibid.

[53]This discussion is primarily concerned with the Aramaic texts in Daniel (Dan 2:4b–7:28) and Ezra (Ezra 4:8–6:18; 7:12–26), but Jer 10:11 also plays an important role here. The two Aramaic words in Gen 31:47 merely preserve the original words of Laban the Aramean. Individual Aramaic words and Aramaisms are not usually considered as members of Biblical Aramaic proper. The occurrence of *bar* in Ps 2:12, however, is a special case due to its possible link to Dan 7:13 (but see also Prov 31:2).

[54]See the discussion in Frank Zimmermann, "The Aramaic Origin of Daniel 8–12," *JBL* 57 (1938): 255–72; James E. Miller ("The Redaction of Daniel," *JSOT* 52 [1991]: 115–24) believes the Hebrew Daniel and the Aramaic Daniel were combined.

[55]E.g., James Montgomery, *A Critical and Exegetical Commentary on the Book of Daniel*, The International Critical Commentary (Edinburgh: T. & T. Clark, 1927), 90–92.

[56]E.g., George A. Barton, "The Composition of the Book of Daniel," *JBL* 17 (1898): 62–86.

[57]E.g., Daniel C. Snell, "Why Is There Aramaic in the Bible?" *JSOT* 18 (1980): 32–51; B. T. Arnold, "The Use of Aramaic in the Hebrew Bible: Another Look at Bilingualism in Ezra and Daniel," *JNSL* 22, no. 2 (1996): 1–16; Jan-Wim Wesselius, "The Literary Nature of the Book of Daniel and the Linguistic Character of Its Aramaic," *AS* 3 (2005): 241–83.

[58]Barton, "The Composition of Daniel," 62–65.

[59]Ibid., 65.

[60]Ibid., 79–83; Barton is undecided as to whether chapter 3 should be assigned to the Babylonian writer or to a fourth writer.

[61]Ibid., 71; the stories of the fiery furnace and the den of lions certainly share more than what Barton finds between chapters 6 and 9.

[62]N. T. Wright, *Christian Origins and the Question of God*, vol. 1, *The New Testament and the People of God* (Minneapolis: Fortress, 1992), 295.

[63]Montgomery, *Daniel*, 90–92; H. J. M. van Deventer ("Testing-Testing, Do We Have a Translated Text in Daniel 1 and Daniel 7?" *JNSL* 31, no. 2 [2005]: 91–106) has shown on the basis of computer-assisted analysis that chapters 1 and 7 do not display certain features of translated texts.

[64]H. H. Rowley, "The Bilingual Problem of Daniel," *ZAW* 50 (1932): 257.

[65]It is interesting to note that the parallel text in Jer 51:15–19 does not have an equivalent to Jer 10:11.

[66]E.g., J. W. Wesselius, "Language and Style in Biblical Aramaic: Observations on the Unity of Daniel II–VI," *VT* 38 (1988): 194–209.

[67]There are links between the adjacent chapters as well such as: the head of gold in chapter 2 and the statue of gold in chapter 3; the den of lions in chapter 6 and the lion in chapter 7.

[68]See Michael B. Shepherd, "Daniel 7:13 and the New Testament Son of Man," *WTJ* 68 (2006): 99–111.

[69]H. H. Rowley, "The Unity of the Book of Daniel," *HUCA* 23 (1950–51): 248.

[70]John H. Sailhamer (*NIV Compact Bible Commentary* [Grand Rapids: Zondervan, 1994], 410) notes three features of the unique contribution of chapter 9 to the book: (1) it contains an interpretation of Scripture rather than a vision or dream of events, (2) God's people are portrayed as rebellious rather than faithful, and (3) the cutting off of the coming messianic figure is introduced, whereas earlier only his victory was in view.

[71]Note how the three friends are worked into the transition to chapter 3 in Dan 2:49.

[72]Cf., the Greek translations (Συριστί) and Ezra 4:7 (ארמית); the blank space before the Aramaic section in 1QDan[a] is weak evidence since the term could have appeared before the space.

[73]John H. Sailhamer, "Biblical Theology and the Composition of the Hebrew Bible," in *Biblical Theology: Retrospect and Prospect*, ed. Scott J. Hafemann (Downers Grove: InterVarsity, 2002), 34–36; see the prologue to Sirach and 4QMMT.

[74]Ibid., 35.

[75]Ibid.

[76]Ibid., 36; earlier in the essay Sailhamer discusses the two final shapes of Jeremiah—the Masoretic Text and the Septuagint (ibid., 27–30); see also Emanuel Tov, *Textual Criticism of the Hebrew Bible*, 2d rev. ed. (Minneapolis: Fortress, 2001), 319–27; Eugene Ulrich, *The Dead Sea Scrolls and the Origins of the Bible* (Grand Rapids: Eerdmans, 1999), passim.

[77]Daniel is often said to be part of that portion of the canon labeled "Prophets" on the basis of its placement in the Greek Bible and on the basis of texts that refer to Daniel as a prophet (4Q174 2:3; Matt 24:15); but the fact that the historical figure Daniel was considered a prophet is not determinative for the canonical placement of the book that bears his name; in a sense, all of Hebrew Scripture is regarded as the product of the prophets (e.g., Rom 1:2; 16:26).

[78]The Hebrew phrase occurs in Dan 10:14.

[79]John H. Sailhamer, *The Pentateuch as Narrative* (Grand Rapids: Zondervan, 1992), 35–37; idem, *Introduction to Old Testament Theology* (Grand Rapids: Zondervan, 1995), 209–12.

[80]Shepherd, "Daniel 7:13," 104.

[81]See Franz Rosenthal, *Die Aramaistische Forschung* (Leiden: Brill, 1964), 63.

[82]Ibid., 63–65.

[83]Ibid., 64.

[84]Segert, *Altaramäische Grammatik*, 444.

[85]Rolf Rendtorff, *The Old Testament: An Introduction*, trans. John Bowden (Philadelphia: Fortress, 1986), 60.

[86]Ibid.

[87]Snell, "Why Is There Aramaic in the Bible?" 34.

[88]Arnold, "The Use of Aramaic," 6.

Chapter Two

Textlinguistic Methodology

The purpose of this chapter is to lay the textlinguistic foundation for distributional analysis. Part of the task here is to distinguish between textlinguistics (the study of written texts as acts of communication) and discourse analysis (the study of written texts as records of spoken communication). The general field of linguistics has truly experienced a boom over the last century. Not only has it branched out into a multitude of various specializations, but also it has come to the center of modern philosophical debate. Linguistics has quite naturally been adopted by those interested in biblical interpretation. From word studies to the analysis of entire texts, exegetes are now benefiting from the advancements in linguistics. After all, the Bible is a linguistic phenomenon.

After a specific exploration of textlinguistics, this chapter will examine the broader backdrop of modern linguistics primarily through the works of Ferdinand de Saussure and Siegfried Schmidt. It will be observed that textlinguistics is in many ways very much an outsider to the trends of modern linguistics. Textlinguistics and distributional analysis are unique in their appropriateness to the study of texts written in what is now dead language. Therefore, discussion of dead languages such as Biblical Hebrew and Biblical Aramaic will form an essential component of this chapter. Finally, the chapter will conclude with the Biblical Hebrew works of Wolfgang Schneider and Wolfgang Richter that serve to a certain extent as models for the Biblical Aramaic research in the subsequent chapters of the present work.

What Is Textlinguistics?

Even if linguists are agreed that textlinguistics is the study of the language of texts, several questions still remain. What is a text? Are "text" and "discourse" interchangeable? Are there different kinds of texts? These questions and many others are raised by the lack of standardized terminology and methodology in the works of those who have claimed textlinguistics.

However the questions are answered, what is clear is that there is a great need for text-immanent and language-specific descriptions of texts, particularly biblical texts. The field of textlinguistics has the greatest potential for producing textual categories for biblical grammar and syntax. Because the Bible is a text written in human language no longer spoken, a textlinguistics is required that is tailored to such an object of study. Therefore, neither a theory of living discourse nor a general theory of sign systems (semiotics) is appropriate to the task here.

Textlinguistics is not so much concerned with what ought to be in a given text as it is with what is actually there. It seeks to describe, not prescribe. Textlinguistics demonstrates how written texts are able to function and produce meaning. In contrast, Gillian Brown and George Yule state, "'Doing discourse analysis' certainly involves 'doing syntax and semantics', but it primarily consists of 'doing pragmatics'."[1] In other words, the primary object of study for discourse analysts is not textual, but extra-textual. To be sure, not all who claim discourse analysis would agree entirely with Brown and Yule, but the choice not to be limited to text-immanent categories is unanimous.

David Dawson, who refers to his work as textlinguistics even though it is really tagmemic discourse analysis, feels perfectly free to acknowledge the roles of human behavior, psycholinguistics, and sociolinguistics.[2] Kirk Lowery, on the other hand, recognizes the different goals of the different pursuits:

> If we wish to understand our psychological nature as we process information, our theory and the hypotheses we derive from them [*sic*] must reflect that concern. If we wish to understand the nature of a certain language, then, of necessity, our theory and goals are going to be substantially different.[3]

The point here is not to condemn study of extra-textual phenomena or to deny external reality. Rather, it is that an approach that combines internal and external factors is fundamentally different from one that looks only at the internal.[4] When it comes to analysis of texts written in either Biblical Hebrew or Biblical Aramaic, the external factors are simply not accessible.

One of the most prominent voices in discourse analysis is that of Robert Longacre. Longacre's work, largely built on the tagmemics of Kenneth Pike, is perhaps best described not as textual, but as "notional."[5] Longacre's concern to identify the semantic value (narrative, procedural, behavioral, expository, etc.) of paragraphs and discourses is fundamentally different from that of textlinguistics.

The extra-textual nature of discourse analysis has led to a basic confusion between spoken discourse and written texts, as if written texts were merely records of spoken communication rather than acts of communication in their own right.[6] The following comments by Peter Cotterell and Max Turner are exemplary:

> The term 'discourse' is used generally for any coherent sequence of strings, any coherent stretch of language. As we have already seen, some linguists would restrict the term to spoken language, but there is no compelling reason for us to do that. A conversation is discourse, but so is a novel or a poem or a dissertation.[7]

No one disagrees that conversations, novels, poems, and dissertations are all examples of coherent language, but so much more can be said about the differences between a conversation and a written text. Failure to distinguish between spoken and written texts results in attempts to import pragmatic meanings into written texts—meanings unintended by authors simply by virtue of the fact that authors are well aware that they are composing and not speaking.[8] On the other hand, it most certainly is correct to examine extra-linguistic features of spoken discourse, because speakers speak with cognizance of audio and visual factors. Speakers take into account sensory perception in a way that authors do not. Authors anticipate reader response with textual elements, not with gestures or with assumptions about the readers' environment or state of being at the point of reading. Too often in discourse analysis the categories derived from analysis of conversation excerpts are transferred directly to analysis of written texts. But textlinguistics requires specifically textual categories for written texts as the objects of study.

Any work in textlinguistics such as that of the present research must have a definition of "text." It is possible to give a very broad, all-inclusive definition,[9] but here the concern is for a definition that fits texts written in human language. Robert-Alain de Beaugrande and Wolfgang Dressler present seven standards of textuality that any given entity must meet in order to be called a text: cohesion, coherence, intentionality, acceptability, informativity, situationality, and intertextuality.[10] They only consider cohesion and coherence to be text-centered.[11] Cohesion is a text's interwoven nature. The parts of a text bear a relationship to one another; they hang together. Cohesion and unity are related, but not synonymous. A text is unified as a result of being cohesive. Coherence, on the other hand, has to do with whether a so-called text makes sense or not. An entity, not a text, could be cohesive without being coherent. The parts of speech in the following "sentence" are apparent, but the "sentence" makes very little sense: the gybytobble kolarded to a shmuffle and ibbitibbied all the errerrmops. The structure words—articles, prepositions, and conjunctions—make the "sentence" cohesive, but the content words—words like nouns and verbs that carry more lexical meaning—are unintelligible. Thus, in order to call something a text, that something must be cohesive and coherent.

Sentences or clauses are good places to start for definitions of texts. Just as it is possible for a word to be a clause in some languages, it is also possible for a clause to constitute a text.[12] Francis Andersen notes, "The traditional definition of a sentence as 'a complete thought expressed in words' fell on evil times when description of language data began with forms rather than ideas."[13] Andersen goes on to give another definition of "sentence": "As a unit in the grammatical component of a language, a sentence may be defined as a construction that is grammatically complete or self-contained; that is, the grammatical functions of all the elements in a given sentence can be described in terms of relationships to other elements within the same sentence."[14] Andersen's working definition of "sentence" is not a bad definition of "text." A text may be said to be made up of many texts—clauses and larger units. This creates a web of textuality or a web of words within and between smaller and larger texts considered as integral parts of whole texts. In an article on analysis of narrative, S. Bar-Efrat defines structure as "the network of relations among the parts of an object or a unit," and he states that "narratives which on the one hand can be considered as self-contained units may be regarded on the other hand as parts of larger wholes."[15] Just as larger texts may be described as cohesive and coherent, so sentences may be said to consist of meaningful relationships. Textlinguistics must take into account both the microstructures and the macrostructures of whole texts.

One of the most salient features of whole texts as opposed to smaller textual units is the fact that whole texts have a beginning and an ending. A clause within a whole text, while distinguishable from other clauses surrounding it, is always at least either preceded or followed by another clause. Single words display a certain amount of cohesion and coherence, but they usually do not stand on their own as whole texts.

In addition to clearly marked boundaries, whole texts written in human language function on a higher level of communication than other "texts"—such as stop signs or clocks—that fall into the broader arena of semiotics. Whole texts (e.g., biblical narratives) have a thematic orientation and a hierarchy of relationships that can vary from text to text.[16]

Texts are often said to be characterized by prominence, although a better term might be "opposition." The following "sentence" does not display prominence: the the the the the the. Everything in this "sentence" is the same. Therefore, it basically says nothing because no relationships are forged. This is not to say that repetition is meaningless, only that repetition needs context in order to be meaningful. Prominence is not the same as emphasis. Emphasis is an author's intentional use of prominence to highlight some aspect of the text. Prominence or "opposition," on the other hand, is a component that is necessary for a text to say anything at all.

In light of the above discussion, it is possible to offer the following provisional definition of a text written in human language: a text written in human language is a thematically oriented unit of communication that exhibits cohesion, coherence, and prominence within clearly marked boundaries. This is, of course, a technical definition meant to describe textual phenomena, not a lexical definition meant to reflect modern English usage of the word "text." But would not this definition fit speech just as well as writing? Speech can be characterized by all, some, or none of the elements of this definition and still be speech. A conversation can easily shift in a number of directions in ways that would be unintelligible in a written text. Speakers and hearers fill in gaps with extra-linguistic communication (e.g., facial expressions), but an author is required to fill in those gaps textually for readers. The following utterance is neither cohesive nor coherent, yet it is exactly the type of expression understood in speech: "I…well…I…uh…you know." The same expression would baffle a reader, especially if it stood on its own.

If a text written in human language is a thematically oriented unit of communication that exhibits cohesion, coherence, and prominence within clearly marked boundaries, then the object of study for textlinguistics is such a unit, not speech. The goal of textlinguistics is text-immanent, linguistic description of whole texts that provides insight into how whole texts function and produce meaning on the micro and macro levels.

According to Noam Chomsky, "only a purely formal basis can provide a firm and productive foundation for the construction of grammatical theory."[17] This statement is particularly true for grammars of texts written in what is now dead language such as those of Biblical Hebrew and Aramaic. The grammarian is not in a position to proceed from preconceived categories of function to the forms of the texts. According to Eep Talstra, "a registration of forms precedes the conclusion of functions."[18] Only the formal features of the texts are accessible for textlinguistic research. A. F. den Exter Blokland has observed that "with ancient texts the signs are all we have—there is no 'language helper' to dialogue with us about their meaning."[19]

For textlinguistic analysis of formal distribution, a computer database is indispensable.[20] Although a full presentation of database analysis of Biblical Aramaic texts is provided in the third chapter of the present work, some preliminary comments are in order here. A computer database offers convenient access to the regularities and irregularities of the language under examination. Provided that the database has been set up well, the retrievals can give feedback that comes as close as possible to that of an "informant." Thus, the computer, not the linguist or grammarian, determines what kind of text grammar is needed for a given language.

Harald Weinrich, whose definition of "text" and understanding of textlinguistics as a syntactical undertaking of the clause level and beyond fit quite well here,[21] has influenced two Hebrew grammarians—Wolfgang Schneider and Alviero Niccacci—who have in turn influenced the work of the present author. In conclusion of this overview of textlinguistics, it may be of help to mention briefly their views of the task at hand. Wolfgang Schneider defines textlinguistics as follows:

> A grammatical description of the language, which goes beyond the clause boundaries and seeks to interpret the constitution and demarcation of texts, has since about 1964 received more and more attention: "Text-Linguistics." Pronouns and other particles, for example, can be described adequately in their function only textlinguistically (author's translation).[22]

Thus, textlinguistics goes beyond clause boundaries and seeks to comprehend the constitution and demarcation of texts.

Niccacci, who is somewhat more sympathetic to discourse analysis, outlines a different model:

> Three different levels of analysis need to be established. Proceeding from the bottom up (from small to broad units), they are: morphological, syntactical, and discourse levels. Morphology is concerned with grammatical analysis of the sentence. Syntax identifies the relationships among sentences and paragraphs in the framework of a text. Discourse analysis brings to the fore macrosyntactic, semantic, and pragmatic devices used by the author to convey his message in a forcible way. I insist that the higher levels be based on the lower ones. Syntax must be based on morphology, and discourse analysis on morphosyntax.[23]

Niccacci's "syntax" and "macrosyntactic devices" are very close to Schneider's "textlinguistics," but it must be said that semantics and pragmatics are two separate disciplines. Pragmatics in particular is not relevant or even accessible for texts written in what is now dead language.

Modern Linguistics

It is possible to characterize the twentieth century in a number of ways, but one distinct possibility is that it was the century of linguistics. For the first time in history, linguistics became recognized as a field separate from grammar and philology. The discipline has since blossomed in a wide variety of directions. Also for the first time in history, linguistics became a major category in philosophy through the works of philosophers like Ludwig Wittgenstein and Jacques Derrida.[24]

If anyone can be called the father of modern linguistics, Ferdinand de Saussure is sure to be at the top of the list.[25] Saussure's posthumous *Cours de linguistique générale*, put together by colleagues mainly from lecture notes taken by students, has stood since 1916 as the first major milestone in modern linguistics. Every subsequent development in linguistics has been in some way a reaction for or against Saussure.

Ferdinand de Saussure

Saussure discusses three phases that preceded modern linguistic study.[26] The first is grammar. According to Saussure, grammar is logical, not scientific or objective. Grammar seeks to prescribe the distinction between correct and incorrect forms. The second phase is philology. Philology is not so much concerned with linguistic structure as it is with interpretation of texts. Saussure's main critique of philology is that it is too preoccupied with written texts to the neglect of living language. The third and final phase is that of comparative philology. Saussure criticizes the comparative philologists for being only comparative and not historical. According to Saussure, such an approach has no basis in reality.[27]

Saussure gives three aims of linguistics: (1) "to describe all known languages and record their history," (2) "to determine the forces operating permanently and universally in all languages," and (3) "to delimit and define linguistics itself."[28] Saussure identifies linguistic structure (*langue*) as the object of study for the linguist.[29] Linguistic structure is not the same as language; rather, it is "a social product of our language faculty."[30]

Speech (*parole*), on the other hand, is an individual act of the will.[31] According to Saussure, linguistic structure (a language system) may be studied independently of speech.[32] The linguistic signs of a language system are not abstractions; thus, they can be fixed in conventional images of writing with the result that dictionaries and grammars can provide a faithful representation of a language.[33] For Saussure, this understanding of linguistic structure places linguistics firmly within the science of semiology.[34]

Since linguistic structure is the proper object of study for linguistics, Saussure suggests the possibility of a separate linguistics of speech.[35] It is odd then that Saussure does not also mention a separate linguistics of texts. He does acknowledge that "[a] language and its written form constitute two separate systems of signs."[36] For Saussure, however, writing only exists to represent speech; and writing represents speech inconsistently.[37] It is true that written language is not an exact replica of spoken language. But this should have been an occasion to introduce a new discipline—textlinguistics. Instead, Saussure focused solely on spoken, living language. This created a ripple effect that has lasted to the present day in modern linguistics. Saussure criticized the philologists for their preoccupation with ancient texts, but modern linguistics is also subject to criticism for its neglect of the same in favor of spoken, living language.

Essential to Saussure's understanding of linguistic structure is the linguistic sign. Linguistic structure is the system of linguistic signs. Speech is the actualization of the system of signs. According to Saussure, the linguistic sign is not merely a mark or an utterance. It is also not a link between a thing and a name; rather, it is a link between a concept and a sound pattern (*image acoustique*).[38] A sound pattern is "the hearer's psychological impression of a sound."[39]

Saussure designates the concept as "signification" and the sound pattern as "signal."[40] The signification and the signal constitute the sign. The relationship between the signification and the signal is arbitrary; therefore, the sign is arbitrary.[41] It may be of help here to mention Saussure's infinitely simpler example in which the relationship between the Latin word *arbor* and a picture of a tree is said to be arbitrary. This example corresponds more with conventional usage of the word "sign." The Latin word *arbor* is the sign, and the picture of the tree is the external referent. The relationship between the two is arbitrary. The Latin word *arbor* is not defined by a description of a tree, but by semantic oppositions with other words within the same semantic field.[42]

Saussure goes on to speak of the invariability and the variability of the sign.[43] In the same context, he also speaks of static (synchronic) linguistics and evolutionary (diachronic) linguistics.[44] Saussure summarizes the discussion as follows:

> A language is a system of which all the parts can and must be considered as synchronically interdependent.
>
> Since changes are never made to the system as a whole, but only to its individual elements, they must be studied independently of the system. It is true that every change has a repercussion on the system. But initially only one point is affected. The change is unrelated to the internal consequences which may follow for the system as a whole.[45]

Saussure uses the example of a game of chess in which any given state of the chess board is totally independent of any previous state.[46] This preference for the synchronic is based on the fact that it is the only reality of which any given community of speakers is aware.[47] Synchronic law "registers a state of affairs."[48]

It goes without saying that Saussure's emphasis on the synchronic has been revolutionary for modern linguistics. Saussure defines synchronic linguistics and diachronic linguistics as follows:

> *Synchronic linguistics* will be concerned with logical and psychological connexions between coexisting items constituting a system, as perceived by the same collective consciousness.
>
> *Diachronic linguistics* on the other hand will be concerned with connexions between sequences of items not perceived by the same collective consciousness, which replace one another without themselves constituting a system.[49]

Synchronic linguistics aims to establish the constitutive principles of any linguistic state.[50] Diachronic linguistics, on the other hand, treats matters such as origin and development.

From the synchronic standpoint, a language is "a system in which all the elements fit together, and in which the value of any one element depends on the simultaneous coexistence of all the others."[51] Each element of the system is compared and contrasted with other elements. This is why there is no one-to-one correspondence in translation. A translated element does not compare and contrast in the same way and with the same set of elements in the target language as the non-translated element does in the source language. The entire mechanism of language depends upon signs that are in opposition to one another.[52] If a sign does not contrast with anything in the system, then it is meaningless.[53]

Saussure discusses two different kinds of relations between linguistic items in a synchronic state: syntagmatic and associative. Syntagmatic relations are a function of the linear nature of language. Syntagmas are combinations based on sequentiality that comprise two or more consecutive units.[54] A unit "acquires its value simply in opposition to what precedes, or to what follows, or to both."[55]

Whereas syntagmatic relations hold *in praesentia*, associative relations hold *in absentia*.[56] Associative relations are groups of connections between words—groups formed by mental association. The connections can be based on form or meaning, or both.[57] Thus, a grammatical paradigm or words that share a formal characteristic can form associative relations as well as words that share the same semantic field.

Saussure's section on synchronic linguistics concludes with some comments about the traditional divisions of grammar.[58] In traditional grammar, morphology and syntax are separate, and both are separate from lexicology, which falls outside of grammar. Saussure contends that the interdependence of form and function causes these divisions to overlap. He suggests that the division between the syntagmatic and the associative is more appropriate. Saussure does not, however, consider the fact that only written forms are available to grammarians working with dead languages.

When Saussure turns to diachronic linguistics, he is not dismissive of it. He only seeks to demonstrate that its object of study is quite different from that of synchronic linguistics. Diachronic linguistics studies "the relations which hold not between the coexisting terms of a linguistic state, but between successive terms substituted one for another over a period of time."[59] Thus, diachronic linguistics does not inform the linguist about the linguistic structure of a synchronic state, and synchronic linguistics does not describe the relations not perceived by the same collective consciousness.[60]

In Saussure's view, "*the only true object of study in linguistics is the language, considered in itself and for its own sake.*"[61] He states, "In linguistics, to *explain a word is to relate it to other words*: for there are no necessary relations between sound and meaning."[62] There is no question that this basic view of linguistics has had a massive influence on the field.[63] Structuralism in particular has claimed Saussure, although Saussure himself was not a structuralist. Structuralism is more the anthropology of Claude Lévi-Strauss than the linguistics of Saussure.

One of the lasting legacies of Saussure has been the emphasis on spoken, living language in modern linguistics. This can be seen in transformational-generative grammar, which examines deep structure and surface structure and states the rules by which kernel sentences generate all the possible sentences (transformations) of a language. It can also be seen in the speech act theory of J. L. Austin and John Searle. Speech act theorists distinguish between three kinds of speech acts: (1) the locutionary act is speech, (2) the illocutionary act is what is done in speech (e.g., promise, command, etc.), and (3) the perlocutionary act is what is accomplished through speech.[64]

It is unfortunate that Saussure never developed a textlinguistics. This would have been of particular value for the study of texts written in what is now dead language. Dead language cannot be examined simply on the analogy of spoken, living language. And whatever may be said to be universal about all languages contributes very little to the understanding of the specific details of any one language.

Siegfried Schmidt

Siegfried Schmidt has provided an introduction to the basic issues of communication-oriented linguistics.[65] One of the most intriguing aspects of Schmidt's contribution is the title of his work *Texttheorie*. Schmidt has alerted linguists to the fact that a text theory is needed. In interaction with the so-called textlinguistics of his day, Schmidt outlines what he considers to be the linguistic foundations of a text theory.

According to Schmidt, there has been a development in the linguistics field from the linguistics of a language system (cf., Saussure) to a text theory of linguistic communication.[66] Schmidt characterizes this in terms of a shift from clause grammar (*Satzgrammatik*) to text grammar (*Textgrammatik*). Text grammar employs a usage-oriented text theory (i.e., a textlinguistics with "pragmatic" components).[67]

For Schmidt, the research task of a text theory is to examine the means and rules by which functioning texts are produced and received; it must plan a model of linguistic communication that presents an ordered system of hypotheses about the "communicative act game" (*kommunikative Handlungsspiel*).[68] From the outset, Schmidt's use of the word "text" is somewhat misleading. He is not necessarily interested in written texts or in speech, but in communication.

Schmidt proposes the communicative act game (cf., Wittgenstein) as the basis of a text theory. He argues that language functions primarily as a communication system, not as a sign system.[69] The communication system of a society becomes determinative for everything. Thus, texts do not refer to "reality," but to the model of reality accepted by the society.[70]

Schmidt defines the term "communicative act game" (*kommunikative Handlungsspiel*) as follows: "A communicative act game is a definable communication 'history' or a temporal and spatial limitable amount of communication acts" (author's translation).[71] According to Schmidt, a communicative act game is a simple social system in which communication partners play within a demarcated realm of perception.[72] Linguistic and non-linguistic constituents constitute communication acts. These communication acts in turn constitute the communication act game in various types of communication situations. The linguistic communication of the communication act game makes social interaction possible.[73]

Within this context, Schmidt offers a theoretical model of the constitution and reception of linguistic meaning. He calls this "semantics of instruction" (*Instruktionssemantik*). The following quote provides a concise explanation of what Schmidt means by this term:

> Lexemes viewed as carriers of semantic instruction can be isolated analytically, but in the actual system of a language the text constituents that occur are never isolated; they are linguistically and systematically integrated in lexematic fields (= subsystems of a lexicon). The position of the lexeme in the lexematic field defines its usage possibilities; in other words, the field context assigns to the lexeme its general possibilities of function in texts, it demarcates and stabilizes them through a web of repeatedly tested connections. The following is the result of what has been developed up to this point for the referential use of lexemes: The individual lexeme does not refer to an extra-linguistic level of correlation, but the particular lexematic field is interpreted as a complex of rules or instructions to a communication partner to refer in communication acts in a certain way to linguistic and non-linguistic factors of the communicative act game or of the system of communication as a whole and to the model of reality validated therein.[74]

Schmidt views "word meaning" in both lexical and textual terms in the framework of a society of speakers.[75] That is, words in some way bring meaning to the context; and the context in some way determines the meaning of the words.

The constituents of a text function in a communication act to interpret the "instructions" manifested in the text.[76] The constituents themselves thus serve as instructions. Only in communication act games do communication partners realize the instruction or meaning of a text.[77] A text isolated from a communication act game has no meaning, only the potential for meaning.[78] For Schmidt, the meaning of a text is only a potentiality to be realized in the dynamic of communication.

Communication partners bring a number of semantic and pragmatic presuppositions to a communicative act game. Certain conditions must be fulfilled with regard to the shared presupposition pool in order for successful communication to take place.[79] A speaker who brings complex assumptions to a communication act is more difficult to understand.[80] Schmidt gives the strong divergences in the interpretation of literary texts as an example. But how much does this apply to literary texts? It is true that authors anticipate a readership. It is also true that readers bring presuppositions to texts. But is the dynamic the same as that of a conversation? Once an author has completed his or her work, the reader has a responsibility to interpret the verbal meaning of the text. For the sake of understanding, the reader must be aligned adequately, though perhaps not absolutely, with the author's intention. Written texts do imply a communication situation, but the author-reader relationship is something quite apart from the speaker-hearer relationship.[81]

Against the consensus of textlinguistics, Schmidt does not view a text as a purely linguistic phenomenon. He prefers to speak of "textuality," which refers to a two-sided structure—one linguistic and one social.[82] Because whole texts function in an extra-linguistic context, Schmidt argues that linguistic criteria alone are not enough for their interpretation. But what about texts for which social data are not accessible? No text occurs in a vacuum, but study of texts written in what is now dead language has only linguistic data (i.e., written forms) at its disposal.

Schmidt defines a text as "each expressed, linguistic integral part of a communication act in a communicative act game, which is thematically oriented and fulfills a recognizable communicative function; that is, it realizes a recognizable potential for illocution" (author's translation).[83] Here the fulfillment of communicative function is equated with the realization of illocution potential. A coherent system in which illocutionary acts can be ordered hierarchically is valid as a text.[84]

The communicative act game serves as the framework for communicative acts.[85] The communicative act provides the organizational structure for texts. Texts organize clauses, and clauses organize the constituents of the language system.[86] As for text production, the activity of a speaker in the framework of a communicative act game can be defined as production of the linguistic constituents of a communication act.[87]

In conclusion, Schmidt's basic concern to highlight the communicative function of texts is surely correct whether or not all of his categories apply to all texts. Written texts imply communication situations. They also display communication levels (e.g., narrative, discourse, etc.). What is needed is a textlinguistics appropriate for dead language texts as acts of communication.

The Study of Dead Language

It is apparent by now that a textlinguistics specific to dead language is required. In the first chapter, it was discovered that the standard grammars for Biblical Aramaic, as well as the alternative to the standard grammars, have not described the Biblical Aramaic verbal system in a manner appropriate to the nature of its language. Up to this point in the present chapter, it has been observed that modern linguistics has offered very little to remedy this situation. Due to its preoccupation with spoken/living language, modern linguistics has not addressed the specific issues of written texts, let alone dead language. Even the communication-oriented linguistics of Schmidt has embraced too many extra-linguistic factors for a proper textlinguistics of dead language.

The two languages of the Hebrew Bible—Biblical Hebrew and Biblical Aramaic—are both dead languages. They are no longer spoken. This can be demonstrated by concise accounts of their respective histories.

A Brief History of the Hebrew Language

Edward Ullendorff has asked the provocative question, "Is Biblical Hebrew a language?"[88] Ullendorff explores whether or not the language of the Hebrew Bible would be adequate for the daily requirements of a normal speech community. He acknowledges that the recognition of a larger vocabulary stock in ancient Hebrew is not new, but he seeks to give a more sustained treatment of the subject.

Ullendorff calculates that out of roughly three hundred thousand words in the Hebrew Bible there are only about eight thousand separate words.[89] He contrasts this number with the twenty-two thousand words of a one-volume dictionary of Biblical, Mishnaic, Medieval, and Modern Hebrew.[90] Ullendorff refers to Theodor Nöldeke's original point that the approximately one thousand five hundred *hapax legomena* of Biblical Hebrew demonstrate that the vocabulary stock of the spoken language was significantly larger.[91] He notes that many of these words are common words of daily life that were frequently used in later Hebrew.[92]

Over against Biblical Hebrew in its "Masoretic garb," Ullendorff suggests that Mishnaic Hebrew contains a better sampling of the colloquial language.[93] He concludes that Biblical Hebrew is no more than a "linguistic fragment."[94] For Ullendorff, this means that post-Biblical Hebrew is essential for understanding the Hebrew Bible.[95] An important caveat, however, is that Mishnaic often imitates Biblical Hebrew.

According to E. Y. Kutscher, the destruction of Jerusalem in A.D. 70 ended the unbroken tradition of Biblical Hebrew as a vehicle of literary expression.[96] This paved the way for the use of the spoken language of Judea—Mishnaic Hebrew.[97] The Second Jewish Revolt (A.D. 132–35) along with the death or enslavement of all Hebrew speakers marked the end of Mishnaic Hebrew as a spoken language.[98] By the fifth century A.D., "Hebrew was not used anywhere as a spoken language, although it was still extensively employed in writing until it was revived three generations ago as a spoken language."[99] The later strata of Hebrew have been a mixture of Biblical Hebrew, Mishnaic Hebrew, and other elements.[100]

Although there was occasional use of Hebrew as a spoken language in the medieval period, the Jews tended to employ the vernacular of the region in which they lived.[101] Modern Hebrew began with a revival of Hebrew writing in the Enlightenment era. According to Kutscher, the adherents of the Enlightenment considered Hebrew to be the most suitable language for the dissemination of their ideas among the Jews.[102] This language was basically a series of quotations from the Hebrew Bible.[103]

It was soon realized that the vocabulary stock of the Hebrew Bible was insufficient for Hebrew writing about contemporary life. New creations, loanwords, and new meanings for Biblical Hebrew words and phrases were provided in order to avoid linguistic strains.[104] With the new force of Zionism, Hebrew literature was in a position to become nationalistic. Kutscher calls Mendele Mokher Sefarim (the pen name of A. S. Abramowitz) the father of Yiddish and Modern Hebrew.[105] The components of Mendele's Modern Hebrew included Biblical Hebrew, Mishnaic Hebrew, Aramaic, Medieval Hebrew, and Yiddish. The tense system of Biblical Hebrew was abandoned in favor of three tenses—past, present participle, and future.[106] This Hebrew, however, was still a literary language; Yiddish was the spoken language in Eastern Europe; Mendele never intended to revive Hebrew as a spoken language.[107]

Kutscher comments that only in Palestine could Hebrew have been revived as a spoken language.[108] Families such as that of Eliezer Ben Yehuda began to raise their children with the knowledge of no language other than

Hebrew.[109] Thus, what was artificial for the first generation was natural for the second and subsequent generations. The Hebrew Language Committee was created in 1889 to supply words for daily life from Hebrew sources, word creations, and other Semitic languages.

In the Jewish State, "Hebrew was established as the language of instruction in every official institution of learning from kindergarten to the universities."[110] This type of language revival was unprecedented. No language that had entirely ceased to be spoken had ever been revived.[111] But what kind of Hebrew was this? It was not Biblical Hebrew: "BH syntax was almost entirely rejected and with it all the morphosyntactic aspects of the verb that are the main features of BH."[112] Nevertheless, this amalgamation of the classical sources became a real, native language. Kutscher relates this to the new developments in the field of linguistics:

> A new school of thought came into being that stressed the synchronic aspect of linguistic research. This school is mainly interested in discovering how a certain language functions as an entity at a given time. In this context it disregards the history of the different parts of the language. It stresses the inter-relationship of the different elements that make up the language. This new linguistic viewpoint reached Israel in the late forties. A new generation of general linguists arose who maintained that all the different sources of IH [Israeli Hebrew] had fused into a new identity, which did not consist simply of its components. Rather, functioning as an identity it willy-nilly created a new *entity* through the interplay of the various old elements.[113]

Kutscher maintains that one of the special features of Modern Israeli Hebrew is that the linguistic chasm between it and Biblical Hebrew is not too great: "Every reader can be his own interpreter and believe that his ilnterpretation [*sic*] of the Bible is the right one."[114] This is somewhat of an odd statement in light of the fact that Modern Hebrew has abandoned the verbal system of Biblical Hebrew. It would be one thing if Modern Hebrew had simply changed the orthography of a few words or something of that nature. But to adopt a completely new verbal system is to alter the very heartbeat of the language.

It is true that the alphabet is the same and that Modern Hebrew speakers can generally decipher the word meanings of the Hebrew Bible. But what can be said about semantic change, archaic forms, and *hapax legomena*? What do Modern Hebrew speakers know about complex syntactical constructions foreign to the spoken language? To be sure, Kutscher is not arguing that Modern Israeli Hebrew and Biblical Hebrew are identical, but it is perhaps still too much to say that knowledge of Modern Hebrew is adequate for proper interpretation of the Hebrew Bible. According to Kutscher's own account, Biblical Hebrew ceased as a literary language toward the end of the first century A.D. The language represented by Biblical Hebrew died as a spoken language even earlier, and it is a dead language to this day.

A Brief History of the Aramaic Language

Zdravko Stefanovic provides the following chronological division of the Aramaic language:

Old Aramaic (900–700 B.C.)
Official Aramaic (700–300 B.C.)
Middle Aramaic (300 B.C.–A.D. 200)
Late Aramaic (A.D. 200–700)
Modern Aramaic (A.D. 700–present)[115]

According to Stefanovic, this division represents a broad consensus among scholars today.

Stefanovic has attempted to relate the first division to a significant representative of the second division—the Aramaic of Daniel. For example, Stefanovic notes that the supposedly free word order of the Aramaic of Daniel is found in Old Aramaic only in texts that are merging or transitioning into Official Aramaic.[116] Some of Stefanovic's conclusions may have implications for an earlier date of the Aramaic of Daniel. As for the Old Aramaic phase itself, Joseph Fitzmyer states that it "is represented by inscriptions on stone and other materials, written in the borrowed Phoenician alphabet and preserving the earliest known forms of the language that we have come to recognize as Aramaic."[117] One of the most recently discovered pieces of Old Aramaic is an inscription from the ninth century B.C. that was found in 1993 at Tell Dan. The inscription has raised interest in the possibility of a "*waw* consecutive" in Old Aramaic.[118]

Official or Imperial Aramaic was the official language of the Persian Empire. Although early grammarians divided Official Aramaic into "Eastern" and "Western,"[119] it has since become customary to reserve that distinction for post-Christian dialects.[120] According to the account in 2 Kgs

18:26, Aramaic was understood by the upper class of Jerusalem at the end of the eighth century B.C., but not by the common people.

The two most outstanding representatives of Official Aramaic are Egyptian Aramaic (primarily Elephantine, fifth century B.C.) and Biblical Aramaic. Franz Rosenthal attributes the linguistic uniformity of the diverse Biblical Aramaic texts to the character of Official Aramaic.[121] S. R. Driver's well-known verdict for the book of Daniel that "the Greek words demand, the Hebrew supports, and the Aramaic permits, a date after the conquest of Palestine by Alexander the Great (332 B.C.)" may require revision in light of the similarity of the Aramaic of Daniel with Egyptian Aramaic texts from the fifth century B.C.[122] The small number of Greek words in Daniel cannot bear the entire weight of what is demanded for the book's date. The Aramaic supports, and the Hebrew permits, a date at least as early as the fifth century B.C.

Even though Biblical Aramaic is firmly established within the Official Aramaic stage, the unique history of the Biblical Aramaic texts places the language in somewhat of a separate category. Fitzmyer only counts Biblical Aramaic among the Official Aramaic texts "minus the Masoretic encrustations."[123] Not only is the Aramaic of the Bible no longer spoken or written, but also the language has an added artificial element. Klaus Beyer explains: "...[S]ince the Masoretic consonantal text of the Old Testament (Biblia Hebraica) was first definitively established along with the canon in the 1st cent. A.D., later orthographic conventions and grammatical forms (as well as a few Hebraisms) were able to penetrate the text..., while the fragments from Qumran...show the usual Hasmonaean orthography of their time."[124] This situation makes the Biblical Aramaic texts ideal for textlinguistics and distributional analysis.

Fitzmyer groups the Middle Aramaic stage into two categories.[125] The dialects of Palestine and Arabia include Nabatean, Qumran, Murabbaʿat, Palestinian inscriptions, Aramaic words in Josephus and the New Testament, and early Palestinian rabbinic literature. The dialects of Syria and Mesopotamia include those of Palmyra, Edessa, Hatra, and the beginnings of early Babylonian rabbinic literature. The language of the Nabatean and Palmyrene inscriptions has been said to be close to that of Biblical Aramaic,[126] but others have been more cautious.[127] Qumran Aramaic also has some affinities with Biblical Aramaic. For example, Stanislav Segert notes that the Prayer of Nabonidus from Qumran Cave 4 shares language and orthography with scrolls of Daniel from Qumran.[128] Some imitation of Biblical Aramaic is to be expected among the Aramaic texts of Qumran.

The early Targums fit within the Middle Aramaic phase. Their language is very close to Official Aramaic.[129] According to Hans Bauer and Pontus Leander, the Targums represent a later form of Biblical Aramaic.[130] The late Targums, however, belong to Late Aramaic. The western dialects of Late Aramaic include Jewish Palestinian Aramaic, Samaritan Aramaic, and Christian Syro-Palestinian Aramaic; the eastern dialects include Syriac (Jacobite and Nestorian), Babylonian Talmudic, and Mandaic.[131] According to Segert, Mandaic best preserved the original Aramaic syntax.[132]

After the Late Aramaic phase, Aramaic was overtaken in the west by Arabic, while the language continued in the east.[133] Modern Aramaic is still spoken today in places like northern Syria, Iran, and Iraq.[134] But what kind of language is Modern Aramaic? The Aramaic language has survived in general, but is there an unbroken link to the language of Old Aramaic or Official Aramaic?

Beyer is confident that Modern Aramaic can shed light on earlier stages of the language.[135] This is primarily because Modern Aramaic is the only stage of the language to which there is access to pronunciation. Beyer also believes that Modern Aramaic may have preserved some very old forms. Fitzmyer, on the other hand, calls Modern Aramaic "a remnant of Aramaic or Syriac, heavily influenced, however, by other modern local languages such as Arabic, Kurdish, or Turkish."[136] Kutscher's assessment is even more striking:

> Modern Syriac has gotten so far away from its parent that a scholar conversant only with Syriac whould [*sic*] not be able to understand one sentence. The entire verbal system has been completely transformed under the impact of Persian and Turkish, and very little is left from the Syriac tenses.
>
> Now, IH [Israeli Hebrew] is much closer to MH [Mishnaic Hebrew] and BH [Biblical Hebrew] than Modern Syriac is to Syriac.[137]

Segert adds that only the Middle and Late stages of Aramaic can provide insight into Old Aramaic and Official Aramaic; Modern Aramaic—with the possible exception of Mandaic—is too far removed.[138]

The earlier stages of the language such as Old Aramaic and Official Aramaic have not been preserved in Modern Aramaic. Thus, the language of the Biblical Aramaic texts stands as a dead language, and it must be treated as such. Unlike Hebrew, Aramaic has always been spoken in some form since its earliest stage. Nevertheless, the massive changes manifested in Modern Aramaic make it clear that no speaker/informant of the language represented by Biblical Aramaic is alive today.

Wolfgang Schneider

The previous two subsections have demonstrated that Biblical Hebrew and Biblical Aramaic are dead languages. The Hebrew language ceased to be spoken for a time and then underwent an unprecedented revival. Modern Hebrew speakers are able to grasp the general meaning of Biblical Hebrew texts through their knowledge of the revived language much like English speakers are able to understand the general meaning of the Hebrew Bible through English translations. But when it comes to the details of Biblical Hebrew, both Modern Hebrew and English translation are inadequate. Even Modern Hebrew speakers must learn the grammar/syntax and semantics of Biblical Hebrew.

Aramaic, on the other hand, never ceased to be spoken, yet Modern Aramaic is even further removed from Biblical Aramaic than Modern Hebrew is from Biblical Hebrew. This is in large part due to the fact that Biblical Hebrew was used to revive the Hebrew language, whereas Biblical Aramaic never had to be consulted for the modern dialects that continued to evolve on their own. Modern Aramaic is now almost unintelligible to scholars who only know Old, Official, Middle, and Late Aramaic.

Biblical Hebrew and Biblical Aramaic are ideal objects of study for textlinguistics and distributional analysis, but only Biblical Hebrew has been made such an object thus far. In these final two subsections of chapter two, the distributional approaches to Biblical Hebrew by Wolfgang Schneider and Wolfgang Richter are discussed in order to show the similarities with the distributional approach to Biblical Aramaic in chapter three.

Wolfgang Schneider has proposed a new understanding of the Biblical Hebrew verbal system based on distributional analysis. Schneider's approach is a textlinguistic approach in that it seeks to relate the parts to the whole.[139] His basic conclusion is that the Biblical Hebrew verb is not employed primarily to indicate time, aspect, or *Aktionsart*, but to orient the reader to the action. In a narrative, a verbal clause (i.e., a clause with a verb in first position) presents the foreground; a nominal clause (i.e., a clause with a nominal form in first position) presents the background.[140]

It may be recalled that traditional Biblical Hebrew grammar has much in common with traditional Biblical Aramaic grammar. For instance, the Biblical Hebrew "perfect" is described as follows: "The perfect serves to express actions, events, or states, which the speaker wishes to represent from the point of view of completion, whether they belong to a determinate past time, or extend into the present, or while still future, are pictured as in their completed state."[141] The so-called imperfect "represents actions, events, or states which are regarded by the speaker at any moment as still continuing, or in process of accomplishment, or even just taking place."[142]

In the midst of this confusion, Schneider provides a simple and comprehensive account of the Biblical Hebrew verbal forms. According to Schneider, the two primary verbal forms in Biblical Hebrew are the *wayyiqtol* (narration) and the *yiqtol* (discourse).[143] The *wayyiqtol* constitutes about 75% of the verbal forms in narration, while the *yiqtol* and *weqatal* each represent approximately 2% of the forms in narration. In contrast, the *yiqtol* predominates in discourse with 50% of the forms,[144] while the *wayyiqtol* represents 5% of the forms in discourse. The *qatal* is a secondary form occurring with moderate consistency in both narration (22%) and discourse (28%). The *wayyiqtol* and *yiqtol* control the main text planes. Their "opposition" forms the basis of Biblical Hebrew syntax.[145] The *qatal* does not serve to progress the narrative; it belongs to the background of narration, and it functions as a back-reference in discourse.[146]

Narration can be narration, narration within discourse, or narration within reported discourse. A narration within discourse or reported discourse will still be carried by *wayyiqtol* (e.g., 2 Sam 12:1–4). A *yiqtol* in narration points ahead or indicates that the narrator is addressing the reader (e.g., Gen 2:24). Discourse can be discourse, reported discourse, or reported discourse within reported discourse. Even psalms can have narration (e.g., the *wayyiqtol* forms in Ps 78) or discourse (e.g., Ps 5:2–4).

It will be observed in the following chapter that a similar pattern emerges from distributional analysis of Biblical Aramaic. The Biblical Aramaic *qtl* (narration) corresponds to the Biblical Hebrew *wayyiqtol* (narration). The Biblical Aramaic *yqtl* (discourse) corresponds to the Biblical Hebrew *yiqtol* (discourse). And the Biblical Aramaic nominal clause with or without a participle (secondary) corresponds to the Biblical Hebrew nominal clause and *qatal* clause (secondary).[147]

An immediate objection to Schneider's theory might be that many *qatal* forms appear in the place of *wayyiqtol* forms. An example might be the use of קרא Gen 1:5a: ויקרא אלהים לאור יום ולחשך קרא לילה ("And God called [ויקרא] the light day, and the darkness he called [קרא] night"). Why are there not two *wayyiqtol* forms here?[148] The answer seems to be that no advancement of the narration is intended in the second clause. The *qatal* form is employed to layer the action upon the preceding *wayyiqtol*. This construction is fairly common in the Hebrew Bible. A *wayyiqtol* clause is followed by an "x + *qatal*" clause in which the verbal root is the same, similar, or opposite. Either the action of one actant is segmented or the action is assigned to more than one actant. This inter-clausal relationship can be forged with a large portion of intervening text. Exodus 20:22 begins: ויאמר יהוה אל משה ("And the LORD said to Moses"). Exodus 24:1 has: ואל משה אמר ("And to Moses he said").[149] Although Biblical Aramaic does not have a *wayyiqtol*, a similar construction occurs between Dan 7:25b (ויתיהבון ["and they will be given"]) and Dan 7:27a (יהיבת ["it was given"]).

Talstra summarizes Schneider's presentation of Biblical Hebrew syntax in a single sentence: "the description of linguistic forms that carry out the process of communication."[150] He comments that Schneider's procession from an inventory of linguistic forms to the grammatical function of those forms serves as a necessary check on interpretation of dead languages, languages such as the biblical languages for which there are no native speakers.[151] But Talstra sounds a warning to exegetes and theologians. Schneider's analysis is linguistic analysis, not literary analysis.[152] Linguistic analysis informs literary analysis, but it does not constitute it. Talstra also states that Schneider's grammar does not transfer directly to poetic and prophetic literature.[153] However much Schneider's theory of the Biblical Hebrew verbal system applies to poetic and prophetic literature, it is agreed that his categories cannot be applied uncritically. Nevertheless, the basic opposition between *wayyiqtol* and *yiqtol* covers more of the Hebrew Bible than any previous theory. This is because it is based on distributional analysis and not on grammatical intuition. Schneider's view is not overwhelmed by a host of exceptions, and the few exceptions can be explained adequately.

Wolfgang Richter

In his work entitled *Grundlagen einer althebräischen Grammatik*, Richter addresses some of the basic issues of a linguistic grammar.[154] He defines language as a system of signs—a means of expression to which contents are attached.[155] The influence of Saussurean linguistics is evident throughout Richter's explanation of his methodology.[156] The main difference between Saussure and Richter is that Richter seeks a linguistics that is appropriate for the dead language of the Hebrew Bible.

According to Richter, the use of language in communication consists of a series of signs. The elements of a language have definite relations with one another.[157] Language has rules, and language has structure. Linguistic signs cannot be combined in just any random order. The connection of content with expression is also according to rules. This does not mean that the goal of text grammar is to construct "correct" rules for the language. Rather, the goal is to register the regularities and irregularities of the actual usage of the language.

Richter makes a proper distinction between spoken and written forms of language.[158] It cannot be assumed that they are the same. When it comes to the ancient Hebrew found in the Bible, there is no link to the speakers of the language; there is no one who can inform competently about the language. Biblical Hebrew is "dead."[159] There is also no competent hearer of the language. All that remains is the reader and the written text. The object of ancient Hebrew linguistics is the written text, not the situations of language participants; and the goal of ancient Hebrew linguistics is the understanding of texts passed down in the ancient Hebrew language.[160]

The significance of Richter's insight here can hardly be overstated. Biblical Hebrew cannot be treated as a living language. It cannot be treated as a spoken language. The Neogrammarians of the nineteenth century thought that they could reconstruct the living language of ancient Israel by means of the Biblical Hebrew texts. This reconstructed living language, not the written texts, became the object of study for them. Modern linguistics with its emphasis on spoken language has applied discourse analysis to the Hebrew Bible, but there is no access to ancient Hebrew discourse.

Universal laws, grammatical intuition, and analogies with spoken/living language are not appropriate for the dead language of the Hebrew Bible. Whatever else may be said about Richter's approach, this is certainly the right starting point. Biblical Hebrew requires textlinguistics, not discourse analysis; it requires distributional analysis, not the application of "correct" grammatical categories from Greek and Latin.

Key to Richter's approach is the distinction between the expression side (*Ausdrucksseite*) of the language, which is the object of grammar, and the content side (*Inhaltsseite*), which is the object of semantics.[161] Richter acknowledges that expression and content cannot be completely separated in a grammar, but he limits the content side in grammar to "function." "Function," as opposed to "meaning," is that which so regularly binds itself to a linguistic sign that it can be formalized in a rule.[162]

It may be asked at this point which comes first, the form or the function. Richter explains:

> The expression side is built out of a limited number of sign elements; its analysis is simple and unequivocal. Therefore, the description of the language begins with it and proceeds to the meaning of the function. With its representation it achieves a preliminary work for the description of the content side in semantics (author's translation).[163]

The simpler analysis of the expression side (i.e., the written forms) precedes conclusions about the complexities of function and meaning. This provides a firm basis for the necessary work of semantics. Procession from function to form, on the other hand, is an exercise in explanation of the known by the unknown.

Because Biblical Hebrew is a dead language, the written texts constitute the expression side. Description of the language proceeds from the expression side to the content side. Because Biblical Hebrew has no living informants, no one can be consulted about the meaning of the content side.[164]

Description of the expression side begins with the dissimilarity of the linguistic signs and their varying combinations.[165] The units that make up the text must be isolated before they can be described. This is not isolation according to function and meaning, but isolation according to formal characteristics. In the texts of the Hebrew Bible, the signs are found in a linear sequence, and they are separated by what Richter calls *Zwischenräume* ("spaces" or "gaps").[166] The "spaces" come only between words. Phrases, clauses, and larger units are not distinguished formally. Therefore, a text is initially understood as a series of words.[167]

The corresponding units of the expression side are to be grouped together so that they can be distinguished from the non-corresponding units. Position and distribution are the fundamental criteria for the isolation and categorization of morphemes (i.e., words or integral parts of words).[168] But beyond graphemes, morphemes, words, and word groups, a higher unit is assumed—the clause.[169] This is apparent from the fact that relations among words and word groups are not all of equal value. The lower units always connect to higher units: graphemes to morphemes, morphemes to words, words to word groups, word groups to clauses, clauses to clause chains, and clause chains to texts.

Richter labels the "regular" members of a clause "syntagmas." Syntagmas and clauses are to be classified according to kind. Within this classification, a hierarchy of relations emerges. Richter proposes the following levels:

Phoneme/Grapheme:	Phonology/Orthography
Morpheme with Lexeme/Logeme and Their Types:	Morphology
Word Groups and Their Types:	Morphosyntax
Clause with Syntagmas and Their Types:	Clause Theory
Clause Chains and Their Types:	Clause Syntax
(Text:	Literary Criticism)[170]

According to Richter, the clause is the central level for grammar. It has been suggested that certain constituents on the text level are regular enough for the inclusion of the text level in grammar.[171] In contrast to the clause level, however, the irregularities of the text level make it more appropriate for stylistics and literary analysis.

On each of the levels are found paradigmatic and syntagmatic relations for which the criteria are correspondence and opposition.[172] A grammatical unit either corresponds to or stands in opposition to another unit. The specific criterion for paradigmatic relations is substitution. For example, the slot "verbal predicate" can be filled by a limited number of related forms in Biblical Hebrew. The relations among these forms are observed in the language system (*langue*), but they do not occur in any realization (*parole*) of the language.[173] Only syntagmatic relations are realized.

Syntagmatic relations are those that occur in real texts. They can be observed in the use of the language. Syntagmatic relations consist between units of paradigmatic series; classes of paradigmatic relations can also be used for the syntagmatic relations.[174] The syntagmatic relations are thus more varied than the paradigmatic. The subject-verb relationship is an example of a syntagmatic relation, but syntagmatic relations can bind larger units even beyond the clause boundaries.[175]

Richter also speaks of the “form system” (*Gestaltsystem*), the analysis of which identifies what builds the boundaries between the units of the language.[176] This analysis has two important criteria: the order of the elements and what Richter calls the *Fügungspotenz* of the elements of a unit.[177] The *Fügungspotenz* is apparently “valency” or “power of attraction.” According to Richter, valency reflects the ranking order or hierarchical structure of the construction of the language.[178] An example of the Biblical Hebrew *Gestaltsystem* at work on the clause level is the importance of the occupant of first position. It has already been observed from Schneider’s grammar that this occupant determines the clause type. A nominal element in first position indicates a nominal clause (background). A verbal element in first position indicates a verbal clause (foreground). Clauses in which a verbal element stands out of first position create a sub-category (*Zusammengesetzte Nominalsätze*).

The isolation of a text into morphemes and graphemes/phonemes is formally possible. For Richter, the analysis and description of the text as a series of morphemes make possible the description and classification of the functions of the elements according to a general knowledge of the content.[179] This leads to the content side (*Inhaltsseite*) of the language. Morphemes are the smallest linguistic units that carry either functions (as grammatical morphemes) or meanings and functions (as lexical morphemes).[180]

Function concerns all linguistic signs and their relationships with one another. Grammatical functions also serve as syntagmatic relations.[181] Function is thus frequently formalized as a content element in the language with an effect on syntax. Function, however, is not always formalized, especially on the higher grammatical levels. This leads Richter to the recognition of two levels: (1) surface structure, which is provided by the relations of the expression side, and (2) deep structure, the abstract grammatical relations—especially the non-formalized ones.[182] The surface structure is the first level, and the deep structure is the second level. A word (e.g., “love”) classed grammatically as a noun in the surface structure might be classed semantically as an action (verb) in the deep structure. Functions are best determined not by a universal set of categories, but by a language-specific system of binary opposition.[183]

The distinction between function and meaning is not always clear. Often nouns and verbs are considered major content words, while prepositions, conjunctions, and adverbs are considered structure words. But lexical and grammatical morphemes are often combined. Thus, the meaning of a lexeme can influence the function of a grammatical morpheme.[184]

For Richter, the problem of the relationship between syntax and lexicon is of utmost importance on the clause level: "The syntactical lexicon classes determine the choice of words and influence the structure of the clause" (author's translation).[185] Beyond the clause is the question of how clauses are connected to one another. Clauses can also be classified according to function. These classifications correspond to word types (e.g., verbal clauses and nominal clauses).[186]

When it comes to semantics proper, meaning is not unlike function in that it stands in relation to the linguistic signs and participates on the levels provided by the expression side of the language.[187] Meanings are bound to lexical morphemes. These are further limited by elements of function. Therefore, analysis of content must include all the grammatical levels.[188] The two basic word classes for Biblical Hebrew are the noun and the verb. Of course, these can be subdivided further, but every element is either a nominal element or a verbal element. The task is to establish language-specific categories for the linguistic choices available to the language participants.[189] Beyond this is the realm of the lexicon. In Richter's view, matters of function and meaning relate to grammar only insofar as they help explicate the expression side of the language.

The most important classes of function are the lexical functions and the grammatical functions.[190] The many features of meaning of a lexical morpheme have little effect on the syntax. If a syntactical function is not formalized, however, it must be carried in the lexical morpheme.[191] On the other hand, grammatical morphemes are usually characterized more by syntactical function than by elements of meaning, although they can indicate lexical classes in connection with lexical morphemes.[192] Thus, grammatical morphemes are more syntactical than semantic in function, and lexical morphemes are more semantic than syntactical in function. Grammatical functions show the "attraction value" (*Fügungswert*) of words within word groups and of certain elements in the clause, while non-formalized grammatical functions on the clause level (i.e., phrases or whole clauses) can refer to lexical morphemes.[193]

Richter is confident that new linguistic methodology for Biblical Hebrew—apart from the uncontrolled assumptions of traditional grammar—can fill the void left by the lack of a living informant.[194] According to Richter, the task is to produce the competence of the primary language participants by description of the four levels: morphology, morphosyntax, clause theory, and clause syntax. The goal of a linguistic grammar of ancient Hebrew is the understanding of texts through the description of clauses.[195] It is not only preparatory for semantics, but also it is foundational for all literary criticism of the Hebrew Bible.[196]

In conclusion, the influence of Richter on the present study will be evident in the following chapter, but only to a certain degree. The relationship between the *Ausdrucksseite* and the *Inhaltsseite* is a complex subject. Nevertheless, three features of Richter's methodology are of particular value here: (1) the recognition of the general implications of dead language for a linguistic grammar, (2) the necessity of a procession from form to function and not vice versa, and (3) the primacy of distributional analysis of the formal features within the written texts.

Notes

[1]Gillian Brown and George Yule, *Discourse Analysis* (Cambridge: Cambridge University Press, 1983), 26.

[2]David Allan Dawson, *Text-Linguistics and Biblical Hebrew*, JSOTSup 177 (Sheffield: Sheffield Academic Press, 1994).

[3]Kirk E. Lowery, "The Theoretical Foundations of Hebrew Discourse Grammar," in *Discourse Analysis of Biblical Literature: What It Is and What It Offers*, ed. Walter R. Bodine (Atlanta: Scholars Press, 1995), 118.

[4]"By definition, text-external factors cannot occur in texts" (David McLain Carr, "Isaiah 40:1–11 in the Context of the Macrostructure of Second Isaiah," in *Discourse Analysis of Biblical Literature: What It Is and What It Offers*, ed. Walter R. Bodine (Atlanta: Scholars Press, 1995), 55.

[5]See Robert E. Longacre, *The Grammar of Discourse* (New York: Plenum, 1983).

[6]It may be added here that there is also considerable confusion between living language and dead language, as if linguists and grammarians were able to act as living informants of dead languages.

[7]Peter Cotterell and Max Turner, *Linguistics and Biblical Interpretation* (Downers Grove: InterVarsity, 1989), 230.

[8]The realm of pragmatics lies outside the control of the author and should not be considered as part of textlinguistics.

[9]"Offensichtlich bedeutet ‚Text' mehr und anderes als eine bloß linguistische Form oder Einheit. Das ging auch daraus hervor, daß der Begriff ‚Text' nicht auf sprachliche Phänomene beschränkbar war, sondern mit Erfolg überall dort angewandt wurde, wo gegliederte mehrheitliche Element-Komplexe mit einer daran gekoppelten übertragbaren Information bzw. Wirkung vorlagen: im Bereich der bildenden Kunst (cf. *M. Bense*, 1962), der Musik, des Tanzes etc." (Siegfried J. Schmidt, *Texttheorie* [Munich: Fink, 1973], 14).

[10]Robert-Alain de Beaugrande and Wolfgang Ulrich Dressler, *Introduction to Text Linguistics*, Longman Linguistics Library 26 (New York: Longman, 1981), 3–12.

[11]Intertextuality is included among the standards external to a text because it involves a text referring to an outside entity—another text; intertextuality is, however, quite different from the other external standards due to the fact that it remains in the world of texts.

[12]Schmidt, *Texttheorie*, 151–52.

[13]Francis I. Andersen, *The Sentence in Biblical Hebrew* (The Hague: Mouton, 1974), 21.

[14]Ibid.

[15]S. Bar-Efrat, "Some Observations on the Analysis of Structure in Biblical Narrative," *VT* 30 (1980): 155–56.

[16]Schmidt, *Texttheorie*, 150–51.

[17]Noam Chomsky, *Syntactic Structures*, 2d ed. (Berlin: Mouton de Gruyter, 2002), 100.

[18]Eep Talstra, "Hebrew Syntax: Clause Types and Clause Hierarchy," in *Studies in Hebrew and Aramaic Syntax*, ed. K. Jongeling, H. L. Murre-Van den Berg, and L. van Rompay (Leiden: Brill, 1991), 180.

[19]A. F. den Exter Blokland, *In Search of Text Syntax: Towards a Syntactic Text-Segmentation Model for Biblical Hebrew* (Amsterdam: VU University Press, 1995), 7.

[20]See Eep Talstra, ed., *Computer Assisted Analysis of Biblical Texts* (Amsterdam: Free University Press, 1989).

[21]"Ein Text ist eine sinnvolle (d. h. kohärente und konsistente) Abfolge sprachlicher Zeichen zwischen zwei auffälligen Kommunikationsunterbrechungen" (Harald Weinrich, *Tempus: Besprochene und erzählte Welt*, 6th new rev. ed. [Munich: Beck, 2001], 22); "Der Linguist *kann*, ausgehend von den Phonemen oder Merkmalen, größere Einheiten als den Satz konstruieren, und umgekehrt *kann* er, absteigend vom Text, die Segmentierung über den Satz hinaus weitertreiben, um kleinere Einheiten zu gewinnen" (ibid., 19).

[22]"Eine grammatische Beschreibung der Sprache, die über die Satzgrenzen hinausgeht und die Konstitution und die Abgrenzung von Texten zu erfassen sucht, hat seit ca. 1964 immer mehr Beachtung gefunden: 'Text-Linguistik'. Pronomina und andere Partikeln z.B. lassen sich in ihrer Funktion adaequat nur textlinguistisch beschreiben" (Wolfgang Schneider, *Grammatik des Biblischen Hebräischen*, 8th ed. [Munich: Claudius, 1993], 231, n. 1); Schneider's grammar, which was originally published in 1974, will be discussed in more detail in the latter part of this chapter.

[23]Alviero Niccacci, "On the Hebrew Verbal System," in *Biblical Hebrew and Discourse Linguistics*, ed. Robert D. Bergen (Dallas: SIL, 1994), 118.

[24]See Kevin J. Vanhoozer, *Is There a Meaning in This Text?* (Grand Rapids: Zondervan, 1998).

[25]Ferdinand de Saussure, *Cours de linguistique générale*, ed. Charles Bally and Albert Sechehaye (Paris: Payothèque, 1916).

[26]Ferdinand de Saussure, *Course in General Linguistics*, ed. Charles Bally and Albert Sechehaye, trans. and ann. Roy Harris (London: Duckworth, 1983; reprint, Chicago and La Salle: Open Court, 1986), 1–5.

[27]At the end of this discussion, Saussure also mentions the Neogrammarians who viewed language as "a product of the collective mind of a linguistic community" (ibid., 5).

[28]Ibid., 6.

[29]Ibid., 9.

[30]Ibid.

[31]Ibid., 13–14.

[32]Ibid., 14; Saussure gives dead language as an example of this, but texts written in what is now dead language do not constitute or provide access to the broader social product of a language system as such; therefore, dead language is more properly the realm of philology and textlinguistics.

[33]Ibid., 15.

[34]Ibid., 15–17.

[35]Ibid., 19.

[36]Ibid., 24.

[37]Ibid., 24–31.

[38]Ibid., 66.

[39]Ibid.

[40]Ibid., 67.

[41]Ibid., 67–69.

[42]James Barr, *The Semantics of Biblical Language* (Oxford: Oxford University Press, 1961; reprint, London: SCM, 1983), 235.

[43]Saussure, *Course*, 71–78.

[44]Ibid., 79–98.

[45]Ibid., 86.

[46]Ibid., 88.

[47]Ibid., 89.

[48]Ibid., 91.

[49]Ibid., 98.

[50]Ibid., 99.

[51]Ibid., 113.

[52]Ibid., 119; Roy Harris comments, "The essential feature of Saussure's linguistic sign is that, being intrinsically arbitrary, it can be identified only by contrast with coexisting signs of the same nature, which together constitute a structured system" (ibid., x).

[53]This has important implications for the evaluation of the standard Biblical Aramaic grammars in the first chapter of the present work; that is, the grammars that present the *qtl* and the *yqtl* as virtually interchangeable have failed to identify any basic opposition in the verbal system; thus, they have in effect rendered the Biblical Aramaic verbal system meaningless.

[54]Ibid., 121.

[55]Ibid.; "The whole depends on the parts, and the parts depend on the whole. That is why the syntagmatic relation between part and whole is just as important as the syntagmatic relation between one part and another" (ibid., 126).

[56]Ibid., 122.

[57]Ibid., 124.

[58]Ibid., 133–35.

[59]Ibid., 139.

[60]One well known example of confusion between synchronic linguistics and diachronic linguistics is popular etymology: "Analogy does not draw upon the substance of the signs it replaces. Popular etymology, on the contrary, reduces to an interpretation of the old form: it is the memory of the old form, confused though it may be, which is the point of departure for the distortion it undergoes" (ibid., 174); "*An analogical form is a form made in the image of one or more other forms according to a fixed rule*" (ibid., 160); that is, forms are "reinterpreted in terms of known forms," not according to unknown origin (ibid., 173).

[61]Ibid., 230.

[62]Ibid., 188.

[63]See, for example, the influence on Barr (*Semantics*, 1) of Saussure's demonstration that linguistic structure does not necessarily reflect the thought structure of a people group (Saussure, *Course*, 221–26).

[64]See J. L. Austin, *How to Do Things with Words*, 2d ed. (Cambridge: Harvard University Press, 1975).

[65]Schmidt, *Texttheorie*.

[66]Ibid., 10.

[67]Ibid.

[68]Ibid., 16.

[69]Ibid., 45; "Wer eine Sprache lernt, erwirbt dabei nicht nur die Regeln für die Verwendung eines Zeichensystems (= Verfahren sprachlicher Sinnkonstitution), sondern zugleich die Regeln sozialer Interaktion in einem komplexen verbalen und nichtverbalen Kommunikationsbereich" (ibid., 44).

[70]Ibid., 45.

[71]"Ein kommunikatives Handlungsspiel ist eine abgrenzbare Kommunikations ‚geschichte' [*sic*] bzw. eine zeitlich und räumlich begrenzbare Menge von Kommunikationsakten" (ibid., 46).

[72]Ibid., 46–49; a key component of this system is the thematic orientation of the communication acts.

[73]Ibid., 49.

[74]"Lexeme sind instruktionssemantisch gesehen zwar analytisch isolierbare, im System einer Sprache aber nie isoliert vorkommende Textkonstituenten; sie sind sprachsystematisch integriert in lexematischen Feldern (= Subsystemen eines Lexikons). Die Stellung des Lexems im lexematischen Feld definiert die Anwendungsmöglichkeiten eines Lexems: m. a. W. der Feld-Kontext weist dem Lexem seine generellen Funktionsmöglichkeiten in Texten zu, begrenzt und stabilisiert sie durch ein Geflecht rekurrent erprobter Anschließbarkeiten. Für den referentiellen Gebrauch von Lexemen folgt aus den bisher entwickelten Vorstellungen (cf. 4.1.): Nicht das einzelne Lexem bezieht sich auf eine außersprachliche Korrelatebene/auf Korrelate, sondern das jeweilige lexematische Feld ist interpretierbar als ein Komplex von Regeln (s. o.)/Instruktionen an Kommunikationspartner, *sich* in Kommunikationsakten in einer bestimmten Weise auf sprachliche und nicht-sprachliche Faktoren des kommunikativen Handlungsspiel bzw. des Kommunikationssystems insgesamt und auf die in ihm geltenden Wirklichkeitsmodelle *zu beziehen*" (ibid., 56); cf., componential/feature analysis.

[75]Ibid., 58–59.

[76]Ibid., 75.

[77]Ibid., 76.

[78]*Textsinn* is the potential for a communicative role, and *Textanweisung* is the realization of the communicative relevance of texts in communicative act games (ibid.).

[79]Ibid., 101–03.

[80]Ibid., 105.

[81]This is especially the case for dead languages for which there is access neither to the author nor to informants of the language; a reader cannot assume that anything about grammar/syntax, semantics, or pragmatics is shared.

[82]Ibid., 144.

[83]"Ein Text ist jeder geäußerte sprachliche Bestandteil eines Kommunikationsaktes in einem kommunikativen Handlungsspiel, der thematisch orientiert ist und eine erkennbare kommunikative Funktion erfüllt, d. h. ein erkennbares Illokutionspotential realisiert" (Ibid., 150).

[84]Ibid.

[85]Ibid., 153.

[86]Schmidt argues that the understanding of long texts and the ability to summarize texts are made possible by deep structure (ibid., 156).

[87]Ibid., 162–63.

[88]Edward Ullendorff, *Is Biblical Hebrew a Language?* (Wiesbaden: Harrassowitz, 1977).

[89]Ibid., 5.

[90]Ibid., 6.

[91]Ibid., 7, 14; out of about six hundred words in Biblical Aramaic, 291 are *hapax legomena* (ibid., 16).

[92]Ibid., 15–16; beyond vocabulary gaps, Ullendorff also observes grammatical gaps such as the dearth of second person feminine forms and syntactical gaps such as the lack of non-literary sentence structures (ibid., 14).

[93]Ibid., 7–11, 16–17; see, however, James Barr's conclusion that the Masoretes registered a tradition that was connected with earlier stages of the Hebrew language (James Barr, *Comparative Philology and the Text of the Old Testament* [Oxford: Oxford University Press, 1968; reprint, Winona Lake, Ind.: Eisenbrauns, 1987], 188–222).

[94]Ullendorff, *Biblical Hebrew*, 16.

[95]Ibid.

[96]E. Y. Kutscher, *A History of the Hebrew Language*, ed. Raphael Kutscher (Jerusalem: Magnes, 1982), 115.

[97]Ibid.

[98]Ibid., 115–16.

[99]Ibid., 148.

[100]Ibid.

[101]Ibid., 149–50.

[102]Ibid., 183.

[103]Ibid., 184.

[104]Ibid., 186–89.

[105]Ibid., 190.

[106]Ibid.

[107]Ibid., 191–92.

[108]Ibid., 193.

[109]Ibid., 193–94.

[110]Ibid., 193.

[111]Ibid., 294.

[112]Ibid., 196.

[113]Ibid., 244.

[114]Ibid., 298.

[115]Zdravko Stefanovic, *The Aramaic of Daniel in the Light of Old Aramaic*, JSOTSup 129 (Sheffield: JSOT, 1992), 16–17.

[116]Ibid., 106.

[117]Joseph A. Fitzmyer, *A Wandering Aramean: Collected Aramaic Essays*, SBL Monograph Series 25 (Missoula, Mont.: Scholars Press, 1979), 60.

[118]See J. A. Emerton, "New Evidence for the Use of *Waw* Consecutive in Aramaic," *VT* 44 (1994): 255–58.

[119]E.g., E. F. Kautzsch, *Grammatik des Biblisch-Aramäischen* (Leipzig: Vogel, 1884), 1; H. L. Strack, *Grammatik des Biblisch-Aramäischen* (Leipzig: Hinrich, 1905), 9.

[120]H. H. Rowley, *The Aramaic of the Old Testament* (London: Oxford University Press, 1929), 15.

[121]Franz Rosenthal, *A Grammar of Biblical Aramaic* (Wiesbaden: Harrassowitz, 1961), 6.

[122]See Rowley, *The Aramaic of the Old Testament*, 11–16.

[123]Fitzmyer, *Wandering Aramean*, 61.

[124]Klaus Beyer, *The Aramaic Language: Its Distribution and Subdivisions*, trans. John F. Healey (Göttingen: Vandenhoeck & Ruprecht, 1986), 19; see also Hans Bauer and Pontus Leander, *Grammaik des Biblisch-Aramäischen* (Halle: Niemeyer, 1927; 4th unrev. reprint, Hildesheim: Georg Olms, 1995), 13.

[125]Fitzmyer, *Wandering Aramean*, 61–62.

[126]Bauer and Leander, *Grammatik*, 8.

[127]"Doch einerseits lassen sich hier Erscheinungen einer weiteren Entwicklung, andererseits die Einflüsse der arabischen Sprache dieser beiden Völkerschaften in den aramäischen Schriftsprachen der Nabatäer und der Palmyrener feststellen, bei der letzteren auch eine Einwirkung des Ostaramäischen. Im Gebiet der östlichen aramäischen Dialekte wurden neue Schriftsprachen gebildet, die immer mehr im Gegensatz zur reicharamäischen Tradition die lokalen Sprach- und Schreibgewohnheiten bevorzugten" (Stanislav Segert, *Altaramäische Grammatik*, 3d ed. [Leipzig: Enzyklopädie, 1986], 50–51.)

[128]Ibid., 47.

[129]Ibid., 49.

[130]Bauer and Leander, *Grammatik*, 6–7.

[131]Fitzmyer, *Wandering Aramean*, 62.

[132]Segert, *Altaramäische Grammatik*, 55.

[133]Carl Brockelmann, *Grundriß der vergleichenden Grammatik der semitischen Sprachen*, vol. 1, *Laut- und Formenlehre* (Berlin: Reuther & Reichard, 1908; 4th reprint, Hildesheim: Georg Olms, 1999), 17–20.

[134]Beyer estimated in the mid-1980s that there were about three hundred thousand speakers of Modern Aramaic (Beyer, *The Aramaic Language*, 53).

[135]Ibid., 54.

[136]Fitzmyer, *Wandering Aramean*, 62.

[137]Kutscher, *A History of the Hebrew Language*, 296.

[138]Segert, *Altaramäische Grammatik*, 55; "Diese modernen Dialekte können nur selten für eine Erklärung der altaramäischen Phase verwendet werden" (ibid.).

[139]Schneider, *Grammatik*, 231, n. 1.

[140]Ibid., 160–61; nominal clauses can contain verbs; a compound nominal clause is any clause whose predicate consists of a whole clause (ibid.); John Cook ("The Semantics of Verbal Pragmatics: Clarifying the Roles of *Wayyiqtol* and *Weqatal* in Biblical Hebrew Prose," *JSS* 49 [2004]: 247–73) has argued that the foreground-background distinction is a psycholinguistic feature, but Schneider is concerned only to identify the correlation between the forms and their locations.

[141]E. F. Kautzsch, ed., *Gesenius' Hebrew Grammar*, trans. A. E. Cowley, 2d ed. (Oxford: Clarendon, 1910), 309.

[142]Ibid., 313.

[143]Schneider, *Grammatik*, 182.

[144]The *weqatal* represents about 20% of the forms in discourse.

[145]"'Opposition' nennt die Sprachwissenschaft das Verhältnis zweier sprachlicher Einheiten, die sich durch mindestens ein distinktives Merkmal voneinander unterscheiden, in ein und demselben sprachlichen Kontext auftreten können und sich—zumindest in diesem Kontext—wechselseitig ausschließen" (ibid., 182–83, n. 2).

[146]Ibid., 185, 188; the *weqatal* works like a *yiqtol* in discourse, or it points forward (ibid., 207); the *qatal* often sets and resets the stage for whole units (ibid., 186).

[147]See Michael B. Shepherd, "The Distribution of Verbal Forms in Biblical Aramaic," *JSS* 52 (2007), 236.

[148]E.g., ויקרא אלהים לאור יום ויקרא לחשך לילה.

[149]See John H. Sailhamer, *The Pentateuch as Narrative* (Grand Rapids: Zondervan, 1992), 56.

[150]Eep Talstra, "Text Grammar and Biblical Hebrew: The Viewpoint of Wolfgang Schneider," *JOTT* 5 (1992): 269.

[151]Ibid., 270.

[152]Ibid., 282–83.

[153]See, however, Diethelm Michel, *Tempora und Satzstellung in den Psalmen* (Bonn: Bouvier, 1960).

[154]Wolfgang Richter, *Grundlagen einer althebräischen Grammatik* (St. Ottilien: EOS, 1978), 3–39.

[155]Ibid., 4.

[156]See Hans Rechenmacher and Christo H. J. van der Merwe, "The Contribution of Wolfgang Richter to Current Developments in the Study of Biblical Hebrew," *JSS* 50 (2005): 59–82.

[157]Richter, *Grundlagen*, 4.

[158]"Man kann nicht von vornherein annehmen, daß die mündliche und schriftliche Form der Sprache voll kongruieren" (ibid., 5).

[159]"Die althebr. Sprache ist zudem "tot"; denn von den Sprachteilnehmern zur Zeit der Abfassung der Texte führt kein kontinuierliches Band bis zu denen in der Gegenwart. Es gibt also keinen kompetenten Sprecher des Althebr. mehr und somit keinen, der competent über diese Sprache informieren könnte ('Informant')" (ibid., 6).

[160]"Gegenstand der althebr. Sprachwissenschaft ist also nur ein Ausschnitt aus der sprachwissenschaftlichen Grammatik: der schriftliche Text. Dieser steht auch im Vordergrund gegenüber den (nicht mehr existierenden) Sprachteilnehmern und deren Situationen" (ibid., 8).

[161]Ibid., 11.

[162]Ibid.

[163]"Die Ausdrucksseite baut sich aus einer begrenzten Zahl von Zeichenelementen auf; ihre Analyse ist einfacher und eindeutiger. Deshalb setzt die Beschreibung der Sprache bei ihr an und schreitet zur Deutung der Funktion weiter. Mit deren Darstellung leistet sie eine Vorarbeit für die Beschreibung der Inhaltsseite in der Semantik" (ibid.).

[164]Ibid., 14.

[165]Ibid.

[166]Ibid., 15; this would not apply, for example, to ancient Greek texts written in *scriptio continua*.

[167]"Alte hebr. Urkunden haben nur Worttrenner; Wortgruppen und Sätze sind also durch Zeichensetzung nicht erkennbar. Da andere Kriterien für eine Satzabgrenzung noch nicht bestehen, ist auch eine Einteilung des Textes nach Sätzen noch nicht möglich. Der Satz ist somit nicht primär gegeben. Der Text wird deshalb zunächst als Wortreihe verstanden" (ibid.).

[168]Ibid., 16.

[169]Ibid., 18–19.

[170]Ibid., 21.

[171]Ibid., 20–21.

[172]Ibid., 21–22; cf., Saussure, *Course*, 121–25.

[173]Ibid., 22; i.e., texts must be compared with other texts; formal paradigms must be distinguished from functional paradigms since one form can have multiple functions.

[174]Ibid., 23.

[175]Ibid.

[176]Ibid.; see also idem, "Verbvalenz und Verbalsatz: Ein Beitrag zur syntaktischen Grundlegung einer atl. Literaturwissenschaft," *JNSL* 4 (1975): 61–69.

[177]Richter, *Grundlagen*, 24.

[178]Ibid.

[179]Ibid., 25

[180]Ibid., 28.

[181]Ibid.

[182]Ibid., 29.

[183]Ibid., 30.

[184]Ibid., 31.

[185]"Die syntaktischen Lexikonklasse bestimmen die Auswahl der Wörter und beeinflussen die Struktur des Satzes" (ibid.).

[186]Ibid.

[187]Ibid., 32; see also Martin T. Pröbstle, "The Advantages of W. Richter's Approach for a Lexical Description of Biblical Hebrew," *JNSL* 21, no. 1 (1995): 95–110.

[188]Richter, *Grundlagen*, 32.

[189]Ibid., 32–33.

[190]Ibid., 34.

[191]Ibid.

[192]Ibid.

[193]Ibid., 34–35.

[194]Ibid., 36–38.

[195]Ibid., 39.

[196]Ibid.

Chapter Three

Database Results and Extra-biblical Parallels

In the first chapter, it was observed that the standard grammars for Biblical Aramaic have not explained the language in language-specific categories. The use of tense, aspect, and *Aktionsart* has not led to the identification of any basic opposition between the *qtl* and the *yqtl*. A new foundation for the study of the verb in Biblical Aramaic was laid in chapter two—textlinguistic methodology. Key to any textlinguistic approach is distributional analysis, which is the subject of this chapter.

It is now time to present the research on the primary sources. First and foremost is the data from the Biblical Aramaic texts. Therefore, the first two sections of this chapter are devoted to an outline of the distributional database approach and to the results of the database analysis. The second half of the chapter shows parallels with extra-biblical Aramaic: Old Aramaic and Modern Aramaic, Egyptian Aramaic, the Targums, and even Aramaic-influenced texts. Distributional analysis is applied only to limited portions of extra-biblical Aramaic.

The Distributional Database Approach

"The goal of distributional analysis is to allow the data about the locations of the forms to speak."[1] This must be done apart from preconceived ideas about the functions and meanings of the forms. The method employed here begins with the creation of a database of tagged clauses. But what is a clause in Biblical Aramaic? Although the traditional definition of a clause is generally satisfactory, there are always exceptions to the rule that make any definition questionable. It does not seem reasonable, however, to abandon the clause altogether; thus, the provisional definition of Stanislav Segert will have to suffice: "A clause is a series of words, which contains a verbal or nominal predicate, which belongs to a subject" (author's translation).[2] A clause contains a "subject" and a "predicate," which in Biblical Aramaic means that a single verb can constitute a clause. There are two main types of clauses in Biblical Aramaic: the verbal clause and the nominal clause. The verbal clause is of immediate interest here, although the nominal clause is not unimportant.

Through the development of multiple kinds of databases for Biblical Aramaic, the present author has found that an indiscriminate tagging of clauses can be quite misleading.[3] For this reason, only the clauses on the main plane of the narration or discourse are entered into the database. Clauses off the main plane (relative/attributive, temporal, causal, conditional, subject, object, purpose, etc.), in a manner similar to prepositional phrases (adverbs and attributes), constitute nominal elements (nouns, adjectives, and adverbs). A clause that stands as a subject or an object is really only part of a larger clause. A clause that modifies a noun or a verb is secondary to the main level of the clause. Only a focused analysis of the primary verbal forms on the main plane of complete grammatical units can give insight into the heart of the verbal system.

For example, the three verbs in the three clauses of Dan 2:4b are all on the main plane of the discourse: "Live," "Tell," and "We will declare." In Dan 2:5b, however, the main clauses are preceded by a conditional clause marked by הֵן ("If you do not make known to me the dream and its interpretation").[4] This clause is not a complete unit. It only serves to modify or put a condition on the verbs in the main clauses: "You will be made into limbs" and "Your houses will be set into a rubbish heap." Another example is the content clause in Dan 2:8a. The king says, "Truly I know that you are buying time." The main clause is "I know." The clause that begins with דִּי ("that you are buying time") only indicates the content of what the king knows. One of the most notorious types of clauses that occur off the main plane is the relative or attributive clause. In Dan 2:24a, the main clause is "Daniel went in to Arioch." What follows is nothing more than a description of Arioch: "whom the king appointed to destroy the wise men of Babylon." This clause is basically an adjective. It cannot be used as data for the primary uses of the verbal forms. Many more examples could be multiplied here, but all the specific questions that pertain to this aspect of the database are addressed in the commentary of the fourth chapter.

A number of database approaches have been outlined for Biblical Hebrew, including those of Wolfgang Richter and Eep Talstra. The following outline is an adaptation of John Sailhamer's approach to Biblical Hebrew narrative.[5] Sailhamer seeks a new system of organization for "the storage and retrieval of relevant information beyond the level of morphology and inner-clausal relationships."[6]

The first clause constituent to be marked is the presence (coordination) or absence (apposition) of the *waw*.[7] This is not the presence or absence of a *waw* anywhere within a clause. Rather, what is marked is whether or not a *waw* stands at the beginning of a clause. The same is true for the second clause constituent—the presence or absence of *edayin*. This constituent does not play a role in Biblical Hebrew, but it is quite prominent in Biblical Aramaic. Some grammarians consider *edayin* to be an adverb,[8] while others take it to be a conjunction.[9] Whatever the case may be, a judgment on the function of *edayin* is held in reserve for the time being. Like *waw*, however, it does seem to play a role in the function of the clause at higher levels. With the possible exception of Ezra 5:16b, it is noteworthy that *waw* and *edayin* never occur together at the beginning of a clause. This initially suggests that *edayin* functions more in the role of a conjunction than in that of an adverb.

The third clause constituent is the occupant of first position. A *waw* or an *edayin* at the beginning of a clause is not a "syntagma" occupying first position; that is, *waw* and *edayin* are not nuclear members of a clause.[10] First position is marked for whether or not it is occupied by a verbal form, and if so the type of verbal form is indicated (*qtl* or *yqtl*). If the clause contains a verbal form out of first position, then it is tagged as in the following example: "x + *qtl*." This does not necessarily indicate that the verbal form is in second position. It only indicates that first position is not occupied by a verbal form and that a verbal form occurs outside of first position. Clauses without a verbal form are marked "nc" for "nominal clause."[11]

Because of the supposed use of the participle as a so-called "verbal predicate" in Biblical Aramaic, the fourth clause constituent is the presence or absence of a participle. But because the participle is technically a verbal adjective, its clauses are marked "nc."[12] This raises the question of what to do with periphrastic constructions in which a verb of being is combined with a participle. One option is to mark the verbal form as the third clause constituent and the participle as the fourth clause constituent. Another option is to mark the entire periphrastic construction as the third clause constituent.

The next category to be tagged is not a clause constituent, but a label for the clause type. There are at least two, and perhaps three, types of clauses in Biblical Aramaic that correspond to the clause types in Biblical Hebrew.

Alviero Niccacci provides a simple, textlinguistic account of the clause types in Biblical Hebrew:

> A sentence that begins with a finite verb form is verbal; any other kind of sentence is nominal. If a sentence contains a finite verb in second position, it is a compound nominal clause; if it does not contain any finite verb form, it is a simple nominal clause. The compound nominal clause and the simple nominal clause basically have the same function.[13]

Gesenius' Hebrew Grammar defines the compound sentence as "[e]very sentence, the subject or predicate of which is itself a full clause."[14] According to this view, a sentence does not require a verb in order to be compound. The following example is given from Nah 1:3: יהוה בסופה דרכו ("the Lord—in the storm is his way").[15] Niccacci's view is closer to that of the Arab grammarians, which was held in previous editions of Gesenius' grammar.[16]

Niccacci's explanation of clause types is easily transferable to Biblical Aramaic because it is based not on what constitutes the subject and the predicate, but on what occupies first position. There is, however, more than one way to indicate what Niccacci calls a "compound nominal clause."[17] Any clause that contains a finite verbal form can be called verbal, if the verb is not preceded by its subject. If the verb is preceded by its subject, the clause is an inverted verbal clause.[18] Inverted verbal clauses and other verbal clauses whose verbs are out of first position are compound nominal clauses in Niccacci's terminology. In the present database, the distinction between verbal clauses whose verbs are in first position and verbal clauses whose verbs are out of first position does not have to be made in the labeling of the clause type. It has already been made in the marking of the third clause constituent (e.g., the difference between "*qtl*" and "x + *qtl*"). Any "x + *qtl* or *yqtl*" clause is a compound nominal clause. All that remains is the indication of whether or not the subject precedes the verb. This can be done with the label "inverted" for the clause type. As for nominal clauses, any clause that does not contain a finite verbal form can be called nominal.

It is only appropriate to acknowledge the literary nature of the biblical texts and their representation of reality.[19] Therefore, Sailhamer tags what Elisabeth Gülich and Wolfgang Raible call "levels of communication" (*Ebenen der Kommunikation*).[20] This is recognition, along with Siegfried Schmidt, of the communicative function of texts. The most basic levels are narration and discourse, but there are six levels in all within the Biblical

Aramaic corpus.[21] Level one is narration (e.g., Ezra 6:13–18), level two is discourse (e.g., Dan 2:36–44), level three is narration within discourse (e.g., Dan 4:1–5), level four is reported discourse (e.g., Dan 7:17–18), level five is narration within reported discourse (e.g., Dan 4:7–11a2), and level six is reported discourse within reported discourse (e.g., Dan 4:11a3–14a2). The communicative function of texts is significant for the treatment of written texts as communicative acts.[22] Levels of communication are text-immanent categories. A full presentation of the clause tagging is provided in the appendix, but for quick reference a small sample is given here:[23]

Verse	**Waw**	**Edayin**	**Clause**	**Ptc**	**Type**	**Nar/Dis**	**Level**
da02:04b1	-	-	x+impv	-	v	dis	2
da02:04b2	-	-	impv	-	v	dis	2
da02:04b3	+	-	x+yqtl	-	v	dis	2
da02:05a1	-	-	nc	+	n	nar	1
da02:05a2	+	-	nc	+	n	nar	1
da02:05b1	-	-	x+yqtl	-	v	dis	2
da02:05b2	+	-	x+yqtl	-	i	dis	2
da02:06a1	+	-	x+yqtl	-	v	dis	1
da02:06b1	-	-	x+impv	-	v	dis	2
da02:07a1	-	-	qtl	-	v	nar	1
da02:07a2	+	-	nc	+	n	nar	1
da02:07b1	-	-	x+yqtl	-	i	dis	2
da02:07b2	+	-	x+yqtl	-	v	dis	2
da02:08a1	-	-	nc	+	n	nar	1
da02:08a2	+	-	nc	+	n	nar	1
da02:08a3	-	-	nc	+	n	dis	2
da02:09a1	-	-	nc	-	n	dis	2
da02:09a2	+	-	x+qtl	-	v	dis	3
da02:09b1	-	-	x+impv	-	v	dis	2
da02:09b2	+	-	yqtl	-	v	dis	2
da02:10a1	-	-	qtl	-	v	nar	1
da02:10a2	+	-	nc	+	n	nar	1
da02:10a3	-	-	nc	-	n	dis	2
da02:11a1	+	-	nc	-	n	dis	2
da02:11a2	+	-	nc	-	n	dis	2
da02:12a1	-	-	x+qtl	-	i	nar	1
da02:12a2	+	-	qtl	-	v	nar	1
da02:12b1	+	-	qtl	-	v	nar	1
da02:13a1	+	-	x+qtl	-	i	nar	1
da02:13a2	+	-	nc	+	n	nar	1
da02:13b1	+	-	qtl	-	v	nar	1

This portion is fairly straightforward. The only question that might arise is the indication of communication level three at Dan 2:9a2. Narration within discourse does not have to be an entire story. It can consist of a single *qtl* within discourse. In this case, the king narrates or recounts the Chaldeans' plan of deception. Examples such as these will be discussed in more detail in the commentary of the fourth chapter.

The Results

Out of 643 clauses in Biblical Aramaic, 365 clauses begin with a *waw*. Only 52 clauses begin with *edayin*. The percentages for these data are presented in Table 1.[24] Although *edayin* is less frequent than *waw*, its concentration in a passage like Daniel 6 is noteworthy. Out of 63 clauses in Daniel 6, *edayin* stands at the beginning of 10 (16%). Such a low number or percentage may seem to be of little significance at first, but these 10 are distributed somewhat evenly from verse 4 through verse 26. This is not unlike the use of "*waw* + *qtl*" in Ezra 6:13–18.[25] From these data, *edayin* looks more like a conjunction than an adverb.[26] That is, its role is to join clauses together in a narrative sequence. Having said this, the *waw* is clearly the more dominant of the two. Special insight into the Aramaic verb can be gained from the fact that the sequence of "*waw* + *qtl*" in Ezra 6:13–18 is continued in Hebrew by a *wayyiqtol* in Ezra 6:19.

Out of 643 clauses, 270 are verbal, 215 are nominal, and 158 are inverted. The percentages for these data are presented in Table 2. 296 clauses are compound clauses in which a *qtl* or *yqtl* occurs outside of first position. A *qtl* or *yqtl* is in first position for 104 clauses. The imperative occurs outside of first position in 18 out of 28 clauses. Minus the clauses that have periphrastic constructions with *itai*, 134 of 215 nominal clauses have at least one participle. There are 37 clauses in which a participle is combined in periphrastic construction with *itai* or with a verb of being.[27]

Table 1: Distribution of *Waw* and *Edayin*

Constituent	Presence	Absence
Waw	57%	43%
Edayin	8%	92%

Table 2: Distribution of Clause Types

Clause Type	Percentage
Verbal	42%
Nominal	33%
Inverted	25%

So-called verbs of being are counted as verbal forms in this database. Their clauses are verbal or inverted, not nominal. Regardless of their meaning, *qtl* and *yqtl* of הוא (or הוה) are verbs in terms of form. This database is a registration of forms, not meanings. Tamar Zewi considers clauses with finite verbs of being to be nominal.[28] For Zewi, verbs of being are not predicates; therefore, clauses with verbs of being are nominal clauses since "[n]ominal sentences do not have verbal predicates."[29] This understanding of what makes a clause nominal is based on what occupies the predicate position. It is not based on what occupies first position. It is also not based on the presence or absence of a conjugated verbal form. A verb of being can be called a copula, a linking verb, or a verb of incomplete predication, but when it comes to formal distribution it is simply a verbal form.[30]

Biblical Aramaic displays a somewhat freer word order than Biblical Hebrew. According to Zdravko Stefanovic, the free word order of the Aramaic of Daniel is eastern and closer to the Akkadian of the bilingual Tell Fakhriyah inscription than to the Aramaic of the same: "The only other OA [Old Aramaic] texts that show this word order are the documents from the 'transitional period,' in which they are merging into OfA [Official Aramaic]."[31] In a study of Egyptian Aramaic texts spanning the fifth century B.C. (e.g., Elephantine), Takamitsu Muraoka and Bezalel Porten also note a free word order: "It is in the nominal clause that the word-order variation indicates some significant functional opposition, which is rather rarely a factor in the verbal clause."[32] Although "[t]he verb often occupies the initial slot" in a verbal clause,[33] the verb-final position is not entirely uncommon:

> This verb-final position, which contradicts the classical Semitic word-order VSO, has generally been attributed to a foreign influence, viz. Akkadian on one hand, which in turn is said to be ultimately influenced by Sumerian, a non-Semitic language, and Persian on the other, also non-Semitic. However, in view of a substantial number of cases in which the verb occupies a non-initial position, it is more accurate to speak of a free word-order in our idiom.[34]

In a study of the language of the *Genesis Apocryphon*, E. Y. Kutscher argues that the syntax of the Qumran scroll is more Semitic than Biblical Aramaic partly because it adheres more to the verb-subject word order.[35]

Modern Aramaic also prefers the subject before the verb. This has been observed in two separate studies by Geoffrey Khan and Robert Hoberman. Their findings in two different dialects of Modern Aramaic coincide with the major changes that have taken place in the Aramaic verb from the ancient Aramaic texts to the modern language. These changes will be discussed in the latter part of this chapter. Geoffrey Khan, in his recent grammar of Neo-Aramaic, states, "When the subject is a full nominal, it normally comes before the verb."[36] Likewise, Robert Hoberman observes, "SVO is statistically the most common order."[37]

Does all of this mean that the subject-verb word order should not be labeled "inverted" for Biblical Aramaic? This is perhaps the case for clauses that have an explicit subject apart from the verbal form. But Biblical Aramaic has 112 more verbal clauses—clauses in which the verb precedes the subject or in which no separate subject is mentioned—than inverted clauses. The word order may be freer, but the subject-verb word order still shows in some way an inversion of what is most common. Therefore, the label "inverted" is retained here.

As noted in the previous section, Biblical Aramaic has a remarkable diversity of communication levels. Table 3 shows the percentage of clauses for each communication level. A glance at the distribution of communication levels reveals that narration (level one) and narration within discourse (level three) have the majority (65%) of Biblical Aramaic clauses. This corresponds to the total number of *qtl* forms (265) in contrast to the total number of *yqtl* forms (137).[38]

Table 3: Distribution of Communication Levels

Level	Percentage of Clauses
1. Narration	34%
2. Discourse	22%
3. Narration in discourse	31%
4. Reported discourse	8%
5. Narration in reported discourse	3%
6. Reported discourse in reported discourse	2%

Table 4: Distribution of Verbal Forms in Narration and Discourse

Levels	*Qtl*	*Yqtl*	Impv	Nc
Levels One, Three, and Five	61%	6%	0%	33%
Levels Two, Four, and Six	0%	53%	13%	34%

Out of 435 clauses that contain some form of narration (levels one, three, and five), 264 clauses have *qtl* as the primary verbal form, 26 have *yqtl*, and 145 are nominal with or without a participle.[39] Out of 208 clauses that contain either discourse or reported discourse (levels two, four, and six), 110 clauses have *yqtl* as the primary verbal form, 28 have an imperative, and 70 are nominal clauses with or without a participle. Thus, in terms of distribution, the *qtl* is the primary verbal form for narration; the *yqtl* is the primary verbal form for discourse; and the nominal clause with or without a participle is secondary for both narration and discourse (see Tables 4 and 5).

It may be recalled from the second chapter that this distribution of verbal forms bears a remarkable resemblance to the distribution of verbal forms in Biblical Hebrew. Wolfgang Schneider has estimated that the *wayyiqtol* constitutes about 75% of the verbal forms in Biblical Hebrew narration, while the *yiqtol* and *weqatal* represent 2%.[40] This corresponds to the percentages for levels one, three, and five in Biblical Aramaic; 61% of the forms are *qtl*, and 6% of the forms are *yqtl*. Schneider has also estimated that 50% of the forms in discourse are *yqtl* and that 5% of the forms are *wayyiqtol*.[41] This corresponds to the percentages for levels two, four, and six in Biblical Aramaic; 53% of the forms are *yqtl*, and 0% of the forms are *qtl*. The *qatal* is a secondary form occurring with moderate consistency in both narration (22%) and discourse (28%).[42] This corresponds to the nominal clause in Biblical Aramaic with or without the participle: levels one, three, and five are 33% nominal clauses; levels two, four, and six are 34%.

Table 5: Distribution of Verbal Forms among the Communication Levels

Level	*Qtl*	*Yqtl*/Impv	Nc
1. Narration	60%	1%	39%
2. Discourse	0%	64%	36%
3. Narration in discourse	64%	10%	26%
4. Reported discourse	0%	71%	29%
5. Narration in reported discourse	32%	21%	47%
6. Reported discourse in reported discourse	0%	77%	23%

It has already been established in the first chapter that the opposition between *qtl* and *yqtl* is not based on tense (past versus future), aspect (perfect versus imperfect), or *Aktionsart*. Now it is apparent from distributional analysis that the linguistic opposition between *qtl* and *yqtl* is based on the opposition between narration and discourse. The verbal clauses present the foreground of the action. The verbal clauses with *qtl* present the foreground of some form of narration. The verbal clauses with *yqtl* present the foreground of some form of discourse. Thus, Biblical Aramaic has a primary verbal form for narration (*qtl*) and a primary verbal form for discourse (*yqtl*).

The nominal clause with or without a participle—much like the nominal clause or "x + *qatal*" clause in Biblical Hebrew—presents the background of the action in both narration and discourse. Distributional analysis does not support the theory that the participle is a primary verbal form in Biblical Aramaic. But the participle does appear to be primary in poetry as a verbal adjective. Stefanovic observes:

> In contrast to Ezra, the Aramaic part of Daniel has several short poetic prayers or hymns of praise. They are scattered evenly through the entire Aramaic text: 2.20–23, 3.28, 3.31–33, 4.31–32 and 6.27–28. Almost all of them, after an introduction, open with praise for the beneficence of God. The succession of participles, noted by Sasson in the beginning of the inscription [Stefanovic refers to the Tell Fakhriyah inscription], is parallel to what one finds in DA [Aramaic of Daniel]. There are four participles in this section of the inscription. In DA texts, the succession of active participles used in the same way and for the same purpose is striking. Here I count only those describing God's activity: five are found in Daniel's praise-hymn (2.21–22), five in Darius's (6.27–28) and three in Nebuchadnezzar's (4.31–34).[43]

This use of the participle, however, does not appear to be language-specific. Hermann Gunkel noted this phenomenon in Hebrew and in several other languages.[44]

Knowledge of the *qtl-yqtl* or narration-discourse opposition can help to disambiguate a text in which the communication levels are more complex. For instance, Dan 4:25 reads as follows: כלא מטא על נבוכדנצר מלכא. If this is understood as a continuation of the reported discourse of Daniel, then it will be rendered in English: "Everything has come upon Nebuchadnezzar the king." But if the *qtl* is interpreted as the verbal form of narration, then it will be rendered: "Everything happened to Nebuchadnezzar the king."

A clue to the basic correctness of the correlation made here between *qtl-yqtl* and narration-discourse is the fact that it does not have a great deal of "cash value." That is, it is more preventative than anything. Notorious are the sermons and commentaries that exploit tense, aspect, and *Aktionsart* in the service of abusive interpretations, which the verbal forms were never meant to bear. This situation is no less real for Biblical Aramaic than it is for Biblical Hebrew and New Testament Greek, although less preachers and scholars are familiar enough with Aramaic to venture into such interpretations.

The *qtl-yqtl*/narration-discourse opposition is aligned with the linguistic axiom that ideas are not communicated on the word level alone. Ideas are communicated at the clause level and beyond. Just as interpretations cannot rest entirely on the meaning of a single noun, so they cannot be built entirely on a perceived nuance of a verbal form. The theory of the Biblical Aramaic verbal system proposed here is not a source for hermeneutical "howlers." Rather, it is a solid textlinguistic foundation for the interpretation of larger units of text.

The number of possible anomalies or exceptions to the *qtl-yqtl*/narration-discourse opposition is remarkably low. Such "exceptions" are to be expected in the study of any language. Indeed, a theory that eradicated all exceptions would be quite suspect. The only significant matter that demands attention in Biblical Aramaic is the percentage of clauses (6%) on levels one, three, and five in which a *yqtl* is the verbal form. The 26 *yqtl* forms for which this is the case is a meager number, but why is the *qtl* not employed in these instances?

Bauer and Leander view the *yqtl* in narration as secondary to the main narrative action ("nicht ein Hauptmoment der Erzählung").[45] This appears to be confirmed by the relatively large number of inverted clauses in this group: 16 out of 26. The *yqtl* in narration functions as background like the nominal clause with or without a participle. That is, the *yqtl* in narration, like the nominal clause with or without a participle, seems to be used for description, establishment, and staging. It does not carry the narration. Biblical Aramaic narration never consists of a significant string of *yqtl* forms. Rather, *yqtl* forms in narration usually occur in isolated pairs (Dan 4:2; 5:21; 7:10, 28) or in isolated groups (Dan 4:8–9, 30–31; 7:14–16).[46] Some of the forms even appear to be "fixed" (Dan 4:2, 16; 5:6; 7:15, 28). The root *bhl* never occurs as a *qtl* in Biblical Aramaic, as if prevented by some sort of linguistic convention.

All of the *yqtl* forms in narration can be explained as descriptions of situations rather than advancements of narration. A few examples will suffice here, and the remainder of the occurrences will be addressed in the commentary of the fourth chapter. In Dan 5:2, it is narrated that Belshazzar and those with him "were drinking" (ישתון) in the vessels that Nebuchadnezzar brought from the temple in Jerusalem. But in Dan 5:23 the same situation is described with the plural participle שתין ("drinking"). Belshazzar's drinking is described in Dan 5:1 also with a participle (שתה). Thus, the *yqtl* form in Dan 5:2 looks like a functional equivalent to the participle. When the advancement of the narration begins in Dan 5:3–4, *qtl* forms are employed: "they brought in" (היתיו), "and they drank" (ואשתיו), "they drank" (אשתיו), "and they praised" (ושבחו).

The same parallel usage of *yqtl* and participle occurs in Dan 7:10: "A river of fire was flowing (ptc) and going out (ptc) from before him; a thousand thousands were serving (*yqtl*) him, and ten thousand ten thousands were standing (*yqtl*) before him." This describes a scene. The continuation of the narration from Dan 7:9a occurs in Dan 7:10b with *qtl* forms: "The judgment sat (*qtl*), and books were opened (*qtl*)." These examples argue in favor of the same usage of the *yqtl* in Dan 6:20: "Then the king arose (*yqtl*) at dawn in the daylight, and he went out (*qtl*) in haste to the den of lions." The *yqtl* sets the stage for the main action expressed in the *qtl*.

When all is said and done, there is little from these 26 occurrences of *yqtl* in narration to suggest an alteration to the thesis that the *qtl* is the primary form for narration and that the *yqtl* is the primary form for discourse. If anything these occurrences strengthen the view that the nominal clause (with or without a participle) and its functional equivalents are secondary (i.e., background).

Parallels

This sampling of extra-biblical Aramaic is intended to be representative and not exhaustive. The texts in this section are from a wide variety of sources whose Aramaic stands in a close relationship to Biblical Aramaic. The subsection on Aramaic-influenced texts is primarily devoted to Ecclesiastes, which is obviously neither Aramaic nor extra-biblical. What emerges from these texts is a striking parallel to the results from the Biblical Aramaic database: the *qtl* is the primary verbal form for narration; the *yqtl* is the primary verbal form for discourse; and the nominal clause with or without a participle is secondary in narration and discourse.

Old Aramaic and Modern Aramaic

Old Aramaic and Modern Aramaic are grouped together here because they contribute the least in terms of parallels to the verbal system of Biblical Aramaic. The amount of extant Old Aramaic is not very extensive, and Modern Aramaic is too far removed from the Official Aramaic stage.

Segert comments that the multi-lingual milieu (Babylonian, Assyrian, Ugaritic, Phoenician, Hebrew, and Arabic) in which Aramaic developed had its effect on the Aramaic language as a whole and on the Aramaic verbal system in particular: "Also the drastic simplification of the Aramaic verbal system may be viewed as a result of an attempt to come to terms with a foreign system" (author's translation).[47] He gives one example from the early Aramaic dialect of Hamat in which the influence of Hebrew or Canaanite can be seen in the use of the "imperfect consecutive."[48]

J. A. Emerton states that the ninth-century inscription from Zkr, king of Hamat, is the only place where a "*waw* consecutive" construction in Aramaic has been widely recognized.[49] He suggests that the newly discovered (1993) ninth-century inscription from Tell Dan may also provide evidence for this construction in Aramaic: "despite the damage to the inscription, it is difficult to see how the verbs in the imperfect after *waw* could be understood other than as narrative verbs in past time."[50]

Victor Sasson has been one of the most enthusiastic scholars about the use of the so-called "*waw* consecutive" in Aramaic. The article in which Sasson first proposed his theory for this usage provides brief comments on the extant Old Aramaic texts: texts from Sefire, the Barhadad inscription, inscriptions from Zinjirli and Barrakib, the Tell Fakhriyah inscription, the Zkr inscription, and the Tell Dan inscription.[51] According to Sasson, only the Zkr inscription and the Tell Dan inscription contain any real narration of past events. These are also the only two texts in which are possible examples of the "*waw* consecutive." It is significant that both of these inscriptions come from the same century (i.e., the ninth century B.C.).

Sasson believes that the "*waw* consecutive" may have been somewhat normal in Old Aramaic texts for which the form was appropriate. His thesis is as follows:

> In the Zakkur and Tell Dan inscriptions (as well as in the Moabite inscription), and also in archaic Biblical Hebrew texts [e.g., Exod 15; Deut 32; Judg 5], the *waw* consecutive with the imperfect is used in contexts of war and war-related events. It

> appears therefore that the *waw* consecutive form, as a linguistic or literary feature, originally emerged in some North-West Semitic languages possibly for the purpose of recounting war/epic/heroic acts, and some other acts connected with them.[52]

The use of the "*waw* consecutive" is scant in Aramaic and Hebrew texts from the tenth and ninth centuries B.C. The form is then pervasive in Biblical Hebrew narration from the eighth century B.C. through the sixth century B.C., only to show a consistent decline in usage from that point.[53] This does not explain, however, why the form never became pervasive in Official Aramaic such as the Aramaic of the Bible. The verbal form of narration in Biblical Aramaic is the *qtl*, not the "*waw* consecutive."

In response to Sasson, T. Muraoka and M. Rogland prefer to view the alleged examples of the "*waw* consecutive" in the Tell Dan and Zkr inscriptions as instances of a *waw* followed by a *yqtl* preterite.[54] This debate is not likely to be settled anytime soon due to the fact that the hard morphological datum of a geminated prefix is neither confirmed nor denied by the texts, since they lack indication of vocalization. Emerton thus walks a middle line between Sasson and Muraoka-Rogland: "The examples of *waw* with the prefix conjugation in Aramaic and the *waw* consecutive construction in Hebrew both have their origin in the preterite, which once existed in North-West Semitic as well as in Accadian, and it seems unjustified to draw a sharp distinction between the phenomena in Aramaic and Hebrew."[55]

As intriguing as this discussion has been, it remains inconclusive. Because the inscriptions of Old Aramaic are in many ways very different from the Aramaic texts of the Bible, and because the so-called "*waw* consecutive" clearly plays no role in Biblical Aramaic, it turns out that the discussion adds little to the understanding of the verbal system of Biblical Aramaic. If the "*waw* consecutive" did exist in Old Aramaic, then it is noteworthy that subsequent stages of the Aramaic language employed the *qtl* as a narration form instead, while Biblical Hebrew continued to use the "*waw* consecutive" for narration on a large scale. For the time being, research in this area awaits future discoveries of Aramaic texts with examples of the "*waw* consecutive."

Modern Aramaic's potential for insight into the verbal system of Biblical Aramaic is even less than that of Old Aramaic.[56] According to Hoberman, it is a pitfall to describe Neo-Aramaic forms in terms of their ancient Aramaic precursors: "A Neo-Aramaic verb has a very large number of inflectional forms."[57] The verb in Modern Aramaic has been influenced by a number of modern languages unknown to speakers of ancient Aramaic. Hoberman labels the five Modern Aramaic stems as follows: O is for Order, J is for Jussive, P is for Preterite, Pt is for Perfect, and C is for Continuous. The relationship of these stems to the older Aramaic forms is striking:

> The older Aramaic forms from which these arose are: O-imperative; J-active participle; P-passive participle, absolute state; Pt-passive participle, determinate state; C-verbal noun. The old perfect and imperfect have disappeared entirely.[58]

The old "perfect" and "imperfect" have disappeared entirely. This is about as far removed from the Biblical Aramaic verbal system as Modern Aramaic could be.

The Modern Aramaic verbal system is built not on the old *qtl* and *yqtl*, but on the participle.[59] Carl Brockelmann has made the same observation:

> Both old Semitic tenses are relinquished here entirely and are replaced by new constructions out of the participle, for which beginnings are found already in old Syriac. The vocabulary stock of these dialects is influenced naturally very strongly by the neighboring, widely more powerful languages of the Arabs, Kurds and Turks (author's translation).[60]

Thus, the participial form, which was supposedly making its way into the Aramaic language as a verbal predicate by the time of Biblical Aramaic, has now become the dominant form.[61] It is not entirely clear why this is the case. Perhaps the participle lends itself more to the spoken language than the literary *qtl-yqtl* opposition. The influence of foreign languages, however, has probably been the greatest factor in the creation of this situation.

Egyptian Aramaic

In their assessment of Egyptian Aramaic texts spanning the fifth century B.C. (e.g., Elephantine), Muraoka and Porten reveal their underlying presuppositions about the verb:

> Our basic assumption is that the distinction between the perfect and the imperfect, the latter excluding the jussive and the energic, is essentially that of tense: the former indicates an action already undertaken or a state which once prevailed, thus preterital, and the latter an action yet to be undertaken or a state which will, may or should prevail, thus roughly future.[62]

This description of the verb in Egyptian Aramaic, which is based on tense, aspect, and *Aktionsart*, is reminiscent of the description of the verb in the standard Biblical Aramaic grammars. The question is whether their "basic assumption" is derived from or brought to the texts.

It is hard to avoid the impression that fresh reevaluation of the verb is not the top priority for Muraoka and Porten. They have accepted the traditional explanation of the Semitic verb and have moved on to other matters. The problem is that the same set of difficulties that was addressed in the first chapter is present here as well. Thus, a perfect can be a simple past, a past perfect, or a future perfect among other things.[63] An imperfect indicates among other things a state or an event in the future.[64]

The grammar of Muraoka and Porten is the fruit of foreign grammatical intuition, at least with regard to the verb. Their approach is not a textlinguistic approach. They have not conducted distributional analysis. Rather, Muraoka and Porten have in effect positioned themselves as living informants of a dead language.

One of the Egyptian Aramaic texts from Elephantine is the Ahiqar text. It is fascinating to contrast Segert's comments on this text not only with the approach of Muraoka and Porten, but also with Segert's own approach to other Aramaic texts:

> The distinctions of the literary forms do not give rise to the use of the verbal forms so much as in a more significant way their relative frequency. This becomes especially clear in the different integral parts of the Ahiqar text from Elephantine from the end of the fifth century B.C.: In the narrative (A 1–78) the perfects predominate, while the use of the imperfect is limited mostly to direct address and to circumstantial clauses; the participles do not occur frequently. On the other hand, in the wisdom sayings (A 79–223) the perfect is fairly seldom, and the most frequent form is the imperfect. The fables, however, which are worked in among the sayings (A 110; 118–121), form an exception; they show a similar frequency of the verbal forms as the narrative (author's translation).[65]

According to Segert, the distinction between the verbal forms in literary texts is manifest in their relative frequency. That is, in this one isolated moment Segert appeals to distributional analysis. Why does Segert not continue with formal distribution in his later explanation of the verbal forms?

Segert observes that the "perfect" predominates in the opening first-person narration of the Ahiqar text; the "imperfect" is for the most part limited to direct address and circumstantial clauses; and the participle does not occur frequently. This is almost identical to the thesis proposed herein for the verbal system of Biblical Aramaic: the *qtl* is the primary form for narration; the *yqtl* is the primary form for discourse; and the nominal clause with or without a participle is secondary.

The wisdom sayings of the Ahiqar text have the "imperfect" as the most frequent form, and the "perfect" is seldom. Only in the fables that have been worked into the sayings do the verbal forms show a frequency similar to that of the opening narration. This pattern of *qtl* in narration and *yqtl* in wisdom sayings is also found in the Aramaic-influenced Hebrew of Ecclesiastes, which is treated in the latter part of this chapter.

The value of Segert's insight here is tremendous. It is amazing that he only hints at a similar pattern in some of the Biblical Aramaic texts.[66] In this brief description of the verb in the Ahiqar text, Segert surpasses in accuracy all of his subsequent discussion of tense, aspect, and *Aktionsart*. If only this informal assessment of verb frequency had been carried out systematically throughout Segert's grammar, the course of Aramaic studies would have been very different. Surely this is not too much to say for a scholar of Segert's stature.

The Egyptian Aramaic grammar of Muraoka and Rogland stands in the same class as the Biblical Aramaic grammar by Bauer and Leander when it comes to their explanation of the verb. Segert's comments on at least one Egyptian Aramaic text—the Ahiqar text—stand closer to textlinguistics and distributional analysis. Segert does not act as a living informant on the Ahiqar text. Distributional analysis of the Ahiqar text confirms Segert's assessment of the verbal forms. Thus, in two major representatives of Official Aramaic—Biblical Aramaic and the Ahiqar text—the verbal system is parallel: the *qtl* is the primary form for narration; the *yqtl* is the primary form for discourse; and the nominal clause with or without a participle is secondary.

Targums

The Targums are notoriously difficult to date. This is due in part to the fact that all extant Targums contain earlier and later elements. Nevertheless, there are boundaries. Thus, even the earliest date does not put a written Targum in the Official Aramaic period; and the latest date does not reach the Modern Aramaic period. But though the Targums fit within the Middle

Aramaic and Late Aramaic stages, their language is that of a later form of Biblical Aramaic.[67]

The earliest extant Targums are the Targums to Leviticus and Job from Qumran.[68] This means that written Targums were being produced at least as early as the first century A.D. and probably earlier. The manuscript known as *Targum Neofiti* is a sixteenth-century A.D. copy of a Palestinian Targum to the Pentateuch. In 1956, it was found by A. Díez Macho miscataloged in the Vatican Library as *Targum Onkelos*. Due to its pre-mishnaic features, Paul Kahle believed that a Palestinian Targum was in circulation by the second century B.C. in essentially the same form as the manuscript discovered by Macho.[69] Kahle's enthusiasm for *Targum Neofiti* was shared by many scholars in the years immediately following Macho's discovery. Reevaluation of the evidence since that time has produced what might be called more sober conclusions. But regardless of the date of the whole Targum for which the sixteenth-century manuscript serves as a copy, many parts of *Targum Neofiti* are arguably pre-Christian.

The final form of the Targum for which *Targum Neofiti* serves as a copy is usually dated to 150–350 A.D.[70] Paul Flesher describes the character of the manuscript:

> The translation is word-for-word, often representing not just every Hebrew word, but every particle, prefix, and suffix as well. Within this literal rendering, the targumist has inserted nontranslation material. These additions, or expansions, are sometimes only a word or two long, other times a paragraph or two. Neofiti's targumist has woven most of the expansions into the translation so that they fit without interruption or break.[71]

On the basis of the literal renderings, the Hebrew *Vorlage* of the Targum represented by *Targum Neofiti* has been said to be non-Masoretic. This is an interesting observation in light of the fact that the literal renderings of the Job Targum from Qumran reflect a decidedly Masoretic Hebrew *Vorlage*.

Cairo Geniza fragments of the Palestinian Targums, some of which are as early as the eighth or ninth century A.D.,[72] bear a close relationship to *Targum Neofiti*. According to Flesher, "where Neofiti has an expansion, so do any extant Geniza fragments, and where Neofiti just translates, so do the existing Geniza fragments."[73] *Targum Neofiti* and the Cairo Geniza fragments seem to have a common source—a proto-Palestinian Targum.

The Babylonian Targum to the Pentateuch, which eventually became the official Targum to the Pentateuch for Judaism, is *Targum Onkelos*. Kahle argued that this Targum originated entirely in Babylonia and was introduced to Palestine only in the medieval period.[74] This explains the eastern elements in *Targum Onkelos*, but it does not explain the western elements. Most scholars now believe that *Targum Onkelos* originated in Palestine and received its final, revised form in Babylonia. The brief expansions in *Targum Onkelos* appear to be truncated versions of the larger expansions found in the Palestinian Targums.

A. D. York has suggested a proto-Palestinian Targum and a proto-Onkelos; in his view, *Targum Onkelos* and the witnesses to the Palestinian Targums both contain old material and evidence of early written Targums.[75] Against Kahle's line of argumentation for the early date of the Targum represented by *Targum Neofiti*, York counters that anti-mishnaic does not necessarily mean pre-mishnaic.[76] He also points out that *Targum Neofiti*, *Targum Onkelos*, and *Targum Jonathan* all have messianic renderings (e.g., Num 24:17; Mic 5:1); so why is *Targum Neofiti* alone considered early on this basis?[77] This more balanced perspective has become something of a modern consensus. Stephen Kaufman has built on York's work to say that "the language of the Palestinian Targum is still our best guide to the spoken dialect of first century Galilee" and that the best picture of written Aramaic antecedents of the New Testament can be gained from the literary dialects of Qumran and *Onkelos-Jonathan*.[78]

Flesher suggests that the *Fragmentary Targum* and *Targum Pseudo-Jonathan* were attempts to supplement *Targum Onkelos* with Palestinian expansions when the formerly Palestinian Targum returned to Palestine in a revised, Babylonian form.[79] There are at least two other possibilities for *Targum Pseudo-Jonathan*. One is that it consists of an old Palestinian base to which *Targum Onkelos* was added; the other is that *Targum Onkelos* was somehow dependent on or derived from *Targum Pseudo-Jonathan*.[80]

The Babylonian Targum to the Prophets—*Targum Jonathan*—also had its origins in Palestine. According to Kahle, "*old* parts can be found in the Targum of the Prophets which go far back into pre-Christian times."[81] *Targum Jonathan* essentially eliminated the Palestinian Targum to the Prophets.

The Targums to the Writings are relatively late, although they may contain some early elements.[82] The Targums to the Megilloth are the most expansive. According to Flesher, the Targums to Psalms and Job share the unique characteristic of having two or more different translations and/or interpretations in a number of verses; Flesher also links together the Targums to Proverbs and Chronicles because of their relationship to the Peshitta versions of these books.[83] There are no Targums for Daniel and Ezra-Nehemiah, the two books in which extensive Aramaic is found.

What kind of Aramaic is found in the Targums? It is not enough to say that the Palestinian Targums have Jewish-Palestinian Aramaic and that the Babylonian Targums have a mix of western and eastern elements. Beyond this, the matter of translation Aramaic as opposed to composed Aramaic must be addressed. The Targums contain literal translation, paraphrase, and interpretive expansions. Sometimes a word, phrase, or comment is inserted directly into the syntax of an otherwise literal translation. In response to the question whether the Targums are translation Aramaic or composed Aramaic, it must be said that they are both or at least that they are neither here nor there.

A common view is that the Aramaic Targums arose, at least in oral form, in the post-exilic period out of a need for translation of Scripture in the vernacular of the people, since Hebrew was no longer spoken or understood. In this view, Aramaic translations of Scripture were required for Aramaic-speaking people just like Greek translations of Scripture were required for Greek-speaking people. But it is highly unlikely that Hebrew was no longer spoken or understood among the Aramaic-speaking populace in the post-exilic period.[84]

According to C. Rabin, the rabbinic literature never limits the reading of Aramaic to those who do not know Hebrew, as it does with the reading of Greek.[85] Rabin believes there is another explanation for the use of Aramaic:

> In the synagogue, explanations had to be brief and clear, and closely linked to each verse; they also had to be complete, as no dialogue between teacher and taught was possible. A paraphrase into Hebrew was impossible, because the uninstructed could easily take the paraphrase as part of the sacred text. The difference between mixed language and pure biblical Hebrew was hardly such that it would assure the clear distinction, at speaking speed, between the two kinds of text. It was therefore an almost ideal way out of the difficulty to provide the explanations in a literary language, transitional Aramaic, which was no doubt widely understood, resembling both spoken mishnaic Hebrew and spoken Aramaic, but almost word for word clearly set off from its Hebrew equivalents.[86]

The transposed Hebrew words, Hebraisms, and midrashic expansions within the Targums all presuppose knowledge of the Hebrew original.[87] Therefore, a Targum has more value as an ancient commentary on the Hebrew text—“a guide to the correct understanding of a Hebrew text for those who already understood the words"—than as a translation.[88] Rabin has not been alone with this perspective,[89] yet he is confronted with at least one difficulty: the explanation of the Scripture reading was already set apart by the fact that it was given not by the reader of Scripture, but by a *meturgeman*. The *meturgeman* was not allowed to read his explanation from a written text, making the separation from the canonical text even more evident.[90] Thus, the change from Hebrew to Aramaic would have only enhanced an already clear distinction, if in fact this was the purpose for the Aramaic. Nevertheless, Rabin's view on the whole is most probably correct. It is certainly difficult to disprove the existence of spoken Hebrew in the post-exilic period; and the fact that the Targums go well beyond mere translation is recognized by all.[91]

A good test for Rabin's view would be a comparison of a Biblical Aramaic text with a Targum of the same text. If the common view is correct that the Targums are only translations for speakers of Aramaic, then there should be no change from the Aramaic of the Bible to the Aramaic of the Targum. The Aramaic has already been provided by the biblical text. The problem is that there are no Targums for Daniel or Ezra-Nehemiah. But there is a Targum for Jer 10:11, the biblical text of which is in Aramaic:

> כדנה תאמרון להום אלהיא די שמיא וארקא לא עבדו יאבדו מארעא ומן תחות שמים אלה
> "Thus you will say to them, 'The gods who did not make the sky and the land, may they perish from the land and from under these heavens'" (author's translation).

The Targum of this verse is more than three times the length of the biblical text:

> דנא פרשגן אגרתא די שלח ירמיה נביא לות שאר סבי גלותא דבבבל
> דאם יימרון לכון עממיא דאתון ביניהון פלחו לטעותא בית ישראל
> כדין תתיבון וכדין תימרון להון
> טעון דאתון פלחין להון טעון דלית בהון צרוך אנין
> מן שמיא לא יכלן לאחתא מטרא ומן ארעא לא יכלן לצמחא פירין
> אינין ופלחיהון ייבדו מארעא וישתיצון מן תחות שמיא אלין
> This is the copy of the letter that Jeremiah the prophet sent to the remainder of the elders of the exiles who were in Babylon: "If the peoples among whom you are say to you, 'Worship the idols, O house of Israel,' thus you will reply, and thus you will say to them, 'Idols that you are worshiping, in which there is no profit, they are not able to bring down rain from the sky, and they are not able to cause fruit to spring from the ground. They and their worshipers will perish from the land, and they will cease from under these heavens'" (author's translation).

The Targum interprets the Aramaic verse as a letter from Jeremiah to the exiles. The Targum begins the letter with a word of provocation from the peoples to worship the idols (interpreted from "gods"). But the Targum does not focus on the fact that the idols did not make the sky and the land. Rather, the focus is on their inability to produce rain from the sky and fruit from the ground. The Targum also includes the idol worshipers along with the idols as those who will perish. The biblical text only speaks of the gods/idols.

Clearly the Targum of Jer 10:11 is a commentary, not a translation. Only the very last part of the Targum passes as a translation of the second half of the verse. If only an Aramaic translation was required, then the Targum went well beyond the call of duty. It seems that Rabin's thesis is thus confirmed at least in this unique instance of a Targum of a Biblical Aramaic text.

What can be said about the Aramaic verb in targumic literature? In short, the use of the *qtl* and the *yqtl* is virtually identical to that of Biblical Aramaic. The following examples are widespread enough to be representative, but they are more or less taken at random. These examples are not handpicked for the purpose of confirming a thesis for Biblical Aramaic to the exclusion of contrary evidence.

The Job Targum from Qumran (11QtgJob) is good place to start for a number of reasons. It is early, literal, and Masoretic; and it preserves a substantial portion of the epilogue narrative (Job 42:1–2, 4–6, 9–12). Here the Targum and the Masoretic Text (MT) are provided for ease of comparison along with the present author's translation:[92]

Job 42:1

11QtgJob — ענא איוב ואמר קדם אלהא

Job answered and said before God,

MT — ויען איוב את יהוה ויאמר

And Job answered the LORD and said,

Job 42:2

11QtgJob — ידעת די כלא תכול למעבד ולא יתבצר מנך תקף וחכמה

"I know that you are able to do anything and that power or wisdom is not withheld from you."

MT — ידעתי כי כל תוכל ולא יבצר ממך מזמה

"I know that you are able (to do) anything and that a plan is not withheld from you."

Job 40:5[93]

11QtgJob — חדה מללת ולא אתיב ותרתין ועליהן לא אוסף

"One thing I speak, and I will not reply; and two things, and I will not add to them."

MT
אחת דברתי ולא אענה ושתים ולא אוסיף
"One thing I speak, and I will not reply; and two things, and I will not add."

Job 42:4

11QtgJob
שמע נא ואנה אמלל אשאלנך והתיבני
"Hear please, and I will speak; I will ask you, and answer me."

MT
שמע נא ואנכי אדבר אשאלך והודיעני
"Hear please, and I will speak; I will ask you, and make me know."

Job 42:5

11QtgJob
למשמע אדן שמעתך וכען עיני חזתך
"With the hearing of an ear I have heard you, and now my eye has seen you."

MT
לשמע אזן שמעתיך ועתה עיני ראתך
"With the hearing of an ear I have heard you, and now my eye has seen you."

Job 42:6

11QtgJob
על כן אתנסך ואתמהא ואהוא לעפר וקטם
"Therefore, I will offer a libation, and I will dissolve myself, and I will become dust and ashes."

MT
על כן אמאס ונחמתי על עפר ואפר
"Therefore, I will reject and repent on dust and ashes."

Job 42:9

11QtgJob
...[ו]עבדו [כל די אמר להון] אלהא ושמע אלהא בקלה די איוב
...[And] they did [all that] God [said to them]; and God heard the voice of Job.

MT
...ויעשו כאשר דבר אליהם יהוה וישא יהוה את פני איוב
...And they did just as the LORD spoke to them; and the LORD lifted up the face of Job.

Job 42:10

11QtgJob
ושבק להון חטאיהון בדילה ותב אלהא לאיוב ברחמין
ויהב לה חד תרין בכל די הוא לה
And he forgave them their sins because of him; and God returned to Job with compassion, and he gave him two times more than all that he had.

MT
ויהוה שב את שבית איוב בהתפללו בעד רעהו
ויסף יהוה את כל אשר לאיוב למשנה
And the LORD restored the fortunes of Job when he prayed on behalf of his friends, and the LORD added double all that belonged to Job.

Job 42:11

11QtgJob
ואתין לות איוב כל רחמוהי וכל אחוהי וכל ידעוהי
ואכלו עמה לחם בביתה
ונחמוהי על כל באישתה די היתי אלהא עלוהי
ויהבו לה גבר אמרה חדה וגבר קדש חד די דהב

And all his friends and all his relatives and all those who knew him came to Job, and they ate bread with him in his house, and they comforted him concerning all the bad that God brought upon him, and they each gave him one sacrificial lamb and one ring of gold.

MT

ויבאו אליו כל אחיו וכל אחיתיו וכל ידעיו לפנים
ויאכלו עמו לחם בביתו
וינדו לו וינחמו אתו על כל הרעה אשר הביא יהוה עליו
ויתנו לו איש קשיטה אחת ואיש נזם זהב אחד

And all his brothers and all his sisters and all those who knew him before came, and they ate bread with him in his house, and they consoled him and comforted him concerning all the bad that the LORD brought upon him, and they each gave him a unit of value (or a lamb) and one ring of gold.

Job 42:12

11QtgJob

ואלהא בר[ך] ית א[יו]ב באח[רי ויהב] ל[ה]...

And God bless[ed] J[o]b after[wards and he gave] to [him]…

MT

ויהוה ברך את אחרית איוב מראשתו ויהי לו...

And the LORD blessed the end of Job more than his beginning, and he had…

The expression “Job answered and said” in the Targum of verse 1 is presumably the same type of double participle construction that is so frequent in Biblical Aramaic. In composed Aramaic, a participle would have been used for “I know” at the beginning of the discourse in verse 2 (cf., Dan 2:8), but the translation provides a formal equivalent for the Hebrew *qatal*.

The proverbial Job 40:5 displays the same pattern found in the proverbial sections of the Ahiqar text in which a saying in *yqtl* is set up by a *qtl*. The main discourse continues in the Targum of Job 42:4 with a chiastic pattern of discourse forms: imperative, *yqtl*, *yqtl*, and imperative. The verbal form of narration (*qtl*) is brought in for verse 5 because Job narrates or recounts that he has heard and seen God. The expected discourse forms continue in verse 6—three *yqtl* forms.

Narration begins in verse 9, and the Targum employs two *qtl* forms to translate the two *wayyiqtol* forms of the Hebrew text. The Targum’s narration continues in verse 10 with three more *qtl* forms. The Targum’s participle at the beginning of verse 11 seems out of place, especially since the Hebrew text has a *wayyiqtol*. The Aramaic participle is used in this way in Dan 3:26b where the three friends come out of the fiery furnace. It sets the stage for the narration that follows. The remainder of verse 11 consists of *qtl* forms that translate *wayyiqtol* forms. The narration concludes in verse 12 with a *qtl*.

Another text from Qumran that possesses at least Targum-like characteristics is the *Genesis Apocryphon*.[94] According to Kutscher, the language of this scroll is in transition from Imperial Aramaic to Middle Aramaic, but Kutscher dates the rise of Middle Aramaic to around A.D. 500.[95] The language also has affinities with *Targum Onkelos* and with Christian Aramaic.[96] As for the date of the scroll, Kutscher leans toward the first century B.C., but includes the first century A.D. as a possibility.[97]

The *Genesis Apocryphon* shares a number of features with Biblical Aramaic texts,[98] but the immediate interest here is its use of the verb. The scroll consists primarily of first-person narration by Noah and Abraham. A good sampling of the use of *qtl* in this type of narration can be seen in columns VI, X–XIII, XIX, and XXI–XXII.[99] These columns contain for the most part long strings of *qtl* forms. Reported discourse is found scattered throughout the scroll. Two brief examples are Abraham's report of his own prayer in 1QapGen 20:12–15 and the report of Lot's words in 1QapGen 20:22–23 where *yqtl* and imperative forms are primary (see also 1QapGen 21:12–14).

The better known Targums provide a similar picture of the Aramaic verbal system. In Genesis 1 of *Targum Neofiti*, for example, the distribution of verbal forms between narration and discourse is decisive. The exclusive verbal form of choice on all levels of narration is the *qtl*. The *yqtl* and imperative are used exclusively for discourse. Nominal clauses with or without participles are secondary. It is puzzling then to read the following comments by David Golomb:

> In a targumic text, the appearance of any given verbal tense is often conditioned on the tense used in the Hebrew base text. In particular, the Targum usually follows the Hebrew in the matter of the perfect tense, less so with the imperfect (which is often translated into the Aramaic by a participial form, or, commonly, by a compound tense of 'to be' + participle).[100]

It is no surprise that the Hebrew base text has had an effect on the Aramaic to a certain extent, but even Golomb admits that it is not "necessary to view the Targum solely as a 'translation' of the Hebrew, and hence as copying the syntax of biblical Hebrew, although this indeed occurs."[101]

Where the Targum does offer a literal translation of the Hebrew, it not only follows the "perfect," but also the *wayyiqtol*. The Hebrew verbal form of narration (*wayyiqtol*) is almost always rendered by the Aramaic verbal form of narration (*qtl*). However much less the Targum follows the "imperfect," it remains true that the Aramaic *yqtl* is very often employed to render the Hebrew *yiqtol*.

The *yqtl* is also used as a discourse form to render *weqatal*. The following excerpt of main plane verbal forms is taken from Moses' speech in Deuteronomy 30 of *Targum Pseudo-Jonathan*:

Deut 30:1	And it will be	*yqtl* for *weqatal*
	And you will turn	*yqtl* for *weqatal*
Deut 30:2	And you will turn	*yqtl* for *weqatal*
Deut 30:3	And he will receive	*yqtl* for *weqatal*
	And he will have compassion on you	*yqtl* for *weqatal*
	And he will turn	*yqtl* for *weqatal*
	And he will gather you	*yqtl* for *weqatal*
Deut 30:4	He will gather you	*yqtl* for *yiqtol*
	And he will draw you near	*yqtl* for *yiqtol*
Deut 30:5	And he will bring you up	*yqtl* for *weqatal*
	And he will be good to you	*yqtl* for *weqatal*
	And he will make you greater	*yqtl* for *weqatal*
Deut 30:6	And he will remove	*yqtl* for *weqatal*
Deut 30:7	And he will let loose	*yqtl* for *weqatal*
Deut 30:8	And you will turn	*yqtl* for *yiqtol*
	And you will receive	*yqtl* for *weqatal*
	And you will do	*yqtl* for *weqatal*
Deut 30:9	And he will preserve you	*yqtl* for *weqatal*
Deut 30:10	You will receive	*yqtl* for *yiqtol*
	You will turn	*yqtl* for *yiqtol*

It is possible that these forms are intended as forward references to actions yet to be realized. But two things are certain: (1) this passage is discourse and (2) the *yqtl* is the primary form for the Aramaic text.

A less "prophetic" passage in which there is a substantial amount of discourse is Joshua 1 of *Targum Jonathan*. The data are as follows: (1) narration consists entirely of *qtl* forms—five in all, (2) discourse consists entirely of *yqtl* and imperative forms—thirty-one in all, (3) narration within discourse consists entirely of *qtl* forms—three in all, and (4) reported discourse consists entirely of *yqtl* and imperative forms—six in all. These are, of course, the forms on the main narration and discourse planes.

One final passage from *Targum Jonathan* will show the consistency with which the *qtl* is used as the verbal form of narration. The Hebrew text of Joshua 11 has several instances in which a *wayyiqtol* is followed (not necessarily immediately) by an "x + *qatal*" clause in which the verb root is the same, similar, or opposite. For example, Josh 11:16 says, "And Joshua took (ויקח) all this land." This *wayyiqtol* form is followed by an "x + *qatal*" clause with the same verb root in Josh 11:19b: "The whole they took (לקחו) in the battle." Another example comes in Josh 11:21: "And he cut off (ויכרת) the Anakim...with their cities Joshua exterminated them (החרימם)." In this latter example, the verb root is not identical, but similar. The action of the "x + *qatal*" clause is layered upon the action of the preceding *wayyiqtol*.

The Targum treats these constructions as functional equivalents. The entirety of the narration in Josh 11:16–23 is given in *qtl* forms:

Josh 11:16	And Joshua took possession	*qtl*
Josh 11:17	He subdued	*qtl*
	And he struck	*qtl*
	And he killed	*qtl*
Josh 11:18	Joshua made war	*qtl*
Josh 11:19	There was not	*qtl*
	They took	*qtl*
Josh 11:20	It was	*qtl*
Josh 11:21	And Joshua came	*qtl*
	And he finished/destroyed	*qtl*
	Joshua completed/destroyed	*qtl*
Josh 11:22	The mighty men did not remain	*qtl*
	They did remain	*qtl*
Josh 11:23	And Joshua took	*qtl*
	And Joshua gave	*qtl*
	And the land was quiet	*qtl*

The Targum does not attempt to introduce nominal clauses with or without participles for these unique "x + *qatal*" clauses. It recognizes everything as narration and employs the verbal form of narration accordingly (i.e., *wqtl* followed by "x + *qtl*").

At this point, it is unnecessary to continue to multiply examples from Targums of the same genre (i.e., non-poetic) as the Biblical Aramaic texts. It is clear by now that the use of the verb in Biblical Aramaic is paralleled not only in other Official Aramaic texts, but also in targumic texts that stem from the Middle Aramaic and Late Aramaic periods. Thus, the thesis proposed here for the verbal system of Biblical Aramaic is not an idiosyncratic one that is limited to Biblical Aramaic alone.[102] Rather, it appears that the Aramaic of the Bible is in sync with other Aramaic texts from within and around the same time period, at least when it comes to the primary usages of the verbal forms.

Aramaic-influenced Texts

Although the heading for this subsection is plural, only one text will be the object of analysis here—that of Ecclesiastes or Qoheleth. The reason for this is that substantiation must be provided for the claim of Aramaic influence, and such substantiation for multiple texts would require too much space. Regardless, the type of Aramaic influence documented here for the language of Ecclesiastes is exemplary for other Hebrew texts whose verbal system has been affected by Aramaic.

The study of the language of Ecclesiastes has enjoyed a rich history. Not only has the book's intriguing content attracted commentators, but also its "unconventional" use of Hebrew has invited a significant number of Semitic scholars to propose theories. The beginning of this study is usually traced back to the famous statement made in 1644 by Hugo Grotius with reference to the exclusion of Solomonic authorship: "As proof of this matter I have many words, which you cannot find anywhere else other than in Daniel, Ezra, and the Chaldean translations" (author's translation).[103] From the earliest point of modern research the influence of Aramaic and Mishnaic Hebrew has been widely recognized. It was even fashionable in the mid-twentieth century to posit an Aramaic original for the book of Ecclesiastes.

The focus of research thus far has been on unusual orthography, peculiar vocabulary, and idiomatic expressions foreign to Hebrew. For those who hold to the translation theory, such oddities reflect mistranslation from the original Aramaic into Hebrew. For others, these linguistic features are the primary marks of Aramaic, Mishnaic, or even Phoenician influence. But is the foreign influence limited to stylistic elements, or does it run much deeper into the larger linguistic structure of the book? Does the influence affect oppositions at higher levels, such as the verbal system as a whole?

In his 1875 commentary, F. Delitzsch announced, "If the book of Koheleth were of old Solomonic origin, then there is no history of the Hebrew language."[104] This was not intended to be an argument per se.

Delitzsch was simply making the point that Ecclesiastes is as good a specimen for post-exilic Hebrew as any extant text. In other words, if Ecclesiastes is not late, what is? It is not only a matter of what is possible. It is also a matter of what is most probable. Of course, Delitzsch was not without evidence. He provided a long list of *hapax legomena* and of other words and forms belonging to a more recent period of the Hebrew language.[105]

According to Francesco Bianchi, "Delitzsch's analysis shaped all the following studies about Qohelet's language."[106] The next major development was the theory that an original Aramaic Ecclesiastes had been translated into Hebrew and subsequently lost. Although the initial idea is usually attributed to F. C. Burkitt, it was Frank Zimmermann who developed and defended the theory.[107] Zimmermann argued from the presence of Aramaic words, the inexact status of nouns, the confusion of *hu'* (*hw'*) and *hawa'* (*hw'*), and from a host of alleged mistranslations that the original language of Ecclesiastes was of the Eastern Aramaic type.[108]

Zimmermann's basic rule for the treatment of linguistic problems in Ecclesiastes was: "retrovert the Hebrew to the underlying Aramaic and nine times out of ten the problem will be laid bare and solved simultaneously."[109] Zimmermann was joined in the translation theory by C. C. Torrey and H. L. Ginsburg. Torrey felt that Zimmermann's own demonstration of the theory was somewhat overdone, but he was persuaded by the fact that Ecclesiastes contains more Aramaic idioms than any other late book of the Hebrew Bible.[110] It is noteworthy that both Zimmermann and Torrey were also advocates for Aramaic originals of other biblical books.

Robert Gordis preferred to speak of Aramaisms and Mishnaisms in Ecclesiastes rather than an Aramaic original. Against Zimmermann, Gordis argued that a difficult text does not presuppose translation.[111] According to Gordis, "...Qohelet was written in Hebrew, by a writer who, like all his contemporaries, knew Aramaic and probably used it freely in daily life."[112] Gordis' position that the syntax and semantics of Ecclesiastes represent Aramaic-influenced Hebrew between Biblical Hebrew and Mishnaic Hebrew seems to have won the day for the most part.[113] Gordis may be said to be in the long tradition of Grotius and Delitzsch. His view has had the advantage of the non-extant status of any Aramaic Ecclesiastes manuscripts and the benefit of the findings from among the Dead Sea Scrolls. For instance, the then recent discovery of an Ecclesiastes scroll at Qumran created an added difficulty for Zimmermann's view. James Muilenberg dated the scroll to the middle of the second century B.C. and commented that "the evidence does not strengthen the view of the proponents of an Aramaic original, but seems rather to support a Hebrew *Vorlage*."[114] Of course, this does not exclude the possibility of an Aramaic original, only the likelihood.

In response to Gordis, Zimmermann clarified that he did not assume stupidity on the part of the translator, only the capacity for error, which was true for all the translators of ancient versions.[115] Zimmermann described the translation process as he understood it:

> Frequently he translates word for word as the text comes to his notice for translation. Ever so often, he comes across a word or a collocation of words that appears quite familiar to him, and he renders according to his best knowledge and most familiar experience. The he makes a slip and falls into error. Instead of sense we get a peculiar translation or non-sense. If it is true that the translator strives to give as perfect a translation as possible and to smooth out the difficulties, *it is equally true that he unconsciously reveals his own defects, inadequacies and limitations*.[116]

In this view, a translator's false sense of security about his own familiarity with a text leads into error. However much Zimmermann may have vindicated his arguments, the fact remains that he did not ultimately prove the existence of an Aramaic original.

At the height of the translation theory, Mitchell Dahood proposed another alternative—Canaanite-Phoenician influence. According to Dahood, the author of Ecclesiastes was "a Jew who wrote in Hebrew but who employed Phoenician spelling, and whose language was heavily influenced by Phoenician vocabulary and style."[117] One of Dahood's primary pieces of evidence for his theory was the absence of *matres lectionis* in Ecclesiastes, but this aspect of his argument was weakened considerably by Gordis and James Barr.[118] Dahood also made reference to the use of a third masculine plural suffix with a feminine plural antecedent (e.g., Eccl 2:6, 10; 10:9; 11:8; 12:1). The third feminine plural suffix is not found at all in Ecclesiastes or Phoenician.[119] Other features of Dahood's presentation, such as the so-called "erratic" use of the article and the presence of unusual vocabulary,[120] could just as easily have been explained as due to the influence of Aramaic or Mishnaic Hebrew. Dahood's theory never attracted a large following. It seems best to say with Gordis that the supposed Phoenician elements are part of the Hebrew literary tradition: biblical language, proto-Mishnaic language, and Aramaic-influenced language.[121] The available evidence does not point to an Aramaic original or to a Phoenician and/or Northern Hebrew influence. Unless new evidence is forthcoming, such as an Aramaic manuscript, the most probable conclusion is that Ecclesiastes is a piece of relatively late, Aramaic-influenced Hebrew.

More recent studies on the language of Ecclesiastes include those of Bo Isaksson, D. C. Fredericks, and A. Schoors.[122] Fredericks argues on the basis of the linguistic data that Ecclesiastes should be dated to the eighth or seventh century B.C. He opts for the priority of grammatical/syntactical comparisons over lexical ones.[123] Michael Fox has criticized Fredericks for taking the allegedly late linguistic features of Ecclesiastes in isolation and showing how each one could have occurred individually at an early date; this procedure does not demonstrate how the phenomenon of the book of Ecclesiastes as a whole could have occurred at such an early date.[124] Thus, while Fredericks' thesis is remotely possible, it is likely not the most plausible solution.

The use of the verb in Ecclesiastes seems very much to be influenced by Aramaic. The *qatal* is the primary form for narration; that is, when Qoheleth recounts the events of his life (narration within discourse), the form of choice is the *qatal*.[125] The use of the *qatal* in Ecclesiastes resembles the use of the *qtl* in Aramaic and has virtually replaced the *wayyiqtol* with the exception of the seemingly out of place occurrences in Eccl 1:17; 4:1, 7. The *yiqtol* is used as the primary verbal form for discourse (e.g., the proverbial sayings) as it is in other Biblical Hebrew texts;[126] this corresponds to the use of the *yqtl* as the primary verbal form for discourse in Aramaic.

Thus, even in the Aramaic-influenced Hebrew of Ecclesiastes the basic distribution of the verbal forms parallels that of Biblical Aramaic. The book of Ecclesiastes finds an even closer parallel in the Ahiqar text. Both Ecclesiastes and the Ahiqar text contain first-person narration in which the *qatal/qtl* is the primary verbal form; and both contain a significant amount of proverbial sayings in which the *yiqtol/yqtl* is the primary verbal form.

After the title of Eccl 1:1 and motto of Eccl 1:2, a question is posed in Eccl 1:3 out of which the poetic unit of Eccl 1:4–11 flows.[127] The heart of the poem (Eccl 1:4–7) is dominated by participles (ptc):

A generation goes (ptc) and a generation comes (ptc),
And the land stands (ptc) forever.
And the sun rises (ptc) and the sun sets (ptc),
Longing (ptc) for its place,

> It is rising (ptc) there.
> Going (ptc) southward,
> And turning (ptc) northward;
> Turning (ptc), turning (ptc), going (ptc) is the wind,
> And upon its circuits the wind returns (ptc).
> All the torrent valleys are going (ptc) to the sea,
> And the sea is not full;
> To the place that the torrent valleys are going (ptc),
> There they are returning (ptc) to go (author's translation).

This parallels the usage of the participle in the poetic units of Daniel (e.g., Dan 2:21–23), Hebrew psalms, and in the poetry of other languages.[128]

When Qoheleth begins to narrate his life in Eccl 1:12–14, the *qatal* form takes over. It is interesting to note that the same expression—"And I gave my heart"—is provided once with *waw* plus *qatal* in Eccl 1:13 and once with *wayyiqtol* in Eccl 1:17. This is a clue to the use of *qatal* in the remainder of the book: it serves as the verbal form of narration just like the *wayyiqtol* in other Biblical Hebrew texts and just like the *qtl* in Aramaic texts. Whenever Qoheleth interjects a proverbial saying into his narration, the verbal form of choice is the *yiqtol* (Eccl 1:15, 18).

In Eccl 2:1–20, the *qatal* is clearly the dominant form and is often fronted in the word order as Qoheleth recounts his wealth, wisdom, and works. Twice Qoheleth utters discourse to himself, once with the imperative (Eccl 2:1) and once with the *yiqtol* (Eccl 2:15). The *yiqtol* is also used in a question in Eccl 2:16.[129] Qoheleth shifts from narration to discourse in Eccl 2:21–26. The *yiqtol* and the nominal clause dominate this latter section, although the *qatal* does occur (e.g., Eccl 2:26).

The poetic interlude about time in Eccl 3:1–8 does not feature the participle as does the poem in Eccl 1:4–7, but the infinitive. The *qatal* is again the primary verbal form for the first-person narration of Eccl 3:9–22, and most of the *yiqtol* forms here are subordinate (Eccl 3:11, 13, 22). The *yiqtol* in Eccl 3:15 comes as part of a transitional proverb, and the *yiqtol* in Eccl 3:17 is Qoheleth's discourse with himself. Verses 9 and 19–21 are verbless.

The distribution of forms in chapter four is quite uneven. It is precisely at this point that the coherence of Qoheleth's words begins to break up. That is, the smaller units bear no relationship to one another in terms of development of thought. This is not to say that the book of Ecclesiastes as a whole is incoherent. It is only to say that the author does not attempt to present

Qoheleth's message as uniform.[130] The "*weqatal…wayyiqtol*" sequences in Eccl 4:1, 7 (cf., Eccl 9:11) stand at the heads of the two larger divisions of Eccl 4:1–12.[131] Qoheleth narrates the macro-level framework of his observations with the *qatal* (Eccl 4:1, 4, 7, 15).[132] At the micro-level are the proverbs in which the *yiqtol* is the primary verbal form (Eccl 4:3, 5–6, 8–14, 16).[133]

Chapter five follows the lead of chapter four in becoming more proverbial in genre. As expected, the *yiqtol* is the primary verbal form for the discourse of Eccl 5:1–11. The two primary *qatal* forms (both ראיתי) in this chapter come at Eccl 5:12, 17, marking two units. The first unit (Eccl 5:12–16) is Qoheleth's observation of a grievous evil. The second unit (Eccl 5:17–19) recounts what Qoheleth has observed about the gift of God to mankind. The use of ראיתי to mark new units continues in Eccl 6:1. Thus, the *qatal* plays an important role in the structure and orientation of Qoheleth's sayings—a structure that defies consistency of theme apart from the repetition of certain terms such as הבל. Although the *yiqtol* is the primary verbal form for the discourse, the *qatal* is employed at the beginning of unit divisions in order to keep the sayings within the context of Qoheleth's reminiscence.

Chapters six and seven are discourse for the most part. When the nominal clause is not employed, the verbal clauses usually have the *yiqtol* (but see Eccl 6:3, 5–6, 10). A significant number of טוב sayings are located in Eccl 7:1–14 (vv. 1–3, 5, 8, 10–11, 14), and the imperative is prominent in Eccl 7:13–14. A new unit, Eccl 7:15–22, is again marked by ראיתי. The *qatal* does become more prominent in Eccl 7:23–29, a section otherwise interspersed with imperatives and with more of Qoheleth's discourse with himself.

Chapter eight alternates units of discourse (Eccl 8:1–8, 12–14) with units of narration (Eccl 8:9–11, 15–17). The *yiqtol* goes with the discourse and the *qatal* with the narration. There is very little mixture of forms here on the main planes of the respective units. As for chapter nine, Eccl 9:1–6 is initially marked by a *qatal* form, but the discourse then begins and moves forward without it. The imperative is the dominant form in the following unit (Eccl 9:7–10). The pattern of initial *qatal* plus *qatal*-less discourse is employed again in Eccl 9:11–12, 16–18. But Eccl 9:13–15 features a story in which the *qatal* is sustained throughout.

Chapter ten opens with discourse (Eccl 10:1–4) followed by narration within discourse (Eccl 10:5–7) before launching into an extended section of proverbial discourse carried by *yiqtol* forms and nominal clauses (Eccl 10:8–20). The discourse of chapter eleven is characterized by imperatives (Eccl 11:1–2, 6, 9–10). Chapter twelve also begins with an imperative ("Remember"). The phrase עד אשר (Eccl 12:1, 2, 6) sustains the thought of this initial imperative through verse 6. After a final word in Eccl 12:7, the motto from Eccl 1:2 is repeated in Eccl 12:8.

The epilogue (Eccl 12:9–14) is a fitting conclusion not only in terms of content, but also in terms of its being a microcosm of the book's verbal system. The third-person narration of Qoheleth's life in Eccl 12:9–11 comes with seven *qatal* forms. The address to the "son" in Eccl 12:12–14, however, features the nominal clause, the imperative, and the *yiqtol*.

All of this is not to say that the *qatal* in Ecclesiastes is a mistranslation of the Aramaic *qtl* for which the *wayyiqtol* would be more appropriate. Rather, the point is that the use of the *qatal* in Ecclesiastes reveals the overwhelming influence of the Aramaic *qtl* on the book's Hebrew. Black's comment, although it is with reference to the Gospels and Acts, is apropos: "Mistranslation of an original is, it is true, the best proof of translation; but it is doubtful if it can ever have scientific value as evidence except in cases where we possess not only the translation but also the original work."[134]

Although there are still exceptions to be explained in Ecclesiastes, the primary uses of the verbal forms parallel what has been observed in this chapter in Official Aramaic (including Biblical Aramaic), Middle Aramaic, and Late Aramaic: the *qtl* is the primary verbal form for narration; the *yqtl* is the primary verbal form for discourse; and the nominal clause with or without a participle is secondary. A text such as Ecclesiastes whose verbal system has been influenced by Aramaic shows the same opposition between narration and discourse.

Notes

[1]Michael B. Shepherd, "The Distribution of Verbal Forms in Biblical Aramaic," *JSS* 52 (2007): 231.

[2]"Als ein Satz gilt eine Reihe von Wörtern, die verbales oder nominales Prädikat enthält, das zu einem Subjekt gehört" (Stanislav Segert, *Altaramäische Grammatik*, 3d ed. [Leipzig: Enzyklopädie, 1986], 399).

[3]Shepherd, "Distribution of Verbal Forms," 232.

[4]"Der Bedingungssatz geht dem Hauptsatz voran, als Verbum finitum steht in beiden der Aorist" (Hans Bauer and Pontus Leander, *Grammatik des Biblisch-Aramäischen* [Halle: Niemeyer, 1927; 4th unrev. reprint., Hildesheim: Georg Olms, 1995] 365).

[5]John H. Sailhamer, "A Database Approach to the Analysis of Hebrew Narrative," *Maarav* 5–6 (1990): 319–35.

[6]Ibid., 319; "Only those constituents of the clause that point beyond the clause itself will be considered in formulating analytical categories for tagging the biblical text" (ibid., 321).

[7]"It has long been recognized that the presence or absence of a WAW with a clause plays an important role in the function of the clause at higher levels" (ibid.).

[8]E.g., Bauer and Leander, *Grammatik*, 252.

[9]E.g., Franz Rosenthal, *A Grammar of Biblical Aramaic* (Wiesbaden: Harrassowitz, 1961), 38.

[10]Sailhamer, "Database Approach," 321, n. 11.

[11]"The simpler approach is merely to mark such clauses as nominal with the notation 'NC,' leaving the question of the identification of the predicate and its location undecided. Such an approach would allow a 'text-level' descriptive tagging of nominal clauses, corresponding to the tagging of verbal clauses, yet without forcing the question of the identification of the nominal predicate" (ibid., 322).

[12]Biblical Aramaic has two verbal forms (*qtl* and *yqtl*), not three; the participle is a nominal form, and the imperative is built on the analogy of the *yqtl*.

[13]Alviero Niccacci, "On the Hebrew Verbal System," in *Biblical Hebrew and Discourse Linguistics*, ed. Robert Bergen (Dallas: SIL, 1994), 121.

[14]E. F. Kautzsch, *Gesenius' Hebrew Grammar*, trans. A. E. Cowley, 2d ed. (Oxford: Clarendon, 1910), 450.

[15]Ibid., 457.

[16]"By the Arab grammarians every clause beginning with an independent subject is regarded as a noun-clause, and every clause beginning with a finite verb as verbal. If a finite verb follows the noun-subject the two together (since the verb comprises its own subject and is thus a complete verbal-clause) form a compound noun-sentence, just as when the predicate consists of an independent noun-clause" (ibid., 451).

[17]Shepherd, "Distribution of Verbal Forms," 233.

[18]Because the subject-verb word order is more frequent in Aramaic, the legitimacy of the label "inverted" will be addressed in the following section on results.

[19]See Erich Auerbach, *Mimesis: The Representation of Reality in Western Literature*, fiftieth-anniversary ed., trans. Willard R. Trask (Princeton: Princeton University Press, 2003).

[20]Sailhamer, "Database Approach," 325–27; Sailhamer also tags text-segment markers that stem from the real world: (1) changes in persons, (2) changes in time, and (3) changes in place (ibid., 327–33); such markers are not relevant for the present database analysis of the Biblical Aramaic verbal system.

[21]See Segert's comments on the diversity of the levels in such a small corpus (*Altaramäische Grammatik*, 373); see also Shepherd, "Distribution of Verbal Forms," 234–35.

[22]Siegfried J. Schmidt, *Texttheorie* (Munich: Fink, 1973), 150.

[23]This portion also appears in Shepherd, "Distribution of Verbal Forms," 240–42.

[24]Percentages are rounded up to the nearest whole number.

[25]"*Edayin* + *qtl*" occurs at Dan 2:35; 3:26; 5:3, 29; 6:13, 14, 19; 7:19; Ezra 4:24; 5:2; the construction "*edayin* + x + *qtl*" is more frequent.

[26]Earlier it was noted that *edayin* is not an occupant of first position, and these data seem to confirm this; *edayin* is followed by an adverb in Ezra 5:4.

[27]In addition to this type of periphrastic construction, there are 11 clauses in which an infinitive completes the idea of a participle or verbal form.

[28]Tamar Zewi, "Time in Nominal Sentences in the Semitic Languages," *JSS* 44 (1999): 195–214.

[29]Ibid., 129.

[30]The fact that nominal clauses do not require verbs of being indicates that there is a difference between nominal clauses and clauses with verbs of being; Carl Brockelmann suggested that this difference had to do with the indication of time by means of a verb of being (Carl Brockelmann, *Grundriß der vergleichenden Grammatik der semitischen Sprachen*, vol. 2, *Syntax* [Berlin: Reuther & Reichard, 1913; 4th reprint, Hildesheim: Georg Olms, 1999], 109), but Biblical Aramaic verbs are timeless; this is not to say that speakers of the language had no concept of time; it is only to say that the verb is not the primary carrier of time and that time is indicated by other linguistic elements.

[31]Zdravko Stefanovic, *The Aramaic of Daniel in the Light of Old Aramaic*, JSOTSup 129 (Sheffield: JSOT, 1992), 106.

[32]Takamitsu Muraoka and Bezalel Porten, *A Grammar of Egyptian Aramaic* (Leiden: Brill, 1998), 285.

[33]Ibid., 296.

[34]Ibid., 299; cf., Brockelmann, *Grundriß*, 2:170–72; Bauer and Leander, *Grammatik*, 332–35, 342–45.

[35]E. Y. Kutscher, "The Language of the 'Genesis Apocryphon'," in *Scripta hierosolymitana*, vol. 4, *Aspects of the Dead Sea Scrolls*, ed. Chaim Rabin and Yigael Yadin, 2d ed. (Jerusalem: Magnes, 1965), 33–34.

[36]Geoffrey Khan, *A Grammar of Neo-Aramaic: The Dialect of the Jews of Arbel* (Leiden: Brill, 1999), 334.

[37]Robert Hoberman, *The Syntax and Semantics of Verb Morphology in Modern Aramaic: A Jewish Dialect of Iraqi Kurdistan*, American Oriental Society 69 (New Haven: American Oriental Society, 1989), 171.

[38]One clause has a compound predicate of two *yqtl* forms (Dan 2:44b1); and one clause has a compound predicate of two *qtl* forms (Dan 4:31a4).

[39]These data are forthcoming in Shepherd, "Distribution of Verbal Forms."

[40]Wolfgang Schneider, *Grammatik des Biblischen Hebräischen*, 8th ed. (Munich: Claudius, 1993), 182.

[41]Ibid; this 5% apparently represents narration within discourse.

[42]Ibid.

[43]Stefanovic, *Aramaic of Daniel*, 41.

[44]Hermann Gunkel, *Einleitung in die Psalmen*, 2d ed. (Göttingen: Vandenhoeck & Ruprecht, 1966), 44–48.

[45]Bauer and Leander, *Grammatik*, 281–83.

[46]See the use of ימטא (*yqtl*) in the account of the dream in Dan 4:8 and the use of מטא (*qtl*) in the interpretation (Dan 4:19); Dan 4:30 is recounted in Dan 5:21.

[47]"Auch die durchgreifende Vereinfachung des aramäischen Verbalsystem darf als Ergebnis einer Auseinandersetzung mit einem fremden System betrachtet werden" (Segert, *Altaramäische Grammatik*, 35).

[48]Ibid., 38.

[49]J. A. Emerton, "New Evidence for the Use of *Waw* Consecutive in Aramaic," *VT* 44 (1994): 255.

[50]Ibid., 257.

[51]Victor Sasson, "Some Observations on the Use and Original Purpose of the *Waw* Consecutive in Old Aramaic and Biblical Hebrew," *VT* 47 (1997): 112–14.

[52]Ibid., 117; see also idem, "The *Waw* Consecutive/*Waw* Contrastive and the Perfect: Verb Tense, Context, and Texture in Old Aramaic and Biblical Hebrew, with Comments on the Deir ʿAlla Dialect and Post-Biblical Hebrew," *ZAW* 113 (2001): 602–17.

[53]Sasson, "*Waw* Consecutive in Old Aramaic and Biblical Hebrew," 123, 126.

[54]T. Muraoka and M. Rogland, "The *Waw* Consecutive in Old Aramaic? A Rejoinder to Victor Sasson," *VT* 48 (1998): 99–104.

[55]J. A. Emerton, "Further Comments on the Use of the Tenses in the Aramaic Inscription from Tel Dan," *VT* 47 (1997): 439.

[56]Segert, *Altaramäische Grammatik*, 55.

[57]Hoberman, *Syntax and Semantics*, 1.

[58]Ibid., 27, n. 20.

[59]See also Khan, *A Grammar of Neo-Aramaic*, 248.

[60]"Die beiden altsemitischen Tempora sind hier ganz aufgegeben und durch Neubildungen aus dem Partizip ersetzt, für die sich schon im Altsyrischen Ansätze finden. Der Wortschatz dieser Dialekte ist natürlich sehr stark von den benachbarten, weit mächtigeren Sprachen der Araber, Kurden und Türken beeinflußt" (Carl Brockelmann, *Grundriß der vergleichenden Grammatik der semitischen Sprachen*, vol. 1, *Laut- und Formenlehre* [Berlin: Reuther & Reichard, 1908; 4th reprint, Hildesheim: Georg Olms, 1999], 20–21).

[61]See Segert, *Altaramäische Grammatik*, 370–71.

[62]Muraoka and Porten, *A Grammar of Egyptian Aramaic*, 192.

[63]Ibid., 193–95; "Our idiom is not sensitive to a distinction which is essential and meaningful to English…" (ibid., 193); it may also be said that the explanation here is not

sensitive to a clear distinction or opposition between *qtl* and *yqtl* that is meaningful to Aramaic.

[64]Ibid., 195–98; "No impf. has been identified which indicates an action in the past, whether punctiliar or durative/iterative/habitual" (ibid., 195).

[65]"Die Unterschiede der literarischen Gattungen bewirken nicht so sehr den Gebrauch der Verbalformen, als vielmehr in bedeutender Weise ihre relative Frequenz. Dies wird besonders klar an den verschiedenen Bestandteilen des Ahiqar-Textes von Elephantine vom Ende des 5. Jh. v. u. Z.: In der Erzählung (A 1–78) überwiegen die Perfekta, während der Gebrauch des Imperfekts meist auf die direkte Rede und auf die Nebensätze beschränkt wird; die Partizipien treten nicht häufig auf. Dagegen ist in den Weisheitssprüchen (A 79–223) das Perfekt ziemlich selten, und die häufigste Form ist das Imperfekt. Eine Ausnahme bilden jedoch die unter die Sprüche eingereihten Fabeln (A 110; 118–121), die eine ähnliche Frequenz der Verbalformen wie die Erzählung aufweisen" (Segert, *Altaramäische Grammatik*, 372).

[66]"Die Urkunden im Esrabuch entsprechen im Gebrauch der Verbalformen etwa den jüdischen Urkunden aus Elephantine, der verbindende historische Text etwa der Ahiqar-Erzählung. Doch die Frequenz der Partizipien und der mit ihnen gebildeten periphrastischen Ausdrücke nimmt zu" (ibid., 372–73).

[67]Bauer and Leander, *Grammatik*, 6–7.

[68]It has also been suggested that the *Genesis Apocryphon* from Qumran is a type of Targum; see the discussion in Joseph A. Fitzmyer, *The Genesis Apocryphon of Qumran Cave I: A Commentary*, 2d ed., Biblica et orientalia 18A (Rome: Biblical Institute Press, 1971), 6–14.

[69]Paul Kahle, *The Cairo Geniza*, 2d ed. (New York: Praeger, 1960), 207–208; "In the Palestinian Targum of the Pentateuch we have in the main material coming from pre-Christian times which must be studied by everyone who wishes to understand the state of Judaism at the time of the birth of Christianity. And we possess this material in a language of which we can say that it is very similar to that spoken by the earliest Christians. It is material the importance of which can scarcely be exaggerated" (ibid., 208); see also the Samaritan Targum (ibid., 200).

[70]According to Martin McNamara, the later additions and recensional emendations are "the exception and do not invalidate the arguments in favour of an early date for the bulk of the material" (Martin McNamara, *The New Testament and the Palestinian Targum to the Pentateuch*, Analecta biblica 27 [Rome: Pontifical Biblical Institute, 1966], 45); for McNamara, this early date is maintained by the relationship of the Targums to the New Testament.

[71]Paul V. McCracken Flesher, "The Targumim in the Context of Rabbinic Literature," in Jacob Neusner, *Introduction to Rabbinic Literature* (New York: Doubleday, 1999), 613.

[72]"[T]he comparatively late date of the manuscripts has nothing to do with the date of the translation" (Matthew Black, *An Aramaic Approach to the Gospels and Acts*, 3d ed. [Oxford: Clarendon, 1967], 22–23).

[73]Flesher, "The Targumim," 614.

[74]Kahle, *The Cairo Geniza*, 191–95.

[75]A. D. York, "The Dating of Targumic Literature," *JSJ* 5 (1974): 56, 60–61.

[76]Ibid., 52–53.

[77]Ibid., 55.

[78]Stephen Kaufman, "On Methodology in the Study of the Targums and their Chronology," *JSNT* 23 (1985): 123.

[79]Flesher, "The Targumim," 615–16.

[80]Martin McNamara, *Targum and Testament, Aramaic Paraphrases of the Hebrew Bible: A Light on the New Testament* (Grand Rapids: Eerdmans, 1972), 180; one early element in *Targum Pseudo-Jonathan* is the mention of John Hyrcanus (135–105 B.C.) at Deut 33:11 (ibid., 179–80).

[81]Kahle, *The Cairo Geniza*, 196; "We have in the Targum of the Prophets, besides the translation of the Hebrew text of the Bible, a great deal of material taken from the Midrash which often contains an interesting commentary on the Bible" (ibid., 197).

[82]See, for example, the Targum of Ps 68:19 and Eph 4:8.

[83]Flesher, "The Targumim," 617; for the relationship of the Syriac Peshitta to the Palestinian Targum see Kahle, *The Cairo Geniza*, 266, 272–73.

[84]See James Barr, *Comparative Philology and the Text of the Old Testament* (Oxford: Oxford University Press, 1968; reprint, Winona Lake, Ind.: Eisenbrauns, 1987), 38–43.

[85]C. Rabin, "Hebrew and Aramaic in the First Century," in *The Jewish People in the First Century*, vol. 2, ed. S. Safrai and M. Stern, CRINT 1 (Philadelphia: Fortress, 1976), 1030.

[86]Ibid.

[87]Ibid., 1031–32.

[88]Ibid., 1032; "The fact that its language differed greatly from the spoken Aramaic of those whom it served, that it was artificial and bristled with semantic difficulties, did therefore not matter" (ibid.).

[89]See, for example, Ernest G. Clarke, "Jacob's Dream at Bethel as Interpreted in the Targums and the New Testament," *SR* 4 (1974–75): 369; Michael G. Steinhauser, "The Targums and the New Testament," *TJT* 2 (1986): 264.

[90]E. Lévine, "The Biography of the Aramaic Bible," *ZAW* 94 (1982): 374; it is possible, however, that the rules for a *meturgeman* and for oral Targums were not established in the early stages of the Targums.

[91]"The Targums, like LXX, followed the Hebrew text verse by verse, but they incorporated in the representation of the text a great deal of explanation and interpretation. Thus the text and its interpretation were woven together, and the interpretation often extended and amplified the text greatly" (John Bowker, *The Targums and Rabbinic Literature: An Introduction to Jewish Interpretations of Scripture* [London: Cambridge University Press, 1969], 8).

[92]The Targum here follows Klaus Beyer, *Die aramäischen Texte vom Toten Meer* (Göttingen: Vandenhoeck & Ruprecht, 1984), 298; the standard chapter and verse are given here rather than the column and line.

[93]Here the Targum replaces Job 42:3 with Job 40:5.

[94]Kahle (*The Cairo Geniza*, 198–200) preferred to call it "The Midrash Book from Qumran I."

[95]Kutscher, "Language of the 'Genesis Apocryphon'," 3–6; the language imitates Biblical Aramaic and Imperial Aramaic, but it also shows traces of Middle Aramaic, specifically Western Aramaic (ibid., 7–9).

[96]Ibid., 9–13.

[97]Ibid., 15–22.

[98]E.g., see the use of *edayin* in column II, the Watchers/Holy Ones in 1QapGen 2:1 (cf., Dan 4:10), the expression "my heart was changed upon me" in 1QapGen 2:2 (cf., Dan 5:9), and the scene with the wise men in 1QapGen 20:19–20 (cf., Dan 2:1–13).

[99]Column XIII has several periphrastic constructions in which a verb of being in *qtl* is combined with a participle; 1QapGen 21:23–22:34 is third-person narration and is quite literal in translation (see Fitzmyer, *Genesis Apocryphon*, 157–58).

[100]David M. Golomb, *A Grammar of Targum Neofiti*, Harvard Semitic Monographs 34 (Chico, Cal.: Scholars Press, 1985), 121.

[101]Ibid., 187; according to Golomb, "Neofiti also differs very often from the biblical Hebrew word order" (ibid.); Golomb's view of the Aramaic verb is based on aspectual (durative and non-durative) and temporal (past and non-past) opposition, not on opposition between narration and discourse.

[102]It may be recalled that this was one of the difficulties with H. B. Rosén's theory, which was reviewed in the first chapter.

[103]"Argumentum eius rei habeo multa vocabula, quae non alibi quam in Daniele, Ezra et Chaldaeis interpretibus reperias" (quoted in F. Delitzsch, *The Book of Ecclesiastes*, trans. M. G. Easton, Keil & Delitzsch Commentary on the Old Testament 6 [Edinburgh: T. & T. Clark, 1866–91; reprint, Peabody, Mass.: Hendrickson, 2001], 637).

[104]Ibid.

[105]Ibid., 637–41.

[106]Francesco Bianchi, "The Language of Qohelet: A Bibliographical Survey," *ZAW* 105 (1993): 212.

[107]Ibid., 213.

[108]Frank Zimmermann, "The Aramaic Provenance of Qohelet," *JQR* 36 (1945–46): 17–45; idem, "The Question of Hebrew in Qohelet," *JQR* 40 (1949–50): 79–102.

[109]Zimmermann, "The Question of Hebrew in Qohelet," 101.

[110]C. C. Torrey, "The Question of the Original Language of Qoheleth," *JQR* 39 (1948–49): 152–53.

[111]Robert Gordis, "The Original Language of Qohelet," *JQR* 37 (1946–47): 69–70.

[112]Ibid., 83; one example of Gordis' line of argumentation comes against Zimmermann's comments about the fluctuating use of the article; Gordis maintained that this fluctuation was not a reflection of an inability to identify what is determinate in Aramaic, but a common feature of Mishnaic Hebrew (ibid., 81–83).

[113]Robert Gordis, "Qoheleth and Qumran—A Study of Style," *Biblica* 41 (1960): 395–96, 408–10.

[114]James Muilenberg, "A Qoheleth Scroll from Qumran," *BASOR* 135 (1954): 27–28; "It goes without saying that the *Hebrew* Book of Qoh. must now be dated before c. 150 B.C., and how much earlier we cannot yet say on the basis of the evidence afforded by the fragments. In any event we must reckon with the possibility that Qoh. had attained canonical status, or

something like it, in the Essene community by the middle of the second century B.C." (ibid., 27); translation theory proponents must explain two phenomena: (1) the canonical status of a Hebrew translation of a late Aramaic original by the year 150 B.C. and (2) the disappearance of a late Aramaic original and of any Aramaic copies.

[115]Zimmermann, "The Question of Hebrew in Qohelet," 80.

[116]Ibid., 82.

[117]Mitchell Dahood, "The Language of Qoheleth," *CBQ* 14 (1952): 227.

[118]Gordis, "Qoheleth and Qumran," 397–98; James Barr, "Hebrew Orthography and the Book of Job," *JSS* 30 (1985): 33.

[119]Dahood, "The Language of Qoheleth," 228; Dahood also claimed that the prefixed relative particle, which is often found in Ecclesiastes, was due to Phoenician influence (ibid., 228–29), but he did not explain why this particle is so frequent in other parts of the Bible (e.g., Pss 122:3–4; 124:1–2, 6 129:6– 7; 133:2–3; 136:23; 137:8–9; 146:3).

[120]Ibid., 231–32.

[121]Robert Gordis, "Was Qoheleth a Phoenician?" *JBL* 74 (1955): 103–14.

[122]Bo Isaksson, *Studies in the Language of Qohelet with Special Emphasis on the Verbal System*, AAU: SSU 10 (Uppsala: Almqvist & Wiksell, 1987); D. C. Fredericks, *Qoheleth's Language: Re-Evaluating Its Nature and Date*, ANETS 3 (Lewiston, N.Y.: Mellen, 1988); A. Schoors, *The Preacher Sought to Find Pleasing Words: A Study of the Language of Qoheleth*, OLA 41 (Leuven: Peeters, 1992).

[123]Fredericks, *Qoheleth's Language*, 27–28; for example, he explains the low number of *wayyiqtol* forms as due not to Aramaic influence, but to the philosophical genre (ibid., 28–32); Schoors, however, points out that literary genre does not explain all of the *qatal* forms in Ecclesiastes (*The Preacher*, 87, 172).

[124]Michael V. Fox, *Qohelet and His Contradictions*, JSOTSup 71 (Sheffield: Almond, 1989), 154.

[125]"The influence of the Aramaic construction of the perfect with וְ as the narrative tense, instead of the Hebrew imperfect consecutive, is certainly to be traced in *Qoheleth*, and sporadically in other very late books, perhaps also in a few passages in the books of Kings, which are open to the suspicion of being due to later interpolation" (Kautzsch, *Gesenius' Hebrew Grammar*, 338).

[126]Imperatives and nominal clauses with or without participles are also common in the discourse of Ecclesiastes.

[127]See Thomas Krüger, *Qoheleth*, trans. O. C. Dean, Jr. (Minneapolis: Fortress, 2004), 45.

[128]See Stefanovic, *The Aramaic of Daniel*, 41; Gunkel, *Einleitung in die Psalmen*, 44–48.

[129]The other *yiqtol* forms in this section are in embedded clauses (i.e., off the main plane).

[130]The author's overall message is held together by the epilogue in Eccl 12:9–14.

[131]A division can be made at Eccl 4:4 due to the occurrence of ראיתי, a common division marker not unlike אמרתי אני בלבי (Eccl 1:13; 3:17; 7:25; 8:9, 16; 9:1).

[132]The infinitive absolute in Eccl 4:2 functions like a *qatal*; the use of ראיתי in Eccl 4:15 comes in the middle of a unit rather than at the beginning.

[133]The enigmatic imperative in Eccl 4:17 anticipates the content of chapter five.

[134]Black, *An Aramaic Approach*, 7.

Chapter Four

Commentary

This chapter is a grammatical commentary on the Biblical Aramaic texts in light of the conclusions from the database about the verbal system. Grammatical presentations are almost always organized around grammatical categories. Examples are usually isolated from their *Sitz im Text* and collected under a given rubric. It can be illuminating to view all the examples of one type together, but such a presentation gives little insight into the language in action. Here the exposition of the corpus is intended to complement the more abstract feedback from the database.

Jeremiah 10:11

Jeremiah 10:11 has already played a major role in the present work. In the excursus of the first chapter, it was suggested that Jer 10:11–12 is a microcosm of the composition of Daniel in which the Aramaic of Jer 10:11 is interpreted by the Hebrew of Jer 10:12. In the third chapter, the Targum of Jer 10:11, which interprets the Aramaic as a letter from Jeremiah to the exiles, provided ample evidence that the Targums are more than translations. This verse has been of interest to Aramaists for other reasons as well, such as the use of the archaic form **ארקא**.

Thus, for such a small piece of Aramaic, Jer 10:11 adds a great deal to the discussion of Biblical Aramaic from a variety of angles. It is now time to examine the use of the verb in this unique text.

It is not immediately clear who the speaker is in Jer 10:11. It is equally unclear who is being addressed. The Targum confidently interprets the verse as a letter from Jeremiah to the exiles, but the immediate context of the biblical text does not identify these characters. What is clear is that a discourse is uttered to a plurality: כדנה תאמרון להום ("Thus you [pl.] will say to them"). The pronoun "them" presumably refers to the "nations" of Jer

10:10. The verbal form in this clause is the *yqtl*—the primary verbal form of discourse elsewhere in Biblical Aramaic.

What follows is the reported discourse not of something said previously, but of what is to be said "to them":

> אלהיא די שמיא וארקא לא עבדו יאבדו מארעא ומן תחות שמיא אלה
> 'The gods who did not make the sky and the land, may they perish from the land and from under these heavens.'

The *qtl* form (עבדו) is only a part of an attributive/relative clause (introduced by די) that describes "the gods." The verb on the main plane of the reported discourse is the short *yqtl* (יאבדו). Even within this brief sample of Biblical Aramaic, there are two communication levels: discourse and reported discourse. The primary verbal form of discourse is employed for both.

Daniel 2:4b–7:28

Daniel 2:4b contains three clauses in discourse.[1] The three verbal forms for these clauses are discourse forms—two imperatives and one *yqtl*. After the introductory formula at the beginning of Dan 2:5 ("The king answered and said"), the king's discourse is carried through Dan 2:6 by one nominal clause, three clauses with *yqtl* forms, and one clause with an imperative. The two conditional clauses in Dan 2:5–6 are not on the main plane of the discourse. The formula at the beginning of Dan 2:7 introduces two clauses in discourse containing one *yqtl* form apiece. Following the introductory formula of Dan 2:8, the discourse contains a nominal clause with a participle. Everything following the particle די is the content of what the king says he knows. The causal clause and the subsequent content clause are off the main plane. After the conditional clause at the outset of Dan 2:9, the main plane of the discourse resumes with a nominal clause.[2] The next clause has a *qtl* form in discourse. This is an isolated example of communication level three (narration within discourse). The king narrates the action of the Chaldeans (cf., Dan 2:23b1, 25b2, 28a2): "And you planned to say a false and corrupted word before me."[3] Of the two remaining clauses of discourse in Dan 2:9, one has an imperative, and the other has a *yqtl* form. Following yet another introductory formula at Dan 2:10, the Chaldeans' discourse is represented by a nominal clause. The די clause (attributive) and the causal clause (Dan

2:10b) are off the main plane. Daniel 2:11 contains two nominal clauses on the main plane of the discourse.[4]

Out of the 17 main clauses of level two discourse in Dan 2:4b–11, 7 have *yqtl* as the primary verbal form, 4 have the imperative, and the remaining clauses are nominal. Even within a short stretch of discourse, the *yqtl* establishes itself as the primary verbal form. The first substantial piece of narration begins at Dan 2:12 where the *qtl* takes over.

Daniel 2:12–14 contains 7 clauses on the main plane of the narration. Out of these 7 clauses, 6 have *qtl* as the primary verbal form, and 1 is a nominal clause with a participle. The די clause at Dan 2:14b is attributive (i.e., off the main plane). Verse 14 also includes the first occurrence of *edayin*.

After the introductory formula at Dan 2:15, Daniel's discourse comes in the form of a nominal clause with a participle. The narration resumes at Dan 2:15b and continues through verse 19 with seven clauses on the main plane, all of which have *qtl* as the primary verbal form. The די clauses at Dan 2:16b, 18b introduce content (Dan 2:16b) and purpose (Dan 2:18b); thus, they are off the main plane of the narration.

The introductory formula of Dan 2:20 ushers in a poetic unit that continues through Dan 2:23a. The unit begins with a periphrastic construction (*yqtl* + participle) and is dominated by participles throughout. It appears the participle can serve as a kind of primary form for poetry in Aramaic:[5]

> And he changes (ptc) times and seasons,
> He removes (ptc) kings and establishes (ptc) kings;
> He gives (gives) wisdom to wise men,
> And knowledge to those who know understanding.
> He reveals (ptc) the deep things and the hidden things;
> He knows (ptc) what is in the darkness,
> And illumination abides (ptc) with him.
> I thank (ptc) and praise (ptc) you, O God of my fathers (Daniel 2:21–23aα; author's translation).[6]

After the conclusion of the poetic unit, Daniel narrates (communication level three) the action of God from Dan 2:19a with a *qtl* form (Dan 2:23b). The following די clauses are off the main plane.

The alternation of *qtl* in narration and *yqtl* in discourse occurs in lock step fashion in Dan 2:24–25. Verse 24 begins with three clauses on the main plane of the narration, each with a *qtl* form.[7] What follows is a *yqtl*-imperative-*yqtl* sequence of three clauses on the main plane of the discourse. The narration resumes at verse 25 with two *qtl* clauses. Arioch's narration (communication level three) of his own action ("I found a man"), which is introduced by די,[8] employs yet another *qtl* form. The די clause that concludes verse 25 is attributive (i.e., off the main plane).

After the introductory formula of Dan 2:26, the discourse consists of a nominal clause with a participle followed by an attributive די clause. Daniel 2:27 is identical grammatically to verse 26—introductory formula followed by a nominal clause with a participle—except for the fact that the attributive די clause comes at the front. The discourse continues in Dan 2:28 with a nominal clause.[9] Daniel then narrates God's action with a *qtl* form ("And he made known to the king")—presumably another reference to Dan 2:19a (cf., Dan 2:23b).[10] Verse 28 concludes with a nominal clause in discourse that prepares the way for a narration within discourse in Dan 2:29.

Daniel 2:29–30a consists of three clauses of narration within discourse, and all three verbs are *qtl* forms.[11] Regular discourse resumes briefly in Dan 2:30b with two *yqtl* clauses—the first is impersonal ("let it be known")—before the extended narration within discourse of Dan 2:31–35 where Daniel narrates the dream of Nebuchadnezzar. The verbal form of choice after the initial description of the image in Dan 2:31–33 is the *qtl* (Dan 2:34–35). The question with Dan 2:31–33 is whether to understand the adjectival relations (i.e., adjectives, verbal adjectives, and constructs with די) as nominal clauses or as descriptive phrases.[12] Daniel 2:34 has three *qtl* clauses,[13] and Dan 2:35 has six.[14] These two verses illustrate well the use of the *qtl* in narration within discourse:

I was looking	*qtl* + ptc
And it smote	*qtl*
And it shattered	*qtl*
Then they were shattered	*qtl*
And they were	*qtl*
And the wind lifted	*qtl*
And no place was found	*qtl*
And the stone was	*qtl*
And it filled	*qtl*

The discourse of Dan 2:36 concludes the dream with a nominal clause ("This is the dream") and transitions to the interpretation with a *yqtl* ("we will tell").

The interpretation of the dream is not narration within discourse, but discourse (communication level two). The discourse of Dan 2:37 is one nominal clause ("You, O king, are the king of kings") followed by an attributive די clause whose description of the king continues through Dan 2:38a. The discourse of Dan 2:38b is also a nominal clause ("You are the head of gold").[15]

Every main clause in the discourse of Dan 2:39–44 has *yqtl* as the primary verbal form:[16]

Another kingdom will rise…, and another third kingdom	*yqtl*
And a fourth kingdom will be strong as iron	*yqtl*
It will shatter	*yqtl*
And it will crush	*yqtl*[17]
A divided kingdom it will be	*yqtl*
And the firmness of iron will be in it	*yqtl*
Part of the kingdom will be strong	*yqtl*
And part of the kingdom will be broken	*yqtl*
They will be mixed	*yqtl* + ptc
And they will not cleave to one another	*yqtl* + ptc
The God of heaven will establish a kingdom	*yqtl*
And the kingdom will not be left	*yqtl*
It will shatter and end all these kingdoms	*yqtl* + *yqtl*
And it will rise forever	*yqtl*

The construction מלכו די לעלמין לא תתחבל (Dan 2:44) can be understood in two different ways: (1) "a kingdom that will not be destroyed forever" and (2) "a kingdom of (or which is) forever; it will not be destroyed." The first option is part of one clause, and the second option introduces an additional clause.

Daniel 2:45–49 is primarily narration dominated by *qtl* forms.[18] The first main clause in Dan 2:45 is narration within discourse: Daniel narrates that God made known "what will be after this" (object clause) to Nebuchadnezzar (cf., Dan 2:28). The two nominal clauses in Dan 2:45b are discourse. The three clauses in Dan 2:46 are all on the main plane of the narration, and each has a *qtl* form. After the introductory formula of Dan 2:47, the construction מן קשט די appears to be an adverbial opening ("Truly") to the nominal clause of the discourse (see Greek and Latin versions).[19] Daniel 2:48a has three *qtl* clauses on the main plane of the narration. The narration of Dan 2:49 has two *qtl* clauses and one nominal clause.

Daniel 3:1 begins the new narration with a *qtl* clause. The two clauses that describe the dimensions of the image of gold could be construed as relative clauses ("whose height was sixty cubits and whose width was six cubits"),[20] but there is no relative pronoun ("Its height was sixty cubits, and its width was six cubits").[21] Daniel 3:2 contains only one clause on the main plane of the narration—a *qtl* clause.

The main clauses for Dan 3:3–4 are all nominal clauses with participles. The first three are narration, and the fourth is the impersonal "it is commanded" in discourse. The discourse from Dan 3:4b continues through Dan 3:6 with three *yqtl* clauses.[22] The narration of Dan 3:7 consists of two main nominal clauses with participles ("falling" and "bowing down"), although these could be interpreted as a single clause.[23] This narration continues through Dan 3:8 with two *qtl* clauses.

After the introductory formula at the beginning of Dan 3:9, the discourse begins with an imperative ("O king, live forever"). In Dan 3:10, the Chaldeans narrate with a *qtl* the king's giving of the decree in Dan 3:4–6 ("You, O king, gave a decree"). Everything that follows די through Dan 3:11 is only the content of the decree. The main plane of the Chaldeans' discourse resumes in Dan 3:12 with a nominal clause ("There are Judean men") followed by an attributive clause. At Dan 3:12b, the Chaldeans narrate the action of the three friends with a *qtl* ("These men did not set judgment concerning you, O king"). It is possible that the final two nominal clauses with participles in this verse are also narration within discourse, but it is more likely that *qtl* forms would have been used for such a purpose. Thus, "they are not worshiping" and "they are not bowing down" are understood here as ordinary discourse.

Daniel 3:13 firmly reestablishes the narration with two "*edayin* + x + *qtl*" clauses. Nebuchadnezzar's discourse is introduced in Dan 3:14. This discourse could be one nominal clause: "Is it true that…?" It could also be three: (1) "Is this true?" (2) "Are you not worshiping?" and (3) "Are you not bowing down?" The main plane of the discourse in Dan 3:15 contains three *yqtl* clauses and one nominal clause.[24]

After the introductory formula of Dan 3:16, the discourse of the three friends begins with a nominal clause with a participle. The majority of Dan 3:17 is a conditional clause, but the main plane is the final *yqtl*. The condition at the beginning of Dan 3:18 is "If not." The main plane is "Let it be (*yqtl*) known (ptc)." Daniel 3:18b is subsumed under די as a content clause.[25]

Daniel 3:19 begins a stretch of narration that extends through the middle of Dan 3:24. The *qtl* is the primary verbal form. Here is a sample from Dan 3:20–24a:

He commanded	*qtl*
Those men were bound	*qtl*
And they were thrown	*qtl*
The flame of the fire killed them	*qtl*
And those men fell	*qtl*
Then Nebuchadnezzar the king was alarmed	*qtl*
And he arose	*qtl*

This string of seven *qtl* clauses is preceded and followed by a pair of nominal clauses with participles. Out of 13 clauses on the main plane of Dan 3:19–24, 9 are *qtl* clauses. This unit also has a number of clauses off the main plane, but these need not distract the grammarian from what is taking place with the primary usages of the verbal forms. It is also noteworthy that the macrostructure of this section is built with *edayin* (Dan 3:19, 21, 24, 26, 30).

The king's discourse in Dan 3:24b comes in the form of a question ("Did we not throw?"), but the *qtl* form is used because the question recounts or narrates the action of Dan 3:21b ("they were thrown"). The following response of the counselors ("Certainly, O king") is more like an interjection, but it can be counted as nominal clause ("[We] certainly [did], O king"). The king's discourse in Dan 3:25 is made up of three nominal clauses, two of which have participles.

The narration advances at the outset of Dan 3:26 with "*edayin* + *qtl*." After Nebuchadnezzar commands the three friends with two imperatives ("Go out and come out"), another "*edayin* + *qtl*" construction might be expected, but instead there is an "*edayin* + participle" construction that is used to describe the three friends coming out of the fiery furnace. Bauer and Leander cite this as an instance of the use of the participle to advance the narration, and H. B. Rosén claims it as key evidence of the use of the participle as a narrative tense.[26] But it appears that the participle is used here to reset the stage rather than to advance the narration. This use of the participle continues through Dan 3:27 where the leaders are "gathered" and "looking."[27]

The stage is now set for the king's discourse in Dan 3:28: "Blessed be the God of Shadrach, Meshach, and Abed-nego."[28] The king then narrates his own giving of a decree with a *qtl* form (Dan 3:29a), and all that follows די is the content of the decree with the exception of the כל קבל די clause in Dan 3:29b. The narration concludes in Dan 3:30 with a *qtl* form.

In Dan 3:31, Nebuchadnezzar begins a correspondence with the peoples (cf., Dan 6:26): "May your peace increase (*yqtl*)." He then recounts to the peoples how "it seemed good" (*qtl*) to tell them about the signs and wonders of God (Dan 3:32). The brief poetic unit of Dan 3:33 is made up entirely of nominal clauses.

Daniel 4:1–5 is first-person narration by Nebuchadnezzar. The primary verbal form is *qtl*, but two *yqtl* forms also appear within this section (Dan 4:2).[29] The second of these two *yqtl* forms is built on the root בהל. This root never occurs as a *qtl* in Biblical Aramaic. When it appears as a purely verbal form, it is always a *yqtl* (Dan 4:2, 16; 5:6; 7:15, 28). This apparently "fixed" form has affected the use of the preceding root דחל as a *yqtl*. In any case, these *yqtl* forms do not advance the narration; they describe Nebuchadnezzar's state of being.

Nebuchadnezzar then reports his discourse with Daniel (Dan 4:6). After a lengthy description of Daniel in Dan 4:6a, the main clause of Dan 4:6b has an imperative ("tell"). Yet another communication level is introduced in Dan 4:7–11a2 where Nebuchadnezzar reports his own narration of his dream. The *qtl* clauses and descriptive nominal clauses are to be expected here, but this section also has a cluster of *yqtl* forms. After the two *qtl* clauses of Dan 4:8 ("The tree grew great [רבה], and it grew strong [תקף]"), a *yqtl* clause appears ("And its height reached [ימטא] to the sky"). This use of the *yqtl* is almost inexplicable, especially when the interpretation of the dream in Dan 4:19 has the *qtl* of the same verb ("And your greatness grew great [רבת], and it reached [מטת] to the sky"). The three *yqtl* clauses in Dan 4:9b are analogous to nominal clauses with participles (cf., Dan 4:18). These clauses do not represent the primary use of the *yqtl*.

Daniel 4:11 introduces communication level six (reported discourse within reported discourse). Since Dan 4:6, Nebuchadnezzar has reported his own discourse and narration. Now a report of the watcher's discourse is found as part of the already reported material. Daniel 4:11a3–14 shows the use of the imperative and the *yqtl* on this level of communication:

Cut down the tree	impv
And cut off its branches	impv
Strip off its foliage	impv
And scatter its fruit	impv

Let the beast flee	*yqtl*
Leave the stump	impv
And let it be wet with the dew of the sky	*yqtl*
And let its portion be with the beast	nc
Let its heart be changed	*yqtl*
And let the heart of a beast be given to it	*yqtl*
And let seven times pass over it	*yqtl*
With the decree of watchers is the word	nc
And with the word of holy ones is the affair	nc

Even with the complexity of the communication levels, the use of the imperative and the *yqtl* is as consistent here as it is on communication level two (discourse).

Nebuchadnezzar reports his own discourse again in Dan 4:15. The first half of the verse is probably a nominal clause ("This is the dream") followed by a relative clause ("that I saw"), but it is possible that it is a *qtl* clause ("I saw this dream"). The second half of the verse is a clause with the imperative "tell" (cf., Dan 4:6).[30]

Daniel 4:16 is third-person narration, but the effect is that Nebuchadnezzar is still telling the story.[31] The first clause has a *qtl* form, and the second has a *yqtl* form.[32] Nebuchadnezzar's discourse is reported with a *yqtl*, and Daniel's discourse is reported with two nominal clauses (Dan 4:16b). The report of Daniel's discourse continues through Dan 4:24.

The next clause after Dan 4:16 is a nominal clause that spans three verses: "The tree that you saw (Dan 4:17)…it is you, O king (Dan 4:19)." The portions that follow these separated parts are off the main plane. The entirety of Dan 4:20 is taken off the main plane by the initial די; it serves only to set up the main nominal clause in Dan 4:21a.[33] The remainder of Daniel's interpretation through Dan 4:24 is characterized by nominal clauses, *yqtl* forms, and one imperative.[34]

The third-person narration resumes in Dan 4:25–26 with *qtl* forms. In the database, this is still counted as narration within discourse since it is framed by Nebuchadnezzar's first-person narration. Either way the *qtl* is used as the primary verbal form for some type of narration here. After the introductory formula of Dan 4:27, the king's discourse comes in the form of a nominal clause ("Is this not Babylon the great?").[35] Daniel 4:28a briefly returns to narration within discourse with a *qtl* clause, but Dan 4:28b is the reported discourse of the voice from the sky.[36] Within this reported discourse is a narration: "The kingdom has passed (*qtl*) from you." The reported discourse resumes in Dan 4:29 with two nominal clauses and two *yqtl* clauses. Daniel 4:29b is temporal (cf., Dan 4:14b, 22b).

Daniel 4:30 narrates the realization of what was announced in Dan 4:29. There are two *qtl* clauses and two *yqtl* clauses here.[37] Daniel 4:31 returns to the first-person narration of the earlier part of the chapter with *qtl* clauses,[38] but a *yqtl* (יתוב) is inserted directly into the middle of the narration. This use of the *yqtl* occurs three more times in Dan 4:33, twice with the same verb.[39] However the use of the *yqtl* here is explained,[40] the *qtl* remains the primary verbal form for narration. Even with the sequence of three *yqtl* forms in Dan 4:33a, the verse concludes with two *qtl* forms (Dan 4:33b). Daniel 4:34 is no longer narration within discourse, but direct discourse. The compound predicate consists of three participles ("I praise and exalt and honor").

Daniel 5:1–7b2 begins a new narration about Belshazzar. The primary verbal form is *qtl*. Out of nine main clauses with verbal forms, seven have *qtl*. The sequence in Dan 5:3–5a1 is exemplary:

Then the vessels were brought in	*qtl*
And they drank	*qtl*
They drank	*qtl*
And they praised	*qtl*
Fingers came out	*qtl*

The *yqtl* form in Dan 5:2b (ישתון) is used like the participle of the same root in Dan 5:23 (שתין). It is followed by two occurrences of the same root in the *qtl* form (Dan 5:3b, 4a).[41]

The discourse of Dan 5:7b begins with a subject clause with two *yqtl* forms ("Whoever reads this writing and tells me its interpretation"). This clause is the subject of the main *yqtl* verb ("let him be clothed"). The relationship of this main verb to what follows is not immediately clear: (1) "let him be clothed with purple and with a necklace of gold on his neck" or (2) "let him be clothed with purple and let a necklace of gold be on his neck." The first option is one clause, and the second option has two clauses. The discourse then concludes with a *yqtl* ("let him rule").

The narration of Dan 5:8–9 is really a description of the state of confusion in which Belshazzar, the wise men, and the nobles find themselves. The scene is thus depicted with four nominal clauses that have participles. The narration is advanced in Dan 5:10 with a *qtl* when the queen comes on to the scene. The queen's discourse, which is introduced in Dan

5:10b, begins with the standard imperative addressed to the king ("O king, live forever"). This is followed by two *yqtl* clauses.

The queen's discourse continues in Dan 5:11 with a nominal clause ("There is a man"). The discourse then shifts to a narration within discourse. The queen recounts what took place with Daniel in the days of Nebuchadnezzar, and this is done with two *qtl* clauses: wisdom was found in him, and Nebuchadnezzar established him as chief. After a lengthy כל קבל די clause at the beginning of Dan 5:12, regular discourse resumes and concludes with two *yqtl* clauses.

The narration in Dan 5:13 of Daniel being "brought in" (*qtl*) only serves as a bridge to the conversation between Daniel and Belshazzar. After the introductory formula, Belshazzar's discourse begins with a nominal clause ("You are that Daniel" or "Are you that Daniel?").[42] Belshazzar then narrates with a *qtl* in Dan 5:14 his hearing of the queen's discourse ("I heard").[43] This narration within discourse continues in Dan 5:15 where Belshazzar recounts how the wise men were "brought in" (*qtl*) before him and how they were unable (nc) to tell the interpretation. Belshazzar returns in Dan 5:16a to what he "heard" (*qtl*) from the queen.[44] Thus, Dan 5:14 narrates Dan 5:11, and Dan 5:16a narrates Dan 5:12. Regular discourse resumes in Dan 5:16b with the same content and "*yqtl*-nc-*yqtl*" sequence of Dan 5:7b.[45]

Daniel 5:17 introduces Daniel's discourse. The use of discourse forms in this verse alone is noteworthy:

Let your gifts be to you	*yqtl*
And give your rewards to another	impv
Nevertheless, I will read the writing to the king	*yqtl*
And I will make known to him the interpretation	*yqtl*

Daniel begins to narrate in Dan 5:18 with *qtl* forms. This narration within discourse continues through Dan 5:28. Out of twenty-nine main clauses in this section, twenty-three have *qtl* as the primary verbal form. The *yqtl* forms in Dan 5:21 are part of a reference to Dan 4:12, 20, 30 where it was observed that the use of the *yqtl* was somewhat abnormal.

Daniel 5:19 features five periphrastic constructions in which a *qtl* is combined with a participle. Daniel 5:20a is temporal and off the main plane.[46] A series of four *qtl* clauses begins in Dan 5:20b and runs through the first part of Dan 5:21a.[47] Although interspersed with nominal clauses and possible level two discourse (Dan 5:25–26), Dan 5:22–28 is an excellent example of the use of the *qtl* in narration within discourse:

You did not humble your heart[48]	*qtl*
You exalted yourself	*qtl*
And the vessels of his house were brought in before you	*qtl*
And you…were drinking	ptc
You praised the gods	*qtl*
You did not honor the God	*qtl*
The palm of the hand was sent	*qtl*
And this writing was inscribed	*qtl*
And this is the writing	nc
This is the interpretation	nc
God has numbered your kingdom	*qtl*
And he has completed it	*qtl*
You have been weighed	*qtl*
And you have been found lacking	*qtl*
Your kingdom has been divided	*qtl*
And it has been given to the Medes and Persians	*qtl*

The use of *qtl* forms continues in Dan 5:29–30, only now the narration is not within discourse. The king's commands (cf., Dan 5:7, 16) are not presented as discourse; rather, the carrying out of his commands is narrated with *qtl* forms.[49] The story concludes in Dan 5:30 with a *qtl* clause that narrates Belshazzar's death.

The narration of Dan 6:1–7a is carried primarily by the *qtl*. Six of ten main clauses have *qtl* as the primary verbal form.[50] As noted in the third chapter of the present work, the use of *edayin* is more prominent in Daniel 6 than in any other portion of Biblical Aramaic. This usage begins in Dan 6:4. The narration of this opening section is broken only momentarily in Dan 6:6 by discourse introduced by די. The *yqtl* ("we will not find") is used in the main clause of this discourse, but the exceptive clause of Dan 6:6b has a *qtl* ("unless we find"). This use of *qtl* has been hailed as the only future *qtl* in all of Biblical Aramaic.[51] But can anything definitive really be said about this usage? It is off the main plane, and nothing like it occurs elsewhere. Whatever the case may be, this occurrence cannot be considered determinative for what is the primary use of the *qtl*, lest the exception be allowed to become the rule.

The discourse of Dan 6:7b begins with the by now familiar address to the king in the imperative ("O king, live forever"). The only main clause in Dan

6:8 has a *qtl* ("All have taken counsel together").[52] This narration within discourse narrates the meeting of the leaders (see Dan 6:5–6). The discourse then proceeds in Dan 6:9 with two *yqtl* clauses.[53] Darius does not respond in the discourse; rather, the narrator simply indicates with a *qtl* that he "signed" the interdict.

Daniel 6:11 opens with a temporal clause ("when he knew"), but the main *qtl* form of the narration is "he went in." Daniel 6:11b contains three participles in a compound predicate. It is possible that the pronoun הוא that precedes these participles is the verb הוה as in some medieval Aramaic manuscripts. This *qtl* would then be the main verb in periphrastic construction with the participles.[54]

The narration continues in Dan 6:12 with two *qtl* clauses (cf., Dan 6:7, 16). Yet another *qtl* clause begins Dan 6:13 before the discourse is introduced. The discourse comes in the form of a question: "Did you not sign (*qtl*) an interdict?" This question narrates or recounts the action of the king from Dan 6:10.[55] After the introductory formula of Dan 6:13b, the king's discourse is a nominal clause ("The word is true"). This interchange paves the way for the leaders to narrate the action of Daniel in Dan 6:14, first with a *qtl* clause and then with a nominal clause that has a participle.[56]

After the opening temporal clause ("when he heard") in Dan 6:15, the king's response is narrated with three *qtl* clauses, the last of which is in periphrastic construction with a participle. This *qtl* chain continues into Dan 6:16a. The discourse of Dan 6:16b1 consists of an imperative ("Know, O king") and the content ("that...") of what the king is to know. The narration of Daniel being thrown into the lions' den (Dan 6:17a) comes in the form of three *qtl* clauses. The king then addresses Daniel with a *yqtl*: "Your God whom you worship continually will save you." The narration of Dan 6:18 consists of three *qtl* clauses as well. The final די clause expresses purpose/result.

Daniel 6:19 contains four *qtl* clauses on the main plane of the narration. The *yqtl* at the beginning of Dan 6:20 ("the king arose") sets up the main action expressed with a *qtl* form ("he went out").[57] The narration continues in Dan 6:21a with another *qtl* clause. After the introductory formula of Dan 6:21b, the king asks a question of Daniel: "Has your God, whom you worship continually, been able (*qtl*) to rescue you from the lions?"[58] The question comes in the form of a narration of a scenario that the king hopes is the reality.

The narrator then informs the reader in Dan 6:22 that Daniel "spoke" (*qtl*) with the king,[59] and the standard imperatival form of address to the king follows ("O king, live forever"). Daniel then narrates his experience in Dan 6:23a with three *qtl* clauses: "My God sent (*qtl*) his angel, and he shut (*qtl*) the mouth of the lions, and they did not harm (*qtl*) me."[60]

The main plane of the narration in Dan 6:24–26a consists of nine *qtl* clauses:[61]

Then the king was very pleased	*qtl*
And he commanded Daniel	*qtl*
And Daniel was brought up	*qtl*
And no harm was found in him	*qtl*
And the king commanded	*qtl*
And those men were brought in	*qtl*
And they were thrown into the lions' den	*qtl*
And they did not reach the bottom of the den	*qtl*
Then Darius the king wrote	*qtl*

Darius opens his letter to the peoples with "may your peace increase (*yqtl*)" (cf., Dan 3:31). He then narrates with a *qtl* that a decree has been set (Dan 6:27). All that follows די in Dan 6:27a is the content of the decree. Daniel 6:27b–28 provides the rationale for the decree to fear the God of Daniel; namely, that he is the living and eternal God who rescues people.[62] The narrator has the final word in Dan 6:29: "And this Daniel prospered (*qtl*) in the kingdom of Darius and in the kingdom of Cyrus the Persian."

Daniel 7 divides evenly into two halves: the vision (Dan 7:1–14) and the interpretation (Dan 7:15–28).[63] These two halves then break down into two main sections each. In the first section of the first half is the appearance of four beasts (Dan 7:1–8), the climax of which is the little horn speaking "great things" (Dan 7:8). In the second section of the first half is the judgment scene (Dan 7:9–14), the climax of which is the appearance of one "like a son of man" (Dan 7:13–14). The second, interpretative half (Dan 7:15–28) has the general explanation of the vision (Dan 7:15–18) and the explanation of the fourth beast and the little horn (Dan 7:19–28).

Bauer and Leander have provided an analysis of the verbal forms in Dan 7:2–14 for the purpose of giving a clear view of the narrative style in Daniel.[64] After walking through the text, they provide the following summary:

> One obtains from the analysis of this section the impression that the narrator portrays longer lasting events or circumstantial clauses in the participle or aorist, on the other hand the major moments (above all, when with verbs of so-called punctiliar or perfective kind of action) in the nominal. Also the same event can appear, if it happens gradually, in the participle, if suddenly, in the nominal: סָלְקָן (V. 3) means that the beasts come out gradually, סִלְקַת (V. 8) on the other hand that the horn shoots out suddenly. A historical (dramatic) present in the true sense we need not to assume in this section, although the participles used here represent the transition to such (author's translation).[65]

In this summary, Bauer and Leander speak of the "narrator." The narrator beginning in Dan 7:2 is Daniel; thus, Dan 7:2–14 is narration within discourse (or first-person narration). The third-person narration in Dan 7:1, however, is what sets the context for the whole chapter.[66] This means that Daniel 7 has two primary levels of communication: (1) narration (Dan 7:1) and (2) narration within discourse (Dan 7:2–28).[67]

Bauer and Leander group the participle and the "aorist" (*yqtl*) together as the forms that express durative or circumstantial action.[68] It is perhaps best to speak of these forms as secondary within any form of narration. Bauer and Leander rightly note that the major moments of the narration are given in the "nominal" (*qtl*). There is no need, however, to label this use of the *qtl* "punctiliar" or "perfective" *Aktionsart*. It is simply the primary verbal form for narration within discourse. It is used to narrate the main action. Thus, Bauer and Leander go beyond the evidence when they say that the little horn comes up "suddenly" due to the use of a *qtl* form in contrast to the participle of the same root used to speak of the four beasts coming up out of the sea. The contrast is not between what is sudden and what is not sudden, but between what is primary and what is secondary. The secondary forms set the stage, and the primary forms give the main action. The *qtl* gives the main action throughout this section, and it would be odd for this one occurrence to express suddenness.

After the third-person narration of Dan 7:1, the formula at the beginning of Dan 7:2 introduces Daniel's narration of his own dream.[69] The stage is set in Dan 7:2b–3a by means of nominal clauses with participles. Nominal clauses with or without participles are used of the beasts for descriptive purposes (Dan 7:4–8), but the main action is always expressed by a *qtl* form. The only discourse in Dan 7:1–14 is the reported discourse of Dan 7:5 where the second beast is commanded, "Arise (impv), eat (impv) much flesh."

After the expression "I was looking" at the beginning of Dan 7:9, the עד די can be interpreted as temporal ("until") or as deictic ("behold").[70] The עד די could go either with both *qtl* clauses ("until/behold thrones were cast and the Ancient of Days sat") or with only the first ("until/behold thrones were cast. And the Ancient of Days sat"). The description of the Ancient of Days in Dan 7:9 is done with nominal clauses, but in Dan 7:10 participles and *yqtl* forms, which appear to be semantically equivalent, are employed. The *qtl* narration in Dan 7:10b ("The judgment sat, and books were opened") picks up where it left off in Dan 7:9a ("And the Ancient of Days sat").[71]

The main plane of Dan 7:11–14a1 is carried entirely by *qtl* clauses:

I was looking	*qtl* + ptc
I was looking[72]	*qtl* + ptc
And its body was destroyed	*qtl*
And it was given to the burning of the fire	*qtl*
Their dominion was removed	*qtl*
And prolonging in life was given to them	*qtl*
I was looking	*qtl* + ptc
One like a son of man was coming	*qtl* + ptc
And he reached to the Ancient of Days	*qtl*
And he was drawn near before him	*qtl*
And dominion was given to him	*qtl*

In light of this consistent use of the *qtl*, the *yqtl* ("they worshiped him") in Dan 7:14a2 seems somewhat out of place. It appears to be the same usage of *yqtl* as that found in Dan 7:10a. The two *yqtl* forms in Dan 7:14b come in attributive clauses. Daniel 7:14b has only one main clause—a nominal clause ("His dominion is an everlasting dominion").[73]

Daniel 7:15–16, which begins the interpretive section, has an interesting pattern of alternation between the *qtl* and the *yqtl*. The *qtl* is always in first position, and the *yqtl* is always out of first position. This suggests that the *qtl* is primary, while the *yqtl* is secondary. Such an understanding yields the following idiomatic translation:

> "My spirit was distressed (*qtl*) within me, as the visions of my head were alarming (*yqtl*) me. I drew near (*qtl*) to one of those standing, requesting (*yqtl*) the truth from him about all this. And he said (*qtl*) to me, making known (*yqtl*) to me the interpretation of the words…" (author's translation).

This understanding of the alternation is as plausible as any other. It makes for one of the clearest examples of the relationship between *qtl* and *yqtl* in narration.

Daniel 7:17 begins the reported discourse that was introduced at the end of Dan 7:16. The syntax of Dan 7:17 can be understood in at least two ways: (1) "These great beasts...are four kings..." or (2) "As for these great beasts...four kings will rise (*yqtl*)." The first option is a nominal clause, and the second option is a *yqtl* clause. The second option fits better with the pattern found in Dan 7:23–24 where the interpreted element is introduced before the interpretation is given in the main clause. This pattern also occurs elsewhere in Daniel (e.g., Dan 5:25–28). The reported discourse continues in Dan 7:18 with two more *yqtl* clauses.

The main plane for Daniel's narration in Dan 7:19–20 is "Then I was inclined (*qtl*) to make certain." The remainder of Dan 7:19 is a description of the fourth beast ("about the fourth beast which..."), and Dan 7:20 is a description of the ten horns and the little horn ("and about the ten horns which...and another which..."). Daniel's narration continues in Dan 7:21 with "I was (*qtl*) looking (ptc)." The two nominal clauses with participles then describe the war scene.[74] The clause "until the Ancient of Days came (*qtl*)" is off the main plane, but it is not clear that "and the judgment was given (*qtl*) to the saints of the Most High" should be included under "until." This raises the question of whether the sitting of the Ancient of Days in Dan 7:9 and the sitting of the judgment in Dan 7:10 is one action or two. However this matter is resolved, it is clear that the narration of Dan 7:22 then concludes with two *qtl* clauses. The reported discourse that begins in Dan 7:23 is introduced with a *qtl* clause: "Thus he said (*qtl*), 'As for the fourth beast....'"

The main plane of the reported discourse in Dan 7:23–26 consists of fourteen *yqtl* clauses:[75]

A fourth kingdom will be in the land[76]	*yqtl*
And it will devour all the land	*yqtl*
And it will trample it	*yqtl*
And it will crush it	*yqtl*
Ten kings will arise	*yqtl*
And another will arise after them	*yqtl*
And he will be different from the first ones	*yqtl*
And he will bring low three kings	*yqtl*
And he will speak words against the Most High	*yqtl*

And he will wear out the saints of the Most High *yqtl*
And he will intend to change times and law *yqtl*
And they will be given into his hand *yqtl*
And the judgment will sit *yqtl*
And his dominion will be removed *yqtl*

The *qtl* form in Dan 7:27a comes initially as a surprise: “And the kingdom…was given (*qtl*) to a people, the saints of the Most High.” It was noted, however, in the second chapter of the present work that this usage is not unlike what is found in a Hebrew construction such as Gen 1:5a: “And God called (ויקרא) the light day, and the darkness he called (קרא) night.” The *wayyiqtol* is followed by an “x + *qatal*” clause in which the verbal root is the same. The action of the *qatal* is thus layered upon the action expressed in the *wayyiqtol*. The same phenomenon takes place between Dan 7:25b2 and Dan 7:27a: “And they were given (ויתיהבון) into his hand…And the kingdom…was given (יהיבת) to a people, the saints of the Most High.” Here the *wyqtl* is followed by an “x + *qtl*” clause in which the verbal root is the same. The action of the *qtl* is layered upon the action expressed in the *wyqtl*; thus, the *qtl* does not stand alone.

The first clause of Dan 7:27b is a nominal clause (“His kingdom is an everlasting kingdom”), and the final clause has a compound predicate (“And all the dominions will worship [*yqtl*] and obey [*yqtl*] him”). Daniel 7:28a returns to narration within discourse with a nominal clause. The use of *yqtl* clauses in Dan 7:28b is not unlike what was observed in Dan 4:2, 16; 5:6; 7:15. Daniel’s first-person narration concludes with a *qtl* clause: “I kept (*qtl*) the matter in my heart.”

Ezra 4:8–6:18

In Ezra 4:8, it is narrated that Rehum and Shimshai “wrote” (*qtl*) a letter about Jerusalem to Artaxerxes. But the letter itself does not begin until Ezra 4:11. The intervening verses (Ezra 4:9–10) are off the main plane; they provide background information about the people behind the letter. In Ezra 4:11, the narrator says, “This is the letter” (nc). This is followed by a relative clause and the letter opening.

The first two main clauses of the letter come in Ezra 4:12–13. These two verses qualify as level two communication (discourse), even though they are from a written letter. Ezra 4:12 begins, "Let it be (*yqtl*) known (ptc) to the king." All that follows is a subject clause; in other words, "Let what the Judeans are doing be known to the king." The same pattern occurs in Ezra 4:13: "Let it be (*yqtl*) known (ptc) to the king" is followed by a subject clause. Thus the translation, "Let the fact that they will not pay tribute be known to the king."

In Ezra 4:14, Rehum and Shimshai narrate the action that they have taken: "Concerning this we have sent (*qtl*) and we have made known (*qtl*) to the king." The lengthy כל קבל די clause at the beginning of Ezra 4:14 is counted as the "x" in the "x + *qtl*" clause of Ezra 4:14a1, which runs past the *athnach*.

Ezra 4:15 begins with a purpose clause ("that he might seek"). It is possible that this includes the following two *yqtl* forms as well, but the use of the *waw* makes it preferable to view these as direct discourse with the king ("And you will find...and you will know"). All that follows די provides the content of what the king is to find and know. In Ezra 4:15b, Rehum and Shimshai offer a brief narration of what happened to Jerusalem: "Because of this that city was destroyed (*qtl*)."

"We are making known (ptc) to the king that..." (Ezra 4:16) is very much like "Let it be made known to the king that..." (Ezra 4:12–13). This concluding remark by Rehum and Shimshai is followed by narration of the fact that the king "sent" (*qtl*) a letter in reply (Ezra 4:17). The king narrates with *qtl* how he has responded to the initial letter (Ezra 4:18–19): the letter was read;[77] a decree was set; they sought; and they found what Rehum and Shimshai reported.[78]

The king's discourse in Ezra 4:21–22 is made up of imperatives and *yqtl* forms. The decree ("Set [impv] a decree") appears to be limited to stopping the men. The statement, "And that city will not be rebuilt (*yqtl*)," is separate.[79] The imperative at the beginning of Ezra 4:22 is combined with a participle in periphrastic construction. A final *yqtl* form occurs in a question (Ezra 4:22b). What takes place after the king's reply is read to Rehum and Shimshai (Ezra 4:23) involves two *qtl* clauses ("they went out" and "and they stopped them"). What is labeled Ezra 4:23a1 runs past the *athnach*. The resumption of Ezra 4:5 at Ezra 4:24 involves two more *qtl* clauses ("then the work stopped" and "and it was ceasing").

The narration beginning at Ezra 5:1–2 is established with three *qtl* clauses. This is where the prophets Haggai and Zechariah support the efforts of Zerubbabel and Jeshua to build the temple. The narration of Ezra 5:1–7 is carried primarily by *qtl* forms.[80] The discourse of Ezra 5:3b is an inquiry that involves a narration: "Who set (*qtl*) a decree for you?" The only other discourse in this section is the nominal clause in Ezra 5:4b. The two *yqtl* forms at the end of Ezra 5:5 are off the main plane because of the עד. It is possible that the nominal clause in Ezra 5:6 is not a clause at all; it is comparable, however, to Ezra 4:11 without the דנה. Ezra 5:7 is comparable to Ezra 4:17.

The discourse of Ezra 5:8 begins, "Let it be (*yqtl*) known (ptc) to the king." Everything that follows די through Ezra 5:16 is the subject (cf., Ezra 4:12–13, 16). In other words, "Let Ezra 5:8–16 be known to the king." This unit can be treated separately, but technically it is all off the main plane in terms of what is happening with the verbal system. Ezra 5:8–10 is narration within discourse (primarily *qtl* forms); Ezra 5:11–14, 16 consists of narration within reported discourse (primarily *qtl* forms); and Ezra 5:15 is reported discourse within reported discourse (two imperatives and one *yqtl*). Ezra 5:17 resumes and concludes the discourse from Ezra 5:8 with two *yqtl* clauses; the conditional clauses are off the main plane.

The narration of Ezra 6:1–2 consists of four *qtl* clauses. Darius' search for the decree of Cyrus is described in terms similar to those of Artaxerxes' search for information about Jerusalem (Ezra 4:19). The scroll about Cyrus begins with a narration within discourse: "Memorandum: In the first year of Cyrus the king, Cyrus the king set (*qtl*) a decree." At this point a די might be expected to introduce the content of the decree (cf., Dan 3:10), but none occurs. This indicates that the reported discourse of Cyrus beginning in Ezra 6:3 is on the main plane: "As for the house of God in Jerusalem, let the house be built (*yqtl*)—a place of sacrificing sacrifices—and let its foundations be raised (ptc)."[81]

The reported discourse of Cyrus continues in Ezra 6:4b–5 with four *yqtl* clauses:

And let the expense be given from the house of the king	*yqtl*
And also let the vessels of the house of God…be returned	*yqtl*[82]
And let him/it go to the temple…	*yqtl*
And you will place in the house of God	*yqtl*

This concludes the report of Cyrus' decree. The very next verse (Ezra 6:6) gives the impression that the preceding material has been part of a letter to Tattenai and Shetar-bozenai. Presumably the contents of the scroll were communicated in some way to these officials. In any case, Ezra 6:6 clearly picks up the correspondence from Ezra 5:17.[83] The verbal form of choice in Darius' letter (Ezra 6:6–12) is the *yqtl*.

Darius' letter begins with two imperatives in Ezra 6:6–7a. The first *yqtl* form occurs in Ezra 6:7b ("let them build"). In Ezra 6:8a, Darius narrates with a *qtl* his giving of a decree.[84] This is followed by two very similar *yqtl* clauses in Ezra 6:8b and Ezra 6:9a: (1) "let the expense be (*yqtl*) given (ptc)" and (2) "let what is needed be (*yqtl*) given (ptc)."[85] Darius then narrates his giving of another decree with a *qtl* form.[86] The discourse resumes in Ezra 6:12a with a *yqtl* clause: "May the God who made his name dwell there overthrow (*yqtl*) any king or people who sends his hand to change to destroy that house of God which is in Jerusalem." After narrating/reiterating the fact that he "gave" (*qtl*) a decree, Darius concludes his letter, "Let it be done (*yqtl*) thoroughly."

Ezra 6:13–15 narrates the response to Darius' letter, and Ezra 6:16–18 narrates the celebration of the people of God. This entire section (Ezra 6:13–18) is made up of one of the most remarkable strings of *qtl* clauses in all of Biblical Aramaic. After the "*edayin* + x + *qtl*" clause in Ezra 6:13 and the nominal clause with two participles in Ezra 6:14a, there is a stretch of six "*waw* + *qtl*" clauses from Ezra 6:14b through Ezra 6:18:

And they built	*qtl*
And they completed	*qtl*
And this house was finished	*qtl*[87]
And they made…a dedication	*qtl*
And they offered	*qtl*
And they appointed the priests	*qtl*

The very next verse (Ezra 6:19), which is in Hebrew, continues the narration with a *wayyiqtol* (see also Ezra 6:20b, 21, 22). This suggests that the bilingual author understands the *qtl* (in this case *wqtl*) and the *wayyiqtol* to be the primary verbal forms of narration for Aramaic and Hebrew respectively.

Ezra 7:12–26

The support from Artaxerxes for Ezra mentioned in this section is not unlike the support from Cyrus and Darius mentioned in Ezra 5:13–16; 6:1–12.[88] This is yet another letter in Aramaic. The letter opening in Ezra 7:12 is not a clause.[89] The first main clause is Artaxerxes' narration of his giving of a decree (Ezra 7:13), which is followed by a די clause indicating the content of the decree. The כל קבל די in Ezra 7:14 subordinates Ezra 7:14–16 to the content clause of Ezra 7:13. This means that everything following "From me a decree was set" in Ezra 7:13 through Ezra 7:16 is off the main plane.

The discourse of the letter begins in Ezra 7:17 with two *yqtl* clauses. Altogether Ezra 7:17–20 has four *yqtl* clauses and one imperative:

You will purchase	*yqtl*
And you will offer them	*yqtl*
And you will do	*yqtl*[90]
Render in full	impv
You will give	*yqtl*

The discourse forms here are consistent with those of the other letters in Ezra.

Ezra 7:21–22 is very much like Ezra 7:13–16. Artaxerxes' narration of his giving of a decree is followed by the content of the decree. As in Ezra 7:17–20, the usual discourse forms occur in Ezra 7:23–26:

Let it be done	*yqtl*[91]
We make known to you[92]	ptc
Appoint magistrates and judges[93]	impv
And you will inform anyone who does not know	*yqtl*
Let the judgment be done	*yqtl*[94]

Thus, the letters in Ezra do not cause any disruption to the theory of the Biblical Aramaic verbal system proposed here. The letters are basically discourse, but they also employ other levels of communication. The *qtl* is the primary verbal form for levels one, three, and five; and the *yqtl* is the primary form for levels two, four, and six. The nominal clause with or without a participle is secondary. The narration in Ezra apart from the letters displays the same distribution of verbal forms as the narration in Daniel.

This chapter has documented a significant number of lengthy sequences of either *qtl* forms in some form of narration (levels one, three, and five) or *yqtl* forms in some form of discourse (levels two, four, and six). The distribution of these sequences over the whole of the Biblical Aramaic corpus shows that the primary patterns observed in the database retrievals do not derive from isolated occurrences. Rather, the patterns emerge immediately from the uses of the forms in any given passage. This is the type of observation that gives impetus to confirmation by database analysis.

No attempt has been made here to establish the original texts of the Biblical Aramaic corpus. Such a pursuit would be very much beside the point. The textual-critical issues of these texts have very little bearing on the verbal system as a whole. For example, the Masoretic Text of Dan 2:4b–7:28 and the reconstructed Aramaic text behind the Old Greek of Dan 2:4b–7:28 do not present two completely different Aramaic verbal systems, however much they may differ in other matters.

The commentary of this chapter has highlighted the importance of the main plane of the communication levels when it comes to determination of the primary uses of the verbal forms. This is not to deny that there are real verbal forms off the main plane. It is only to affirm that the primary uses and the secondary uses are two different objects of study. Conclusions about the secondary uses cannot be allowed to override conclusions about the primary uses, and vice versa.

Notes

[1]An earlier version of the commentary on Dan 2:4b–28 can be found in Michael B. Shepherd, "The Distribution of Verbal Forms in Biblical Aramaic," *JSS* 52 (2007): 237–39.

[2]The particle די at the beginning of Dan 2:9 is not given much weight here; it may add to the content clause at the end of Dan 2:8, or it may be causal.

[3]This *qtl* clause is followed by a temporal/adverbial clause that is off the main plane.

[4]The following די clause (attributive) and exceptive clause (Dan 2:11b) are off the main plane (see Hans Bauer and Pontus Leander, *Grammatik des Biblisch-Aramäischen* [Halle: Niemeyer, 1927; 4th unrev. reprint, Hildesheim: Georg Olms, 1995], 366).

[5]See Zdravko Stefanovic, *The Aramaic of Daniel in the Light of Old Aramaic*, JSOTSup 129 (Sheffield: JSOT, 1992), 41; Hermann Gunkel, *Einleitung in die Psalmen*, 2d ed. (Göttingen: Vandenhoeck & Ruprecht, 1966), 44–48.

[6]The די that begins the following clause, which contains a *qtl* form, could be a coordinating conjunction—like כי in Hebrew or γάρ in Greek—but it is usually understood as a subordinating conjunction (see Bauer and Leander, *Grammatik*, 360–65).

[7]The די clause is attributive and off the main plane.

[8]See Bauer and Leander, *Grammatik*, 364.

[9]The participle "revealing" is attributive.

[10]The following די clause is an object/content clause off the main plane.

[11]The two די clauses in Dan 2:29 are object/content clauses.

[12]The expression הוא צלמא (Dan 2:32) is normally understood as "This image," not as "This is the image"; also, the suffixed pronoun before די in the constructs with די normally refers as a prolepsis to the noun after די (e.g., שמה די אלהא ["his name of God" is "the name of God" in Dan 2:20]), but expressions like ראשה די דהב in Dan 2:32 could be understood as nominal clauses: "its head was of gold" (see Bauer and Leander, *Grammatik*, 312–14).

[13]There is perhaps a fourth *qtl* clause on the main plane if the temporal "until" (עד די) is understood as "behold" (see Bauer and Leander, *Grammatik*, 287); it is also possible that the last two *qtl* clauses in this verse should be subsumed under the עד די.

[14]The די clause in Dan 2:35b is attributive.

[15]Here the pronoun הוא is used as a copula (see Bauer and Leander, *Grammatik*, 268).

[16]There are, of course, clauses off the main plane in this section such as the כל קבל די clauses.

[17]It is possible that the verbs "shatter" and "crush" at the end of Dan 2:40 form a compound predicate rather than two separate clauses, but the candidate for their shared object is the preceding "all these," which probably goes with the participle "crushes": "…iron shatters and smashes everything, and as iron that crushes all these, it will shatter and it will crush"; the compound predicate in Dan 2:44b ("It will shatter and end") is clearly followed by a shared object ("all these kingdoms").

[18]The first three verbal forms in Dan 2:45 are subsumed under כל קבל די.

[19]The די clause in Dan 2:47b is off the main plane.

[20]Bauer and Leander, *Grammatik*, 355; Carl Brocklemann, *Grundriß der vergleichenden Grammatik der semitischen Sprachen*, vol. 2, *Syntax* (Berlin: Reuther & Reichard, 1913; 4th reprint, Hildesheim: Georg Olms, 1999), 556.

[21]Cf., Daniel 4:9.

[22]Daniel 2:5 has a couple of די clauses off the main plane, and Dan 2:6 begins with a subject clause ("And whoever does not fall and bow down") that goes with the main verb ("will be thrown").

[23]It goes without saying that כל קבל דנה (introduces a main plane clause) is not the same as כל קבל די (introduces a clause off the main plane); in Dan 3:7, this introductory phrase is separated from the participles in Dan 3:7b by a temporal clause.

[24]These are preceded by a nominal conditional clause and by a temporal clause with a *yqtl* form.

[25]For some reason this content clause has one participle (פלחין) and one *yqtl* (נסגד) where either two participles or two *yqtl* forms might be expected.

[26]Bauer and Leander, *Grammatik*, 294–95; H. B. Rosén, "On the Use of the Tenses in the Aramaic of Daniel," *JSS* 6 (1961): 185.

[27]Everything following די is off the main plane.

[28]The remainder of the verse is off the main plane.

[29]Daniel 4:4 has three nominal clauses with participles.

[30]Everything after כל קבל די is off the main plane.

[31]See Dan 4:31.

[32]See comment at Dan 4:2.

[33]Thus, in the tagging Dan 4:20a1 and Dan 4:21a1 are grouped together.

[34]By now it is unnecessary to mention every די clause that is off the main plane; the conditional clause in Dan 4:24b is off the main plane.

[35]See Bauer and Leander, *Grammatik*, 268; Daniel 4:27b is off the main plane.

[36]The participle of this nominal clause is impersonal ("it is said"); see also the impersonal use of the participle and the *yqtl* in Dan 4:29.

[37]The use of the *yqtl* here is not unlike what was observed in the account of the dream and its interpretation earlier in the chapter.

[38]The last two *qtl* forms of Dan 4:31a appear to form a compound predicate with a shared object.

[39]Everything after the די of Dan 4:31b through Dan 4:32 is off the main plane.

[40]It is possible that the fact that this narration is within discourse has had some effect on the choice of forms; indeed, half of the "anomalous" uses of the *yqtl* in Biblical Aramaic occur right here in the fourth chapter where the communication levels are the most complex.

[41]The *yqtl* form at Dan 5:6a is explained under the comment for Dan 4:2.

[42]This is followed by two attributive clauses.

[43]All that follows די in Dan 5:14 is the content of what Belshazzar heard from the queen.

[44]Like Dan 5:14, the די clause of Dan 5:16a is the content of what Belshazzar heard from the queen.

[45]The conditional clause is off the main plane.

[46]In the database, Dan 5:20a is the "x" in the "x + *qtl*" listed for Dan 5:20a1; the main verbal form falls after the athnach.

[47]A nominal clause stands between this series of *qtl* clauses and the *yqtl* forms mentioned above.

[48]The כל קבל די clause of Dan 5:22b is concessive.

[49]The final די clause of Dan 5:29 is the content of the proclamation concerning Daniel.

[50]Once again, it goes without saying that the די clauses and כל קבל די clauses are off the main plane in a unit such as this; detailed discussion of these clauses is important, but preoccupation with them misses the big picture of the verbal system.

[51]See Brockelmann, *Grundriß*, 2:153.

[52]The די clause of Dan 6:8b gives the content of the proposed statute/interdict.

[53]Daniel 6:9b expresses purpose.

[54]The כל קבל די clause is off the main plane.

[55]The די clause of Dan 6:13a gives the content of the interdict signed by the king.

[56]Daniel 6:14 also contains several attributive די clauses.

[57]"Der Nebenumstand braucht aber nicht immer der Haupthandlung zu folgen, sondern kann auch vorangehen" (Bauer and Leander, *Grammatik*, 283).

[58]Cf., Dan 6:17.

[59]It is noteworthy that מלל is found here rather than the usual ענה ואמר.

[60]Everything after כל קבל די in Dan 6:23b is off the main plane.

[61]The די clauses are, of course, off the main plane.

[62]This rationale is placed off the main plane by the initial די; the unit, however, can be analyzed by itself apart from its syntactical relationship to the context.

[63]See Michael B. Shepherd, "Daniel 7:13 and the New Testament Son of Man," *WTJ* 68 (2006): 100.

[64]Bauer and Leander, *Grammatik*, 297.

[65]"Man gewinnt aus der Analyse dieses Abschnittes den Eindruck, daß der Erzähler länger andauernde Vorgänge oder Nebenumstände im Part. oder Aorist darstellt, dagegen die Hauptmomente (vor allem, wenn bei Verbis von sog. punktueller oder perfektiver Aktionsart) im Nominal. Auch kann derselbe Vorgang, wenn er allmählich erfolgt, im Partizip, wenn plötzlich, im Nominal erscheinen: סָלְקָן (V. 3) besagt, daß die Tiere nach und nach herauskommen, סִלְקַת (V. 8) dagegen, daß das Horn plötzlich hervorschießt. Ein histor. (dramatisches) Präsens im eigentlichen Sinne brauchen wir in diesem Abschnitt nicht anzunehmen, wenngleich die hier gebrauchten Partt. den Übergang zu einem solchen darstellen" (ibid., 298–99); Bauer and Leander add, "Man darf wohl sagen, daß der Aramäer mit seinen bescheidenen Mitteln auch die subjektiven Zeitstufen, soweit es auf diese ankommt, mit nahezu derselben Genauigkeit bezeichnen kann als andere Sprachen mit einem viel reicheren Vorrat der Tempusformen. Diese sind ja vielfach, wie auch die Fülle anderer Flexionsformen, nur ein überflüssiger Luxus, der für die wirkliche Ausdrucksfähigkeit einer Sprache wenig oder nichts bedeutet" (ibid., 299).

[66]This opening narration consists of three *qtl* clauses.

[67]The chapter also contains a significant amount of reported discourse, particularly in Dan 7:23–27.

[68]The *yqtl* only occurs three times in Dan 7:2–14 (Dan 7:10, 14).

[69]The expression "I was looking" is used frequently in this chapter (Dan 7:2, 4, 7, 9, 11, 13, 21).

[70]Bauer and Leander, *Grammatik*, 286–87.

[71]See Dan 7:22, 26.

[72]The use of עד די here entails the same issues as the usage in Dan 7:9.

[73]"And his kingdom which will not be destroyed" seems to involve an ellipsis: "And his kingdom (is an everlasting kingdom) which will not be destroyed"; it could be an added note about the "dominion," or it could be a nominal clause in its own right: "And his kingdom is that which will not be destroyed."

[74]This is a vision embedded within the interpretative section; it receives its own interpretation in Dan 7:25.

[75]Each one of these clauses begins with a *waw*.

[76]The די clause is attributive and off the main plane.

[77]See Brockelmann, *Grundriß*, 2:354.

[78]The content of what was found as indicated in Ezra 4:19–20 is off the main plane.

[79]The עד clause is off the main plane.

[80]The Masoretic Text of Ezra 5:4a has "we said" (אמרנא), which indicates first-person narration; but one Aramaic manuscript reads "they said" (אמרו), a reading reflected in the Septuagint and Syriac versions; of course, it is possible that the third-person reading arose within the versions themselves—which then influenced the later Aramaic manuscript—but the Septuagint and the Syriac were not dependent upon one another; rather, they were both translations of Hebrew texts (Ernst Würthwein, *The Text of the Old Testament*, 2d ed., trans. Erroll F. Rhodes [Grand Rapids: Eerdmans, 1995], 86); the third-person reading better fits the context, but the Masoretic reading is more difficult and is better able to account for the origin of the other reading, unless the Masoretic reading is explained as an extract from Ezra 5:9.

[81]At least two options present themselves with the syntax of Ezra 6:3b: (1) it could be a non-clause ("its height sixty cubits and its width sixty cubits") or (2) it could consist of two nominal clauses ("its height should be sixty cubits, and its width should be sixty cubits"); see Bauer and Leander, *Grammatik*, 329; the same issue is encountered in Ezra 6:4a.

[82]The two *qtl* forms in Ezra 6:5a are embedded within a relative clause.

[83]Cf., Ezra 4:21–22.

[84]The content of the decree is given in the די clause.

[85]Ezra 6:10 expresses purpose (די); it is off the main plane.

[86]Once again, all that follows די within the verse is the content of the decree.

[87]This form is not passive in the Masoretic Text (lit., "he finished this house"); the ἐτέλεσαν ("they finished") of the Septuagint may reflect a more original Aramaic reading (שיציו); normally a plural form is used in Aramaic for the impersonal.

[88]For Ezra's commission, see Rolf Rendtorff, *The Old Testament: An Introduction*, trans. John Bowden (Philadelphia: Fortress, 1986), 68.

[89]Cf., Ezra 4:10–11.

[90]The object of this verb is the clause at the beginning of Ezra 7:18 ("whatever seems good to you and to your brothers…"); the same syntax occurs in Ezra 7:19 with the imperative and again in Ezra 7:20 with a *yqtl*.

[91]Cf., the syntax of Ezra 7:18; the די clause in Ezra 7:23b is off the main plane.

[92]The following די introduces the content of what they are making known.

[93]This is followed by a relative clause with a periphrastic construction.

[94]Cf., the syntax of Ezra 7:18, 23.

Chapter Five

Conclusion

This final chapter provides a summary of the preceding chapters and a statement of the significance of the presented research. No new material appears here. Rather, this chapter is a snapshot of the whole work—a kind of extended abstract. It is only appropriate then to begin with a restatement of the basic thesis: Biblical Aramaic has a primary verbal form for narration (*qtl*) and a primary verbal form for discourse (*yqtl*).[1] This thesis has been defended from a variety of angles, most of all from database analysis of formal distribution.

The introduction and first chapter express indebtedness to the standard grammars of Biblical Aramaic.[2] The survey of these grammars shows the tremendous amount of work that went into their formulation of the Biblical Aramaic verbal system. Modern study of the verb had to begin somewhere, and these grammars have given today's grammarians something to evaluate and something on which to build. Whatever criticism is due the standard grammars, the debt of gratitude that is owed to their authors must not be forgotten.

The standard grammars work with the foreign (i.e., Greek and Latin) categories of tense (time), aspect (how the action is viewed), and *Aktionsart* (the kind of action) in their description of the Biblical Aramaic verb. Thus, the authors act as living informants who are able to apply known categories of function to the written forms. Biblical Aramaic is not treated in these grammars as a dead language for which a procession from form to function would be more appropriate.

If all that is required is an explanation of how the Biblical Aramaic verb translates into German or English, then the standard grammars will suffice. That is, the authors are in a sense living informants of how the Biblical Aramaic verb translates into their native language. German and English verbs have tense, aspect, and *Aktionsart*; and translation into those languages demands those categories. But if an explanation of how the Biblical Aramaic verb is used in Biblical Aramaic is required, then the standard grammars must be set aside.

A description of the Biblical Aramaic verb on the basis of tense, aspect, and *Aktionsart* fails to indicate any fundamental opposition between the *qtl* and the *yqtl*. According to the traditional view, these forms are virtually interchangeable. Both can be past, present, or future; and both can be perfective or imperfective. However well this system works for translation, it renders the verb meaningless within Biblical Aramaic.[3] Why would the only two verbal forms be used interchangeably? Is there nothing to distinguish these forms from one another? If there is, it must be something beyond tense, aspect, and *Aktionsart*.

The only significant departure from the traditional view of the verb has been produced by H. B. Rosén.[4] It is easy to be sympathetic with Rosén's dissatisfaction with the traditional view, but ultimately he himself does little more than reshuffle the labels of the standard grammars. Like the traditional grammarians, Rosén begins with preconceived categories of function rather than analysis of formal distribution, and he displays a great deal of creativity in his role as a living informant of a dead language.

Rosén prefers to speak of the *yqtl* and the participle as the narrative tenses in the Aramaic of Daniel.[5] "Point aspect" verbs have the participle for a narrative tense, and "linear aspect" verbs have the *yqtl* as the narrative tense.[6] The problem, however, is that the *yqtl* and the participle never sustain a passage of narration. The form that does sustain every sizeable passage of narration is the *qtl*, yet this is the one form that Rosén does not allow as a narrative tense, despite the fact that it "serves as a narrative tense...in other types of Aramaic and Semitic."[7]

This review of what has been done thus far with the Biblical Aramaic verb leaves the modern grammarian looking for something more. This something more must begin with a correct understanding of the object of study. That is why the first chapter of the present work concludes with an excursus on the presence of Aramaic in the Bible. The Biblical Aramaic texts are authentic Aramaic texts—not translated or forged texts. The distribution of verbal forms in these authentic texts is the object of study.

The second chapter follows this clarification of the object of study with an introduction to textlinguistic methodology. This moves beyond reorganization of traditional categories to the establishment of new text-immanent categories. Textlinguistics is the study of written texts as acts of communication.[8] It describes how whole texts are able to function and produce meaning on the micro and macro levels. Textlinguistics begins with registration of formal distribution and allows the data to inform conclusions about the functions and meanings of the forms. Thus, the process is exactly the opposite of the methodology employed by the standard grammars and Rosén.

Textlinguistics is particularly appropriate for texts written in what is now dead language. For such texts there is no access to native speakers or to text-external factors. Only the written forms are accessible. But modern linguistics for the most part has not been concerned with these kinds of texts. Ferdinand de Saussure, for example, was primarily interested in the study of spoken, living language.[9] This emphasis has been continued in transformational-generative grammar, speech act theory, and discourse analysis. Textlinguistics has barely been able to find a voice at all in this environment. This is evidenced by the fact that the term "textlinguistics" is often used interchangeably with "discourse analysis."

Siegfried Schmidt has provided in his text theory an alternative to the linguistics of a language system—a linguistics of communication.[10] In Schmidt's view the basis of a text theory is the "communicative act game" (*kommunikative Handlungsspiel*). But Schmidt's linguistics is not specifically oriented to written texts. For Schmidt, textuality has both a linguistic dimension and a social (pragmatic) dimension.[11] The difficulty is that the social data with which Schmidt works are not accessible for texts written in what is now dead language. Such texts have communicative functions and communication situations, but they must be described in text-immanent categories.

The language of the Hebrew Bible—whether Biblical Hebrew or Biblical Aramaic—is dead language. Edward Ullendorff has concluded that Biblical Hebrew is a "linguistic fragment," albeit a very important one.[12] However much Biblical Hebrew has played a role in the revival of Hebrew as a spoken language, Modern Hebrew is not the same language as Biblical Hebrew. Even E. Y. Kutscher, who highlights the close relationship between Modern Hebrew and Biblical Hebrew, admits, "BH syntax was almost entirely rejected and with it all the morphosyntactic aspects of the verb that are the main features of BH."[13] The language represented by Biblical Hebrew died as a spoken language with the rise of Mishnaic Hebrew, and it remains today a dead language for which there are no living informants.

Biblical Aramaic is also a dead language,[14] but Modern Aramaic is even further removed from Biblical Aramaic than Modern Hebrew is from Biblical Hebrew. This can be accounted for by the fact that Biblical Aramaic, unlike Biblical Hebrew, never had to be reused to revive the Aramaic language. Aramaic has survived as a spoken language, but it has developed into something quite different from what is found in ancient Aramaic texts.[15] This is especially true of the verb.[16] Thus, no speaker of the kind of Aramaic found in the Bible is alive today.

Two Hebrew grammarians who have been sensitive to the nature of dead language and to the need for textlinguistic methodology are Wolfgang Schneider and Wolfgang Richter.[17] Schneider has concluded on the basis of distributional analysis that the two primary verbal forms for Biblical Hebrew are the *wayyiqtol* (narration) and the *yiqtol* (discourse). A thesis not unlike the one proposed herein for Biblical Aramaic. And Richter, perhaps more than anyone else, has stressed that Biblical Hebrew is a dead language for which there are no living informants and that a distinction must be made between spoken and written forms of the language. This has led Richter to proceed from the *Ausdrucksseite* (form) to the *Inhaltsseite* (function and meaning), not vice versa.

The backbone of textlinguistic methodology is distributional analysis. Here a database approach to such analysis has been adapted from John Sailhamer's work on Biblical Hebrew narrative.[18] This approach develops a computer database of tagged clauses; that is, all of the clauses in Biblical Aramaic are tagged according to text-immanent categories. This includes marking of clause constituents (e.g., the occupant of first position) as well as the labeling of clause types (e.g., "verbal") and communication levels (e.g., "narration," "discourse," etc.). The database provides a way to store and retrieve information about inner-clausal relationships and beyond.

The possibilities for retrieval are many with this type of database, but one of the most important for the thesis of the present work is the distribution of verbal forms among the various communication levels. Out of 435 clauses that contain some form of narration (levels one, three, and five), 264 clauses have *qtl* as the primary verbal form, 26 have *yqtl*, and 145 are nominal with or without a participle. Out of 208 clauses that contain either discourse or reported discourse (levels two, four, and six), 110 clauses have *yqtl* as the primary verbal form, 28 have an imperative, and 70 are nominal clauses with or without a participle. Thus, in terms of distribution, the *qtl* is the primary verbal form for narration; the *yqtl* is the primary verbal form for discourse; and the nominal clause with or without a participle is secondary for both narration and discourse. The linguistic opposition between *qtl* and *yqtl* is not based on tense, aspect, and *Aktionsart*, but on the opposition between narration and discourse. Exceptions like the use of the *yqtl* in narration, which are few and far between, can be easily explained.

Extra-biblical Aramaic parallels to what has been observed in the verbal system of Biblical Aramaic are not hard to find. Egyptian Aramaic texts from approximately the same time period and texts such as the Targums are especially fruitful. Segert's analysis of the Ahiqar text from Elephantine (fifth century B.C.) is a good place to start: "In der Erzählung (A 1–78) überwiegen die Perfekta, während der Gebrauch des Imperfekts meist auf die direkte Rede und auf die Nebensätze beschränkt wird; die Partizipien treten nicht häufig auf."[19] This is almost identical to the proposed thesis for the verbal system of Biblical Aramaic.

The Targums (Middle to Late Aramaic) are a mixture of literal translation, paraphrase, and interpretive expansions. They are more than translations; they are ancient commentaries on the biblical text.[20] The earliest, sizable extant texts that can be called "targumic" in some sense are the Job Targum from Qumran (11QtgJob) and the *Genesis Apocryphon* from Qumran Cave 1. Both texts feature the use of the *qtl* in narration and the use of the *yqtl* in discourse. The *Genesis Apocryphon* in particular possesses a number of long strings of *qtl* forms within first-person narration (i.e., narration within discourse). Other Targums such as *Targum Neofiti*, *Targum Onkelos*, *Targum Jonathan*, and *Targum Pseudo-Jonathan* follow suit. Passages can be chosen at random, and the same patterns observed in Biblical Aramaic emerge.

Thus, the proposed thesis for Biblical Aramaic does not appear to be an idiosyncratic view that is limited to one small corpus. Even Aramaic-influenced texts display the same patterns. The book of Ecclesiastes has long been viewed as an Aramaic-influenced text due to its unusual orthography, peculiar vocabulary, and idiomatic expressions—even to the point that an Aramaic original of Ecclesiastes has been posited. The use of the Hebrew verb in Ecclesiastes also shows Aramaic influence.[21] The Hebrew *qatal* resembles the Aramaic *qtl* in its use as the primary verbal form for narration; it has virtually replaced the *wayyiqtol*. The Hebrew *yiqtol* corresponds to the

Aramaic *yqtl* as it does in other Biblical Hebrew texts. The nominal clause with or without a participle is secondary.

In addition to parallels from outside the Biblical Aramaic corpus, the abstract feedback from the database is also complemented by a grammatical commentary in the fourth chapter. Instead of grouping examples together from all over the Biblical Aramaic corpus under various headings, this commentary gives an exposition of what is happening with the verb as the text is being read. It documents a significant number of lengthy sequences of either *qtl* forms in some type of narration (levels one, three, and five) or *yqtl* forms in some type of discourse (levels two, four, and six). Thus, the database has not produced a test tube verbal system. Rather, it has fed back that which is in accord with real usage of the language. The commentary also shows the value of analysis of the verbal forms on the main plane over against mixed analysis of primary and secondary (i.e., off the main plane) uses.

A simple and comprehensive account of the primary uses of the verbal forms in Biblical Aramaic has been attempted here. The simplicity is not to the neglect of complex details, and the comprehensiveness does not entail an endless list of qualifications. The *qtl* is the primary verbal form for narration, and the *yqtl* is the primary verbal form for discourse. This view does not provide a lot of "cash value" for the interpretation of individual verbal forms, and therein is its strength. It does not give footing to the kinds of abusive interpretations that are so often built on non-existent nuances of individual forms. Rather, this view offers a solid linguistic foundation for interpretation of whole texts.

The significance of this research is at least threefold. First, it has met the need for an identification of the basic opposition between the *qtl* and the *yqtl*. In order for these forms to be meaningful in Aramaic, there must be a fundamental linguistic opposition that exists between them. It was observed in the first chapter that the categories of the standard grammars—tense, aspect, and *Aktionsart*—were insufficient for the identification of this opposition. The standard grammars have provided ways to translate the Aramaic verb, but they have not shown what distinguishes the forms. On the other hand, database analysis has revealed that the basic opposition between the *qtl* and the *yqtl* is an opposition between narration and discourse.

Second, the present research has demonstrated the value of working with full acknowledgement of the fact that Biblical Aramaic is a dead language.

Grammarians of Biblical Aramaic are not in a position to work as living informants of the language. A textlinguistic methodology is required, a methodology of distributional analysis that works from form to function. Until now, Biblical Aramaic has not been treated as a dead language, and the verb has seen little in the way of distributional analysis.

Third, in view of the nature of Biblical Aramaic and in line with a proper textlinguistics, the scope of the database research here has been limited to text-immanent categories. This has important implications for the larger field of modern linguistics. Beyond the reductionism of structuralism, there is an essential place for text-immanent description of texts, especially texts written in what is now dead language. Modern linguistics with its emphasis on spoken language has yet to address the special needs of these texts. How is it that entire books on linguistics and text theory can be written without the slightest mention of dead language?

Research on the verb in Biblical Aramaic does not end here. Refinements are always in demand. Perhaps the next step is distributional analysis of all the verbal forms that occur off the main plane of the narration and discourse. Supplementary to this would be analysis of all the nominal clauses. The nominal clauses are beyond the realm of the verbal system, but their interplay with verbal clauses cannot be ignored.

The extra-biblical parallels presented in the third chapter also show promise for future research. For example, Segert's brief analysis of the Ahiqar text could be applied to all the Egyptian Aramaic texts from Elephantine. And although it would be a massive undertaking, all the clauses of the Targums could be tagged and entered into a database. Such a database would provide statistics for the whole of the corpus like those recorded for individual passages.

A database could also be created for Ecclesiastes and other Aramaic-influenced texts. This would perhaps include a book like Job or texts written in Aramaic-influenced Mishnaic Hebrew. It is also possible that this type of analysis could extend to Aramaic-influenced texts of the Greek New Testament.

One final suggestion for future research is the genre of grammatical commentary. It seems that this mode of exposition is at least a helpful supplement to the usual presentation of grammars. This is certainly not a popular type of commentary, but one that may prove to be very useful for scholarly research. If the genre is employed more and more, it will surely be improved in ways that have yet to be envisioned.

Notes

[1]Thus, the *qtl* is secondary in discourse, and the *yqtl* is secondary in narration; throughout the present work, it has also been observed that the nominal clause with or without a participle is secondary in narration and discourse.

[2]I.e., E. F. Kautzsch, *Grammatik des Biblischen-Aramäischen* (Leipzig: Vogel, 1884); Hans Bauer and Pontus Leander, *Grammatik des Biblisch-Aramäischen* (Halle: Niemeyer, 1927; 4th unrev. reprint, Hildesheim: Georg Olms, 1995); Stanislav Segert, *Altaramäische Grammatik*, 3d ed. (Leipzig: Enzyklopädie, 1986).

[3]See Ferdinand de Saussure, *Course in General Linguistics*, ed. Charles Bally, and Albert Sechehaye, trans. and ann. Roy Harris (London: Duckworth, 1983; reprint, Chicago and La Salle: Open Court, 1986), 119.

[4]H. B. Rosén, "On the Use of the Tenses in the Aramaic of Daniel," *JSS* 6 (1961): 183–203.

[5]Ibid., 183–85.

[6]Ibid., 192.

[7]Ibid., 185.

[8]This is in contrast to discourse analysis, which is the study of written texts as records of spoken communication.

[9]Ferdinand de Saussure, *Cours de linguistique générale*, ed. Charles Bally and Albert Sechehaye (Paris: Payothèque, 1916); the second chapter of the present work highlights some of Saussure's main contributions to the field of linguistics: (1) the relation between *langue* and *parole*, (2) the linguistic sign, (3) the difference between synchronic linguistics and diachronic linguistics, and (4) syntagmatic and associative relations; particularly important for textlinguistics is Saussure's theory of linguistic opposition.

[10]Siegfried Schmidt, *Texttheorie* (Munich: Fink, 1973).

[11]Ibid., 144.

[12]Edward Ullendorff, *Is Biblical Hebrew a Language?* (Wiesbaden: Harrassowitz, 1977), 16.

[13]E. Y. Kutscher, *A History of the Hebrew Language*, ed. Raphael Kutscher (Jerusalem: Magnes, 1982), 196.

[14]Biblical Aramaic is, as is pointed out in the second chapter, usually included among a body of texts that belong to a stage of Aramaic known as Imperial Aramaic.

[15]"Diese modernen Dialekte können nur selten für eine Erklärung der altaramäischen Phase verwendet werden" (Segert, *Altaramäische Grammatik*, 55).

[16]Robert Hoberman, *The Syntax and Semantics of Verb Morphology in Modern Aramaic: A Jewish Dialect of Iraqi Kurdistan*, American Oriental Society 69 (New Haven: American Oriental Society, 1989), 27, n. 20.

[17]Wolfgang Schneider, *Grammatik des Biblischen Hebräischen*, 8th ed. (Munich: Claudius, 1993); Wolfgang Richter, *Grundlagen einer althebräischen Grammatik* (St. Ottilien: EOS, 1978).

[18]John H. Sailhamer, "A Database Approach to the Analysis of Hebrew Narrative," *Maarav* 5–6 (1990): 319–35.

[19]Segert, *Altaramäische Grammatik*, 372.

[20]See John Bowker, *The Targums and Rabbinic Literature: An Introduction to Jewish Interpretations of Scripture* (London: Cambridge University Press, 1969), 8; C. Rabin, "Hebrew and Aramaic in the First Century," in *The Jewish People in the First Century*, vol. 2, ed. S. Safrai and M. Stern, CRINT 1 (Philadelphia: Fortress, 1976), 1030–32; see also, for example, the Targum of the Biblical Aramaic text Jer 10:11.

[21]A good, brief sample of this influence is the epilogue (Eccl 12:9–14): the third-person narration of Qoheleth's life in Eccl 12:9–11 comes with seven *qatal* forms; the address to the "son" in Eccl 12:12–14, however, features the nominal clause, the imperative, and the *yiqtol*.

Appendix

Verse	Waw	Edayin	Clause	Ptc	Type	Nar/Dis	Level
jr10:11a1	-	-	x+yqtl	-	v	dis	2
jr10:11a2	-	-	x+yqtl	-	i	dis	4
da02:04b1	-	-	x+impv	-	v	dis	2
da02:04b2	-	-	impv	-	v	dis	2
da02:04b3	+	-	x+yqtl	-	v	dis	2
da02:05a1	-	-	nc	+	n	nar	1
da02:05a2	+	-	nc	+	n	nar	1
da02:05b1	-	-	x+yqtl	-	v	dis	2
da02:05b2	+	-	x+yqtl	-	i	dis	2
da02:06a1	+	-	x+yqtl	-	v	dis	1
da02:06b1	-	-	x+impv	-	v	dis	2
da02:07a1	-	-	qtl	-	v	nar	1
da02:07a2	+	-	nc	+	n	nar	1
da02:07b1	-	-	x+yqtl	-	i	dis	2
da02:07b2	+	-	x+yqtl	-	v	dis	2
da02:08a1	-	-	nc	+	n	nar	1
da02:08a2	+	-	nc	+	n	nar	1
da02:08a3	-	-	nc	+	n	dis	2
da02:09a1	-	-	nc	-	n	dis	2
da02:09a2	+	-	x+qtl	-	v	dis	3
da02:09b1	-	-	x+impv	-	v	dis	2
da02:09b2	+	-	yqtl	-	v	dis	2
da02:10a1	-	-	qtl	-	v	nar	1
da02:10a2	+	-	nc	+	n	nar	1
da02:10a3	-	-	nc	-	n	dis	2
da02:11a1	+	-	nc	-	n	dis	2
da02:11a2	+	-	nc	-	n	dis	2
da02:12a1	-	-	x+qtl	-	i	nar	1
da02:12a2	+	-	qtl	-	v	nar	1
da02:12b1	+	-	qtl	-	v	nar	1

Verse	Waw	Edayin	Clause	Ptc	Type	Nar/Dis	Level
da02:13a1	+	-	x+qtl	-	i	nar	1
da02:13a2	+	-	nc	+	n	nar	1
da02:13b1	+	-	qtl	-	v	nar	1
da02:14a1	-	+	x+qtl	-	i	nar	1
da02:15a1	-	-	nc	+	n	nar	1
da02:15a2	+	-	nc	+	n	nar	1
da02:15a3	-	-	nc	+	n	dis	2
da02:15b1	-	+	x+qtl	-	v	nar	1
da02:16a1	+	-	x+qtl	-	i	nar	1
da02:16a2	+	-	qtl	-	v	nar	1
da02:17a1	-	+	x+qtl	-	i	nar	1
da02:17b1	+	-	x+qtl	-	v	nar	1
da02:19a1	-	+	x+qtl	-	i	nar	1
da02:19b1	-	+	x+qtl	-	i	nar	1
da02:20a1	-	-	nc	+	n	nar	1
da02:20a2	+	-	nc	+	n	nar	1
da02:20a3	-	-	yqtl+ptc	-	v	dis	2
da02:21a1	+	-	nc	+	n	dis	2
da02:21a2	-	-	nc	+	n	dis	2
da02:21a3	+	-	nc	+	n	dis	2
da02:21b1	-	-	nc	+	n	dis	2
da02:22a2	-	-	nc	+	n	dis	2
da02:22b1	-	-	nc	+	n	dis	2
da02:22b2	+	-	nc	+	n	dis	2
da02:23a1	-	-	nc	++	n	dis	2
da02:23b1	+	-	x+qtl	-	v	dis	3
da02:24a1	-	-	x+qtl	-	i	nar	1
da02:24b1	-	-	qtl	-	v	nar	1
da02:24b2	+	-	x+qtl	-	v	nar	1
da02:24b3	-	-	x+yqtl	-	v	dis	2
da02:24b4	-	-	impv	-	v	dis	2
da02:24b5	+	-	x+yqtl	-	v	dis	2
da02:25a1	-	+	x+qtl	-	i	nar	1
da02:25b1	+	-	x+qtl	-	v	nar	1
da02:25b2	-	-	x+qtl	-	v	dis	3
da02:26a1	-	-	nc	+	n	nar	1

Verse	Waw	Edayin	Clause	Ptc	Type	Nar/Dis	Level
da02:26a2	+	-	nc	+	n	nar	1
da02:26b1	-	-	nc	+	n	dis	2
da02:27a1	-	-	nc	+	n	nar	1
da02:27a2	+	-	nc	+	n	nar	1
da02:27b1	-	-	nc	+	n	dis	2
da02:28a1	-	-	nc	-	n	dis	2
da02:28a2	+	-	qtl	-	v	dis	3
da02:28b1	-	-	nc	-	n	dis	2
da02:29a1	-	-	x+qtl	-	i	dis	3
da02:29b1	+	-	x+qtl	-	i	dis	3
da02:30a1	+	-	x+qtl	-	i	dis	3
da02:30b1	-	-	x+yqtl	-	v	dis	2
da02:30b2	+	-	x+yqtl	-	v	dis	2
da02:31a1	-	-	x+ptc+qtl	-	i	dis	3
da02:31a2	+	-	nc	-	n	dis	3
da02:31a3	-	-	nc	-	n	dis	3
da02:31a4	+	-	nc	-	n	dis	3
da02:31a5	-	-	nc	+	n	dis	3
da02:31b1	+	-	nc	+	n	dis	3
da02:32a1	-	-	nc	-	n	dis	3
da02:32a2	-	-	nc	-	n	dis	3
da02:32b1	-	-	nc	-	n	dis	3
da02:33a1	-	-	nc	-	n	dis	3
da02:33b1	-	-	nc	-	n	dis	3
da02:34a1	-	-	ptc+qtl	-	v	dis	3
da02:34a2	+	-	qtl	-	v	dis	3
da02:34b1	+	-	qtl	-	v	dis	3
da02:35a1	-	+	qtl	-	v	dis	3
da02:35a2	+	-	qtl	-	v	dis	3
da02:35a3	+	-	qtl	-	v	dis	3
da02:35a4	+	-	x+qtl	-	i	dis	3
da02:35b1	+	-	x+qtl	-	i	dis	3
da02:35b2	+	-	qtl	-	v	dis	3
da02:36a1	-	-	nc	-	n	dis	2
da02:36a2	+	-	x+yqtl	-	v	dis	2
da02:37a1	-	-	nc	-	n	dis	2

Verse	Waw	Edayin	Clause	Ptc	Type	Nar/Dis	Level
da02:38b1	-	-	nc	-	n	dis	2
da02:39a1	+	-	x+yqtl	-	v	dis	2
da02:40a1	+	-	x+yqtl	-	i	dis	2
da02:40b1	+	-	x+yqtl	-	v	dis	2
da02:40b2	+	-	yqtl	-	v	dis	2
da02:41a1	+	-	x+yqtl	-	i	dis	2
da02:41a2	+	-	x+yqtl	-	v	dis	2
da02:42a1	+	-	x+yqtl	-	i	dis	2
da02:42b1	+	-	x+yqtl	-	i	dis	2
da02:43a1	-	-	x+ptc+yqtl	-	v	dis	2
da02:43a2	+	-	x+yqtl+ptc	-	v	dis	2
da02:44a1	+	-	x+yqtl	-	v	dis	2
da02:44a2	+	-	x+yqtl	-	i	dis	2
da02:44b1	-	-	yqtl+yqtl	-	v	dis	2
da02:44b2	+	-	x+yqtl	-	i	dis	2
da02:45a1	-	-	x+qtl	-	i	dis	3
da02:45b1	+	-	nc	-	n	dis	2
da02:45b2	+	-	nc	+	n	dis	2
da02:46a1	-	+	x+qtl	-	i	nar	1
da02:46a2	+	-	x+qtl	-	v	nar	1
da02:46b1	+	-	x+qtl	-	v	nar	1
da02:47a1	-	-	nc	+	n	nar	1
da02:47a2	+	-	nc	+	n	nar	1
da02:47a3	-	-	nc	-	n	dis	2
da02:48a1	-	+	x+qtl	-	i	nar	1
da02:48a2	+	-	x+qtl	-	v	nar	1
da02:48a3	+	-	qtl	-	v	nar	1
da02:49a1	+	-	x+qtl	-	i	nar	1
da02:49a2	+	-	qtl	-	v	nar	1
da02:49b1	+	-	nc	-	n	nar	1
da03:01a1	-	-	x+qtl	-	i	nar	1
da03:01a2	-	-	nc	-	n	nar	1
da03:01a3	-	-	nc	-	n	nar	1
da03:01b1	-	-	qtl	-	v	nar	1
da03:02a1	+	-	x+qtl	-	i	nar	1
da03:03a1	-	+	nc	+	n	nar	1

Verse	Waw	Edayin	Clause	Ptc	Type	Nar/Dis	Level
da03:03b1	+	-	nc	+	n	nar	1
da03:04a1	+	-	nc	+	n	nar	1
da03:04b1	-	-	nc	+	n	dis	2
da03:05a1	-	-	x+yqtl	-	v	dis	2
da03:05b1	+	-	yqtl	-	v	dis	2
da03:06a1	+	-	x+yqtl	-	i	dis	2
da03:07a1	-	-	nc	+	n	nar	1
da03:07b1	-	-	nc	+	n	nar	1
da03:08a1	-	-	x+qtl	-	v	nar	1
da03:08b1	+	-	qtl	-	v	nar	1
da03:09a1	-	-	qtl	-	v	nar	1
da03:09a2	+	-	nc	+	n	nar	1
da03:09b1	-	-	x+impv	-	v	dis	2
da03:10a1	-	-	x+qtl	-	i	dis	3
da03:12a1	-	-	nc	-	n	dis	2
da03:12b1	-	-	x+qtl	-	i	dis	3
da03:12b2	-	-	nc	+	n	dis	2
da03:12b3	+	-	nc	+	n	dis	2
da03:13a1	-	+	x+qtl	-	i	nar	1
da03:13b1	-	+	x+qtl	-	i	nar	1
da03:14a1	-	-	nc	+	n	nar	1
da03:14a2	+	-	nc	+	n	nar	1
da03:14a3	-	-	nc	-	n	dis	2
da03:14b1	-	-	nc	+	n	dis	2
da03:14b2	+	-	nc	+	n	dis	2
da03:15a1	-	-	x+yqtl	-	v	dis	2
da03:15a2	+	-	yqtl	-	v	dis	2
da03:15a3	+	-	x+yqtl	-	v	dis	2
da03:15b1	+	-	nc	-	n	dis	2
da03:16a1	-	-	qtl	-	v	nar	1
da03:16a2	+	-	nc	+	n	nar	1
da03:16b1	-	-	nc	+	n	dis	2
da03:17a1	-	-	x+yqtl	-	v	dis	2
da03:18a1	+	-	x+ptc+yqtl	-	v	dis	2
da03:19a1	-	+	x+qtl	-	i	nar	1
da03:19a2	+	-	x+qtl	-	i	nar	1

Verse	Waw	Edayin	Clause	Ptc	Type	Nar/Dis	Level
da03:19b1	-	-	nc	+	n	nar	1
da03:19b2	+	-	nc	+	n	nar	1
da03:20a1	+	-	x+qtl	-	v	nar	1
da03:21a1	-	+	x+qtl	-	i	nar	1
da03:21b1	+	-	qtl	-	v	nar	1
da03:22a1	-	-	x+qtl	-	v	nar	1
da03:23a1	+	-	x+qtl	-	i	nar	1
da03:24a1	-	+	x+qtl	-	i	nar	1
da03:24a2	+	-	qtl	-	v	nar	1
da03:24b1	-	-	nc	+	n	nar	1
da03:24b2	+	-	nc	+	n	nar	1
da03:24b3	-	-	x+qtl	-	v	dis	3
da03:24b4	-	-	nc	+	n	nar	1
da03:24b5	+	-	nc	+	n	nar	1
da03:24b6	-	-	nc	-	n	dis	2
da03:25a1	-	-	nc	+	n	nar	1
da03:25a2	+	-	nc	+	n	nar	1
da03:25a3	-	-	nc	+	n	dis	2
da03:25a4	+	-	nc	-	n	dis	2
da03:25b1	+	-	nc	+	n	dis	2
da03:26a1	-	+	qtl	-	v	nar	1
da03:26a2	-	-	nc	+	n	nar	1
da03:26a3	+	-	nc	+	n	nar	1
da03:26a4	-	-	x+2impv	-	v	dis	2
da03:26b1	-	+	nc	+	n	nar	1
da03:27a1	+	-	nc	+	n	nar	1
da03:27a2	-	-	nc	+	n	nar	1
da03:28a1	-	-	nc	+	n	nar	1
da03:28a2	+	-	nc	+	n	nar	1
da03:28a3	-	-	nc	+	n	dis	2
da03:29a1	+	-	x+qtl	-	v	dis	3
da03:30a1	-	+	x+qtl	-	i	nar	1
da03:31a1	-	-	x+yqtl	-	i	dis	2
da03:32a2	-	-	x+qtl	-	v	dis	3
da03:33a1	-	-	nc	-	n	dis	2
da03:33a2	+	-	nc	-	n	dis	2

Verse	Waw	Edayin	Clause	Ptc	Type	Nar/Dis	Level
da03:33b1	-	-	nc	-	n	dis	2
da03:33b2	+	-	nc	-	n	dis	2
da04:01a1	-	-	x+qtl	-	i	dis	3
da04:02a2	-	-	x+qtl	-	v	dis	3
da04:02a2	+	-	yqtl	-	v	dis	3
da04:02b1	+	-	x+yqtl	-	i	dis	3
da04:03a1	+	-	x+qtl	-	v	dis	3
da04:04a1	-	+	nc	+	n	dis	3
da04:04b1	+	-	nc	+	n	dis	3
da04:04b2	+	-	nc	+	n	dis	3
da04:05a1	+	-	x+qtl	-	v	dis	3
da04:05b1	+	-	x+qtl	-	v	dis	3
da04:06a1	-	-	x+impv	-	i	dis	4
da04:07a1	+	-	x+ptc+qtl	-	v	dis	5
da04:07b1	+	-	nc	-	n	dis	5
da04:07b2	+	-	nc	-	n	dis	5
da04:08a1	-	-	qtl	-	v	dis	5
da04:08a2	+	-	qtl	-	v	dis	5
da04:08b1	+	-	x+yqtl	-	i	dis	5
da04:08b2	+	-	nc	-	n	dis	5
da04:09a1	-	-	nc	-	n	dis	5
da04:09a2	+	-	nc	-	n	dis	5
da04:09a3	+	-	nc	-	n	dis	5
da04:09b1	-	-	x+yqtl	-	v	dis	5
da04:09b2	+	-	x+yqtl	-	v	dis	5
da04:09b3	+	-	x+yqtl	-	v	dis	5
da04:10a1	-	-	ptc+qtl	-	v	dis	5
da04:10b1	+	-	nc	+	n	dis	5
da04:11a1	-	-	nc	+	n	dis	5
da04:11a2	+	-	nc	+	n	dis	5
da04:11a3	-	-	impv	-	v	dis	6
da04:11a4	+	-	impv	-	v	dis	6
da04:11a5	-	-	impv	-	v	dis	6
da04:11a6	+	-	impv	-	v	dis	6
da04:11b1	-	-	yqtl	-	v	dis	6
da04:12a1	-	-	x+impv	-	v	dis	6

Verse	Waw	Edayin	Clause	Ptc	Type	Nar/Dis	Level
da04:12b1	+	-	x+yqtl	-	v	dis	6
da04:12b2	+	-	nc	-	n	dis	6
da04:13a1	-	-	x+yqtl	-	i	dis	6
da04:13a2	+	-	x+yqtl	-	i	dis	6
da04:13b1	+	-	x+yqtl	-	i	dis	6
da04:14a1	-	-	nc	-	n	dis	6
da04:14a2	+	-	nc	-	n	dis	6
da04:15a1	-	-	nc	-	n	dis	4
da04:15b1	+	-	x+impv	-	i	dis	4
da04:16a1	-	+	x+qtl	-	i	dis	3
da04:16a2	+	-	x+yqtl	-	i	dis	3
da04:16b1	-	-	nc	+	n	dis	3
da04:16b2	+	-	nc	+	n	dis	3
da04:16b3	-	-	x+yqtl	-	i	dis	4
da04:16b4	-	-	nc	+	n	dis	3
da04:16b5	+	-	nc	+	n	dis	3
da04:16b6	-	-	nc	-	n	dis	4
da04:16b7	+	-	nc	-	n	dis	4
da04:17a1	-	-	nc	-	n	dis	4
da04:20a1	+	-	nc	-	n	dis	4
da04:21b1	+	-	nc	-	n	dis	4
da04:22a1	+	-	nc	+	n	dis	4
da04:22a2	+	-	x+yqtl	-	v	dis	4
da04:22a3	+	-	x+yqtl	-	v	dis	4
da04:22a4	+	-	nc	+	n	dis	4
da04:22a5	+	-	x+yqtl	-	i	dis	4
da04:23a1	+	-	nc	-	n	dis	4
da04:24a1	-	-	x+yqtl	-	i	dis	4
da04:24a2	+	-	x+impv	-	v	dis	4
da04:25a1	-	-	x+qtl	-	v	dis	3
da04:26a1	-	-	x+ptc+qtl	-	v	dis	3
da04:27a1	-	-	nc	+	n	dis	3
da04:27a2	+	-	nc	+	n	dis	3
da04:27a3	-	-	nc	-	n	dis	4
da04:28a1	-	-	x+qtl	-	i	dis	3
da04:28b1	-	-	nc	+	n	dis	4

Verse	Waw	Edayin	Clause	Ptc	Type	Nar/Dis	Level
da04:28b2	-	-	x+qtl	-	i	dis	5
da04:29a1	+	-	nc	+	n	dis	4
da04:29a2	+	-	nc	-	n	dis	4
da04:29a3	-	-	x+yqtl	-	v	dis	4
da04:29a4	+	-	x+yqtl	-	i	dis	4
da04:30a1	-	-	x+qtl	-	i	dis	3
da04:30a2	+	-	x+qtl	-	v	dis	3
da04:30a3	+	-	x+yqtl	-	v	dis	3
da04:30a4	+	-	x+yqtl	-	i	dis	3
da04:31a1	+	-	x+qtl	-	i	dis	3
da04:31a2	+	-	x+yqtl	-	i	dis	3
da04:31a3	+	-	x+qtl	-	v	dis	3
da04:31a4	+	-	x+qtl+qtl	-	v	dis	3
da04:33a1	-	-	x+yqtl	-	i	dis	3
da04:33a2	+	-	x+yqtl	-	i	dis	3
da04:33a3	+	-	x+yqtl	-	i	dis	3
da04:33b1	+	-	x+qtl	-	i	dis	3
da04:33b2	+	-	x+qtl	-	i	dis	3
da04:34a1	-	-	nc	+++	n	dis	2
da05:01a1	-	-	x+qtl	-	i	nar	1
da05:01b1	+	-	nc	+	n	nar	1
da05:02a1	-	-	x+qtl	-	i	nar	1
da05:02b1	+	-	yqtl	-	v	nar	1
da05:03a1	-	+	qtl	-	v	nar	1
da05:03b1	+	-	qtl	-	v	nar	1
da05:04a1	-	-	qtl	-	v	nar	1
da05:04b1	+	-	qtl	-	v	nar	1
da05:05a1	-	-	x+qtl	-	v	nar	1
da05:05a2	+	-	nc	+	n	nar	1
da05:05b1	+	-	nc	+	n	nar	1
da05:06a1	-	+	x+qtl	-	i	nar	1
da05:06a2	+	-	x+yqtl	-	i	nar	1
da05:06b1	+	-	nc	+	n	nar	1
da05:06b2	+	-	nc	+	n	nar	1
da05:07a1	-	-	nc	+	n	nar	1
da05:07b1	-	-	nc	+	n	nar	1

Verse	Waw	Edayin	Clause	Ptc	Type	Nar/Dis	Level
da05:07b2	+	-	nc	+	n	nar	1
da05:07b3	-	-	x+yqtl	-	i	dis	2
da05:07b4	+	-	nc	-	n	dis	2
da05:07b5	+	-	x+yqtl	-	v	dis	2
da05:08a1	-	+	nc	+	n	nar	1
da05:08b1	+	-	nc	+	n	nar	1
da05:09a1	-	+	nc	+	n	nar	1
da05:09a2	+	-	nc	+	n	nar	1
da05:09b1	+	-	nc	+	n	nar	1
da05:10a1	-	-	x+qtl	-	i	nar	1
da05:10b1	-	-	qtl	-	v	nar	1
da05:10b2	+	-	qtl	-	v	nar	1
da05:10b3	-	-	x+impv	-	v	dis	2
da05:10b4	-	-	x+yqtl	-	v	dis	2
da05:10b5	+	-	x+yqtl	-	i	dis	2
da05:11a1	-	-	nc	-	n	dis	2
da05:11a2	+	-	x+qtl	-	i	dis	3
da05:11b1	+	-	x+qtl	-	i	dis	3
da05:12a1	-	-	x+yqtl	-	i	dis	2
da05:12b1	+	-	x+yqtl	-	v	dis	2
da05:13a1	-	+	x+qtl	-	i	nar	1
da05:13b1	-	-	nc	+	n	nar	1
da05:13b2	+	-	nc	+	n	nar	1
da05:13b3	-	-	nc	-	n	dis	2
da05:14a1	+	-	qtl	-	v	dis	3
da05:15a1	+	-	x+qtl	-	v	dis	3
da05:15b1	+	-	nc	+	n	dis	3
da05:16a1	+	-	x+qtl	-	i	dis	3
da05:16b1	-	-	x+yqtl	-	v	dis	2
da05:16b2	+	-	nc	-	n	dis	2
da05:16b3	+	-	x+yqtl	-	v	dis	2
da05:17a1	-	+	nc	+	n	nar	1
da05:17a2	+	-	nc	+	n	nar	1
da05:17a3	-	-	x+yqtl	-	i	dis	2
da05:17a4	+	-	x+impv	-	v	dis	2
da05:17b1	-	-	x+yqtl	-	v	dis	2

Verse	Waw	Edayin	Clause	Ptc	Type	Nar/Dis	Level
da05:17b2	+	-	x+yqtl	-	v	dis	2
da05:18a1	-	-	x+qtl	-	i	dis	3
da05:19a1	+	-	x+qtl+2ptc	-	i	dis	3
da05:19b1	-	-	x+qtl+ptc	-	i	dis	3
da05:19b2	+	-	x+qtl+ptc	-	i	dis	3
da05:19b3	+	-	x+qtl+ptc	-	i	dis	3
da05:19b4	+	-	x+qtl+ptc	-	i	dis	3
da05:20a1	+	-	x+qtl	-	v	dis	3
da05:20b1	+	-	x+qtl	-	v	dis	3
da05:21a1	+	-	x+qtl	-	v	dis	3
da05:21a2	+	-	x+qtl	-	i	dis	3
da05:21a3	+	-	nc	-	n	dis	3
da05:21a4	-	-	x+yqtl	-	v	dis	3
da05:21a5	+	-	x+yqtl	-	v	dis	3
da05:22a1	+	-	x+qtl	-	i	dis	3
da05:23a3	+	-	x+qtl	-	v	dis	3
da05:23a2	+	-	x+qtl	-	v	dis	3
da05:23a3	+	-	nc	+	n	dis	3
da05:23a4	+	-	x+qtl	-	v	dis	3
da05:23b1	+	-	x+qtl	-	v	dis	3
da05:24a1	-	+	x+qtl	-	v	dis	3
da05:24b1	+	-	x+qtl	-	i	dis	3
da05:25a1	+	-	nc	-	n	dis	3
da05:26a1	-	-	nc	-	n	dis	3
da05:26b1	-	-	qtl	-	v	dis	3
da05:26b2	+	-	qtl	-	v	dis	3
da05:27b1	-	-	qtl	-	v	dis	3
da05:27b2	+	-	qtl	-	v	dis	3
da05:28b1	-	-	qtl	-	v	dis	3
da05:28b2	+	-	qtl	-	v	dis	3
da05:29a1	-	+	x+qtl	-	v	nar	1
da05:29a2	+	-	qtl	-	v	nar	1
da05:29a3	+	-	nc	-	n	nar	1
da05:29b1	+	-	qtl	-	v	nar	1
da05:30a1	-	-	x+qtl	-	v	nar	1
da06:01a1	+	-	x+qtl	-	i	nar	1

Verse	Waw	Edayin	Clause	Ptc	Type	Nar/Dis	Level
da06:02a1	-	-	qtl	-	v	nar	1
da06:02a2	+	-	qtl	-	v	nar	1
da06:03a1	+	-	nc	-	n	nar	1
da06:04a1	-	+	x+qtl+ptc	-	i	nar	1
da06:04b1	+	-	nc	+	n	nar	1
da06:05a1	-	+	x+qtl+ptc	-	i	nar	1
da06:05b1	+	-	nc	+	n	nar	1
da06:06a1	-	+	nc	+	n	nar	1
da06:06a2	-	-	x+yqtl	-	v	dis	2
da06:07a1	-	+	x+qtl	-	i	nar	1
da06:07b1	+	-	nc	+	n	nar	1
da06:07b2	-	-	x+impv	-	v	dis	2
da06:08a1	-	-	qtl	-	v	dis	3
da06:09a1	-	-	x+yqtl	-	v	dis	2
da06:09a2	+	-	yqtl	-	v	dis	2
da06:10a1	-	-	x+qtl	-	i	nar	1
da06:11a1	+	-	x+qtl	-	i	nar	1
da06:11a2	+	-	nc	+	n	nar	1
da06:11b1	+	-	nc	+++	n	nar	1
da06:12a1	-	+	x+qtl	-	i	nar	1
da06:12a2	+	-	qtl	-	v	nar	1
da06:13a1	-	+	qtl	-	v	nar	1
da06:13a2	+	-	nc	+	n	nar	1
da06:13a3	-	-	x+qtl	-	v	dis	3
da06:13b1	-	-	nc	+	n	nar	1
da06:13b2	+	-	nc	+	n	nar	1
da06:13b3	-	-	nc	-	n	dis	2
da06:14a1	-	+	x+qtl	-	v	nar	1
da06:14a2	+	-	nc	+	n	nar	1
da06:14a3	-	-	x+qtl	-	i	dis	3
da06:14b1	+	-	nc	+	n	dis	3
da06:15a1	-	+	x+qtl	-	i	nar	1
da06:15a2	+	-	x+qtl	-	v	nar	1
da06:15b1	+	-	x+qtl+ptc	-	v	nar	1
da06:16a1	-	+	x+qtl	-	i	nar	1
da06:16b1	+	-	nc	+	n	nar	1

Verse	Waw	Edayin	Clause	Ptc	Type	Nar/Dis	Level
da06:16b2	-	-	impv	-	v	dis	2
da06:17a1	-	+	x+qtl	-	i	nar	1
da06:17a2	+	-	qtl	-	v	nar	1
da06:17a3	+	-	qtl	-	v	nar	1
da06:17b1	-	-	nc	+	n	nar	1
da06:17b2	+	-	nc	+	n	nar	1
da06:17b3	-	-	x+yqtl	-	i	dis	2
da06:18a1	+	-	qtl	-	v	nar	1
da06:18a2	+	-	qtl	-	v	nar	1
da06:18b1	+	-	qtl	-	v	nar	1
da06:19a1	-	+	qtl	-	v	nar	1
da06:19a2	+	-	qtl	-	v	nar	1
da06:19a3	+	-	x+qtl	-	v	nar	1
da06:19b1	+	-	x+qtl	-	i	nar	1
da06:20a1	-	+	x+yqtl	-	i	nar	1
da06:20b1	+	-	x+qtl	-	v	nar	1
da06:21a1	+	-	x+qtl	-	v	nar	1
da06:21b1	-	-	nc	+	n	nar	1
da06:21b2	+	-	nc	+	n	nar	1
da06:21b3	-	-	x+qtl	-	i	dis	3
da06:22a1	-	+	x+qtl	-	i	nar	1
da06:22b1	-	-	x+impv	-	v	dis	2
da06:23a1	-	-	x+qtl	-	i	dis	3
da06:23a2	+	-	qtl	-	v	dis	3
da06:23a3	+	-	x+qtl	-	v	dis	3
da06:24a1	-	+	x+qtl	-	i	nar	1
da06:24a2	+	-	x+qtl	-	v	nar	1
da06:24b1	+	-	qtl	-	v	nar	1
da06:24b2	+	-	x+qtl	-	i	nar	1
da06:25a1	+	-	qtl	-	v	nar	1
da06:25a2	+	-	qtl	-	v	nar	1
da06:25a3	+	-	x+qtl	-	v	nar	1
da06:25b1	+	-	x+qtl	-	v	nar	1
da06:26a1	-	+	x+qtl	-	i	nar	1
da06:26a2	-	-	x+yqtl	-	i	dis	2
da06:27a1	-	-	x+qtl	-	v	dis	3

Verse	Waw	Edayin	Clause	Ptc	Type	Nar/Dis	Level
da06:29a1	+	-	x+qtl	-	i	nar	1
da07:01a1	-	-	x+qtl	-	i	nar	1
da07:01b1	-	+	x+qtl	-	v	nar	1
da07:01b2	-	-	x+qtl	-	v	nar	1
da07:02a1	-	-	nc	+	n	nar	1
da07:02a2	+	-	nc	+	n	nar	1
da07:02a3	-	-	ptc+qtl	-	v	dis	3
da07:02b1	+	-	nc	+	n	dis	3
da07:03a1	+	-	nc	++	n	dis	3
da07:04a1	-	-	nc	-	n	dis	3
da07:04a2	+	-	nc	-	n	dis	3
da07:04b1	-	-	ptc+qtl	-	v	dis	3
da07:04b2	+	-	qtl	-	v	dis	3
da07:04b3	+	-	x+qtl	-	v	dis	3
da07:04b4	+	-	x+qtl	-	i	dis	3
da07:05a1	+	-	nc	+	n	dis	3
da07:05a2	+	-	x+qtl	-	v	dis	3
da07:05a3	+	-	nc	-	n	dis	3
da07:05b1	+	-	nc	+	n	dis	3
da07:05b2	-	-	impv	-	v	dis	4
da07:05b3	-	-	impv	-	v	dis	4
da07:06a1	-	-	x+ptc+qtl	-	v	dis	3
da07:06a2	+	-	nc	-	n	dis	3
da07:06a3	+	-	nc	-	n	dis	3
da07:06b1	+	-	nc	-	n	dis	3
da07:06b2	+	-	x+qtl	-	i	dis	3
da07:07a1	-	-	x+ptc+qtl	-	v	dis	3
da07:07a2	+	-	nc	+	n	dis	3
da07:07a3	+	-	nc	-	n	dis	3
da07:07a4	-	-	nc	++	n	dis	3
da07:07a5	+	-	nc	+	n	dis	3
da07:07b1	+	-	nc	+	n	dis	3
da07:07b2	+	-	nc	-	n	dis	3
da07:08a1	-	-	ptc+qtl	-	v	dis	3
da07:08a2	+	-	x+qtl	-	i	dis	3
da07:08a3	+	-	x+qtl	-	i	dis	3

Verse	Waw	Edayin	Clause	Ptc	Type	Nar/Dis	Level
da07:08b1	+	-	nc	-	n	dis	3
da07:09a1	-	-	ptc+qtl	-	v	dis	3
da07:09a2	+	-	x+qtl	-	i	dis	3
da07:09b1	-	-	nc	-	n	dis	3
da07:09b2	+	-	nc	-	n	dis	3
da07:09b3	-	-	nc	-	n	dis	3
da07:09b4	-	-	nc	-	n	dis	3
da07:10a1	-	-	nc	++	n	dis	3
da07:10a2	-	-	x+yqtl	-	i	dis	3
da07:10a3	+	-	x+yqtl	-	i	dis	3
da07:10b1	-	-	x+qtl	-	i	dis	3
da07:10b2	+	-	x+qtl	-	i	dis	3
da07:11a1	-	+	ptc+qtl	-	v	dis	3
da07:11b1	-	-	ptc+qtl	-	v	dis	3
da07:11b2	+	-	qtl	-	v	dis	3
da07:11b3	+	-	qtl	-	v	dis	3
da07:12a1	+	-	x+qtl	-	v	dis	3
da07:12b1	+	-	x+qtl	-	i	dis	3
da07:13a1	-	-	ptc+qtl	-	v	dis	3
da07:13a2	+	-	x+ptc+qtl	-	v	dis	3
da07:13b1	+	-	x+qtl	-	v	dis	3
da07:13b2	+	-	x+qtl	-	v	dis	3
da07:14a1	+	-	x+qtl	-	v	dis	3
da07:14a2	+	-	x+yqtl	-	i	dis	3
da07:14b1	-	-	nc	-	n	dis	3
da07:15a1	-	-	qtl	-	v	dis	3
da07:15b1	+	-	x+yqtl	-	i	dis	3
da07:16a1	-	-	qtl	-	v	dis	3
da07:16a2	+	-	x+yqtl	-	v	dis	3
da07:16b1	+	-	qtl	-	v	dis	3
da07:16b2	+	-	x+yqtl	-	v	dis	3
da07:17a1	-	-	x+yqtl	-	i	dis	4
da07:18a1	+	-	yqtl	-	v	dis	4
da07:18b1	+	-	yqtl	-	v	dis	4
da07:19a1	-	+	x+qtl	-	v	dis	3
da07:21a1	-	-	ptc+qtl	-	v	dis	3

Verse	Waw	Edayin	Clause	Ptc	Type	Nar/Dis	Level
da07:21a2	+	-	nc	+	n	dis	3
da07:21b1	+	-	nc	+	n	dis	3
da07:22a1	+	-	x+qtl	-	i	dis	3
da07:22b1	+	-	x+qtl	-	i	dis	3
da07:22b2	+	-	x+qtl	-	v	dis	3
da07:23a1	-	-	x+qtl	-	v	dis	3
da07:23a2	-	-	x+yqtl	-	i	dis	4
da07:23b1	+	-	yqtl	-	v	dis	4
da07:23b2	+	-	yqtl	-	v	dis	4
da07:23b3	+	-	yqtl	-	v	dis	4
da07:24a1	+	-	x+yqtl	-	i	dis	4
da07:24b1	+	-	x+yqtl	-	i	dis	4
da07:24b2	+	-	x+yqtl	-	i	dis	4
da07:24b3	+	-	x+yqtl	-	v	dis	4
da07:25a1	+	-	x+yqtl	-	v	dis	4
da07:25a2	+	-	x+yqtl	-	v	dis	4
da07:25b1	+	-	yqtl	-	v	dis	4
da07:25b2	+	-	yqtl	-	v	dis	4
da07:26a1	+	-	x+yqtl	-	i	dis	4
da07:26b1	+	-	x+yqtl	-	v	dis	4
da07:27a1	+	-	x+qtl	-	i	dis	5
da07:27b1	-	-	nc	-	n	dis	4
da07:27b2	+	-	x+yqtl+yqtl	-	i	dis	4
da07:28a1	-	-	nc	-	n	dis	3
da07:28b1	-	-	x+yqtl	-	i	dis	3
da07:28b2	+	-	x+yqtl	-	i	dis	3
da07:28b3	+	-	x+qtl	-	v	dis	3
er04:08a1	-	-	x+qtl	-	i	nar	1
er04:11a1	+	-	nc	-	n	nar	1
er04:12a1	+	-	x+ptc+yqtl	-	v	dis	2
er04:13a1	-	-	x+ptc+yqtl	-	v	dis	2
er04:14a1	-	-	x+qtl	-	v	dis	3
er04:14b1	+	-	qtl	-	v	dis	3
er04:15a1	+	-	yqtl	-	v	dis	2
er04:15a2	+	-	yqtl	-	v	dis	2

Verse	Waw	Edayin	Clause	Ptc	Type	Nar/Dis	Level
er04:15b1	-	-	x+qtl	-	i	dis	3
er04:16a1	-	-	nc	+	n	dis	2
er04:17a1	-	-	x+qtl	-	v	nar	1
er04:18a1	+	-	x+qtl	-	i	dis	3
er04:19a1	+	-	x+qtl	-	v	dis	3
er04:19a2	+	-	qtl	-	v	dis	3
er04:19a3	+	-	qtl	-	v	dis	3
er04:21a1	-	-	x+impv	-	v	dis	2
er04:21b1	+	-	x+yqtl	-	i	dis	2
er04:22a1	+	-	ptc+impv	-	v	dis	2
er04:22b1	-	-	x+yqtl	-	v	dis	2
er04:23a1	-	+	x+qtl	-	v	nar	1
er04:23b1	+	-	qtl	-	v	nar	1
er04:24a1	-	+	x+qtl	-	v	nar	1
er04:24b1	+	-	qtl+ptc	-	v	nar	1
er05:01a1	+	-	qtl	-	v	nar	1
er05:02a1	-	+	qtl	-	v	nar	1
er05:02a2	+	-	qtl	-	v	nar	1
er05:02b1	+	-	nc	+	n	nar	1
er05:03a1	-	-	x+qtl	-	v	nar	1
er05:03b1	+	-	nc	+	n	nar	1
er05:03b2	-	-	x+qtl	-	i	dis	3
er05:04a1	-	+	x+qtl	-	v	nar	1
er05:04b1	-	-	nc	-	n	dis	2
er05:05a1	+	-	x+qtl	-	i	nar	1
er05:05a2	+	-	x+qtl	-	v	nar	1
er05:06a1	-	-	nc	-	n	nar	1
er05:07a1	-	-	x+qtl	-	v	nar	1
er05:07b1	+	-	x+qtl	-	v	nar	1
er05:08a1	-	-	ptc+yqtl	-	v	dis	2
er05:17a1	+	-	x+yqtl	-	v	dis	2
er05:17b1	+	-	x+yqtl	-	i	dis	2
er06:01a1	-	+	x+qtl	-	i	nar	1
er06:01b1	+	-	qtl	-	v	nar	1
er06:02a1	+	-	qtl	-	v	nar	1
er06:02b1	+	-	x+qtl	-	v	nar	1

Verse	Waw	Edayin	Clause	Ptc	Type	Nar/Dis	Level
er06:03a1	-	-	x+qtl	-	i	dis	3
er06:03a2	-	-	x+yqtl	-	i	dis	4
er06:03a3	+	-	nc	+	n	dis	4
er06:04b1	+	-	x+yqtl	-	i	dis	4
er06:05a1	+	-	x+yqtl	-	i	dis	4
er06:05b1	+	-	yqtl	-	v	dis	4
er06:05b2	+	-	yqtl	-	v	dis	4
er06:06a1	-	-	x+impv	-	v	dis	2
er06:07a1	-	-	impv	-	v	dis	2
er06:07b1	-	-	x+yqtl	-	i	dis	2
er06:08a1	+	-	x+qtl	-	v	dis	3
er06:08b1	+	-	x+yqtl+ptc	-	i	dis	2
er06:09a1	+	-	x+yqtl+ptc	-	i	dis	2
er06:11a1	+	-	x+qtl	-	v	dis	3
er06:12a1	+	-	x+yqtl	-	i	dis	2
er06:12b1	-	-	x+qtl	-	i	dis	3
er06:12b2	-	-	x+yqtl	-	v	dis	2
er06:13a1	-	+	x+qtl	-	i	nar	1
er06:14a1	+	-	nc	++	n	nar	1
er06:14b1	+	-	qtl	-	v	nar	1
er06:14b2	+	-	qtl	-	v	nar	1
er06:15a1	+	-	qtl	-	v	nar	1
er06:16a1	+	-	qtl	-	v	nar	1
er06:17a1	+	-	qtl	-	v	nar	1
er06:18a1	+	-	qtl	-	v	nar	1
er07:13a1	+	-	x+qtl	-	v	dis	3
er07:17a1	-	-	x+yqtl	-	v	dis	2
er07:17b1	+	-	yqtl	-	v	dis	2
er07:18a1	+	-	x+yqtl	-	v	dis	2
er07:19a1	+	-	x+impv	-	v	dis	2
er07:20a1	+	-	x+yqtl	-	v	dis	2
er07:21a1	+	-	x+qtl	-	v	dis	3
er07:23a1	-	-	x+yqtl	-	i	dis	2
er07:24a1	+	-	nc	+	n	dis	2
er07:25a1	+	-	x+impv	-	i	dis	2

Verse	Waw	Edayin	Clause	Ptc	Type	Nar/Dis	Level
er07:25b1	+	-	x+yqtl	-	i	dis	2
er07:26a1	+	-	x+yqtl+ptc	-	i	dis	2

Bibliography

Books

Andersen, Francis I. *The Sentence in Biblical Hebrew*. The Hague: Mouton, 1974.

Auerbach, Erich. *Mimesis: The Representation of Reality in Western Literature*, fiftieth anniversary ed. Translated by Willard R. Trask. Princeton: Princeton University Press, 2003.

Austin, J. L. *How to Do Things with Words,* 2d ed. Cambridge: Harvard University Press, 1975.

Barr, James. *The Semantics of Biblical Language*. Oxford: Oxford University Press, 1961. Reprint, London: SCM, 1983.

———. *Comparative Philology and the Text of the Old Testament*. Oxford: Oxford University Press, 1968. Reprint, Winona Lake, Ind.: Eisenbrauns, 1987.

Bauer, Hans, and Pontus Leander. *Grammatik des Biblisch-Aramäischen*. Halle: Niemeyer, 1927. Fourth Unrevised Reprint, Hildesheim: Georg Olms, 1995.

Beaugrande, Robert-Alain de, and Wolfgang Ulrich Dressler. *Introduction to Text Linguistics*. Longman Linguistics Library 26. New York: Longman, 1981.

Beyer, Klaus. *Die aramäischen Texte vom Toten Meer*. Göttingen: Vandenhoeck & Ruprecht, 1984.

———. *The Aramaic Language: Its Distribution and Subdivisions*. Translated by John F. Healey. Göttingen: Vandenhoeck & Ruprecht, 1986.

Black, M. *An Aramaic Approach to the Gospels and Acts*, 3d ed. Oxford: Clarendon, 1967.

Blokland, A. F. den Exter. *In Search of Text Syntax: Towards a Syntactic Text-Segmentation Model for Biblical Hebrew*. Amsterdam: VU University Press, 1995.

Bowker, John. *The Targums and Rabbinic Literature: An Introduction to Jewish Interpretations of Scripture*. London: Cambridge University Press, 1969.

Brockelmann, Carl. *Laut-und Formenlehre*. Vol. 1, *Syntax*. Berlin: Reuther & Reichard, 1908. Fourth Reprint, Hildesheim: Georg Olms, 1999.

———. *Grundriß der vergleichenden Grammatik der semitischen Sprachen*. Vol. 2, *Syntax*. Berlin: Reuther & Reichard, 1913. Fourth Reprint, Hildesheim: Georg Olms, 1999.

Brown, Gillian, and George Yule. *Discourse Analysis*. Cambridge: Cambridge University Press, 1983.

Carr, David McLain. "Isaiah 40:1–11 in the Context of the Macrostructure of Second Isaiah." In *Discourse Analysis of Biblical Literature: What It Is and What It Offers*, ed. Walter R. Bodine, 51–65. Atlanta: Scholars Press, 1995.

Chomsky, Noam. *Syntactic Structures*, 2d ed. Berlin: Mouton de Gruyter, 2002.

Cotterell, Peter, and Max Turner. *Linguistics and Biblical Interpretation*. Downers Grove: Intervarsity, 1989.

Dawson, David Allan. *Text-Linguistics and Biblical Hebrew*. Journal for the Study of the Old Testament: Supplement Series 177. Sheffield: Sheffield Academic, 1994.

Delitzsch, F. *The Book of Ecclesiastes*. Translated by M. G. Easton. Keil & Delitzsch Commentary on the Old Testament 6. Edinburgh: T. & T. Clark, 1866–91. Reprint, Peabody, Mass.: Hendrickson, 2001.

Fitzmyer, Joseph A. *The Genesis Apocryphon of Qumran Cave I: A Commentary,* 2d ed. Biblica et orientalia 18A. Rome: Biblical Institute Press, 1971.

———. *A Wandering Aramean: Collected Aramaic Essays*. SBL Monograph Series 25. Missoula, Mont.: Scholars Press, 1979.

Flesher, Paul V. McCracken. "The Targumim in the Context of Rabbinic Literature." In Jacob Neusner, *Introduction to Rabbinic Literature*. New York: Doubleday, 1999.

Fredericks, D. C. *Qoheleth's Language: Re-Evaluating Its Nature and Date*. ANETS 3. Lewiston, NY: Mellen, 1988.

Golomb, David M. *A Grammar of Targum Neofiti*. Harvard Semitic Monographs 34. Chico, Cal.: Scholars Press, 1985.

Fox, Michael V. *Qohelet and His Contradictions*. Journal for the Study of the Old Testament: Supplement Series 71. Sheffield: Almond, 1989.

Gunkel, Hermann. *Einleitung in die Psalmen,* 2d ed. Göttingen: Vandenhoeck & Ruprecht, 1966.

Hoberman, Robert. *The Syntax and Semantics of Verb Morphology in Modern Aramaic: A Jewish Dialect of Iraqi Kurdistan*, American Oriental Society 69. New Haven: American Oriental Society, 1989.

Isaksson, B. *Studies in the Language of Qohelet with Special Emphasis on the Verbal System*. AAU, SSU 10. Uppsala and Stockholm: Almqvist & Wiksell, 1987.

Johns, Alger F. *A Short Grammar of Biblical Aramaic*, rev. ed. Berrien Springs, Mich.: Andrews University Press, 1972.

Kahle, Paul E. *The Cairo Geniza*, 2d ed. New York: Praeger, 1960.

Kautzsch, E. F. *Grammatik des Biblischen-Aramäischen*. Leipzig: Vogel, 1884.

———, ed. *Gesenius' Hebrew Grammar*. Translated by A. E. Cowley, 2d ed. Oxford: Clarendon, 1910.

Khan, Geoffrey. *A Grammar of Neo-Aramaic: The Dialect of the Jews of Arbel*. Leiden: Brill, 1999.

Kutscher, E. Y. "The Language of the 'Genesis Apocryphon'." In *Scripta hierosolymitana*. Vol. 4, *Aspects of the Dead Sea Scrolls*, ed. Chaim Rabin and Yigael Yadin, 2d ed., 1–35. Jerusalem: Magnes, 1965.

———. "Aramaic" (1971). In *Hebrew and Aramaic Studies*, ed. Zeev Ben-Hayyim, Aharon Dotan, and Gad Sarfatti, 347–404. Jerusalem: Magnes, 1977.

———. *A History of the Hebrew Language*. Edited by Raphael Kutscher. Jerusalem: Magnes; Leiden: Brill, 1982.

Krüger, Thomas, *Qoheleth.* Translated by O.C. Dean, Jr. Minneapolis: Fortress, 2004.

Longacre, Robert E. *The Grammar of Discourse*. New York: Plenum, 1983.

Lowery, Kirk E. "The Theoretical Foundations of Hebrew Discourse Grammar." In *Discourse Analysis of Biblical Literature: What It Is and What It Offers*, ed. Walter R. Bodine, 103–30. Atlanta: Scholars Press, 1995.

McNamara, Martin. *Targum and Testament*. Shannon, Ireland: Irish University Press, 1972.

———. *The New Testament and the Palestinian Targum to the Pentateuch.*

Michel, Diethelm. *Tempora and Satzstellung in den Psalmen*. Bonn: H. Bouvier u. Co., 1960.

Montgomery, James. *A Critical and Exegetical Commentary on the Book of Daniel.* The International Critical Commentary. Edinburgh: T. & T. Clark, 1927.

Muraoka, Takamitsu, and Bezalel Porten. *A Grammar of Egyptian Aramaic*. Leiden: Brill, 1998.

Niccacci, Alviero. "On the Hebrew Verbal System." In *Biblical Hebrew and Discourse Linguistics*, ed. Robert Bergen, 117–31. Dallas: SIL, 1994.

Rabin, C. "Hebrew and Aramaic in the First Century." In *The Jewish People in the First Century*, vol. 2, ed. S. Safrai and M. Stern, 1007–37. Compendia Rerum Iudaicarum ad Novum Testamentum 1. Philadelphia: Fortress, 1976.

Rendtorff, Rolf. *The Old Testament: An Introduction.* Translated by John Bowden. Philadelphia: Fortress, 1986.

Richter, Wolfgang. *Grundlagen einer althebräischen Grammatik.* St. Ottilien: EOS, 1978.

Rosenthal, Franz. *A Grammar of Biblical Aramaic*. Wiesbaden: Harrassowitz, 1961.

———. *Die Aramaistische Forschung*. Leiden: Brill, 1964.

Rowley, H. H. *The Aramaic of the Old Testament.* London: Oxford University Press, 1929.

Sailhamer, John H. *The Pentateuch as Narrative*. Grand Rapids: Zondervan, 1992.

———. *The NIV Compact Bible Commentary.* Grand Rapids: Zondervan, 1994.

———. *Introduction to Old Testament Theology*. Grand Rapids: Zondervan, 1995.

———. "Biblical Theology and the Composition of the Hebrew Bible." In *Biblical Theology: Retrospect and Prospect*, ed. Scott J. Hafemann, 25–37. Downers Grove: InterVarsity, 2002.

Saussure, Ferdinand de. *Cours de linguistique générale*. Edited by Charles Bally and Albert Sechehaye. Paris: Payothèque, 1916.

———. *Course in General Linguistics*. Edited by Charles Bally and Albert Sechehaye. Translated and annotated by Roy Harris. London: G. Duckworth, 1983. Reprint, Chicago and La Salle: Open Court, 1986.

Schmidt, Siegfried J. *Texttheorie*. Munich: Fink, 1973.

Schneider, Wolfgang. *Grammatik des Biblischen Hebräischen*, 8th ed. Munich: Claudius, 1993.

Schoors, A. *The Preacher Sought to Find Pleasing Words: A Study of the Language of Qoheleth*. Orientalia lovaniensis analecta 41. Leuven: Departement Orientalistiek and Peeters, 1992.

Segert, Stanislav. *Altaramäische Grammatik*, 3d ed. Leipzig: Enzyklopädie, 1986.

Stefanovic, Zdravko. *The Aramaic of Daniel in the Light of Old Aramaic*. Journal for the Study of the Old Testament: Supplement Series 129. Sheffield: JSOT, 1992.

Strack, H.L. *Grammatik des Biblisch-Aramäischen.* Leipeig: Hinrich, 1905.

Talstra, E., ed. *Computer Assisted Analysis of Biblical Texts*. Amsterdam: Free University Press, 1989.

———. "Hebrew Syntax; Clause Types and Clause Hierarchy." In *Studies in Hebrew and Aramaic Syntax*, ed. K. Jongeling, H. L. Murre-Van den Berg, and L. van Rompay, 180–93. Leiden: Brill, 1991.

Tov, Emanuel. *Textual Criticism of the Hebrew Bible,* 2d rev. ed. Minneapolis: Fortress, 2001.

Ullendorff, Edward. *Is Biblical Hebrew a Language? Studies in Semitic Languages and Civilizations*. Wiesbaden: Harrassowitz, 1977.

Ulrich, Eugene. *The Dead Sea Scrolls and the Origins of the Bible.* Grand Rapids, Eerdmans, 1999.

Vanhoozer, Kevin J. *Is There a Meaning in This Text?* Grand Rapids: Zondervan, 1998.

Weinrich, Harald. *Tempus: Besprochene und erzählte Welt*, 6th new rev. ed. Munich: C. H. Beck, 2001.

Wright, N.T. *Christian Origins and the Question of God.* Vol. 1, *The New Testament and the People of God.* Minneapolis: Fortress, 1992.

Würthwein, Ernst. *The Text of the Old Testament,* 2d ed. Translated by Erroll F. Rhodes. Grand Rapids: Eerdmans, 1995.

Journals

Arnold, B. T. "The Use of Aramaic in the Hebrew Bible: Another Look at Bilingualism in Ezra and Daniel." *Journal of Northwest Semitic Languages* 22/2 (1996): 1–16.

Bar-Efrat, S. "Some Observations on the Analysis of Structure in Biblical Narrative." *Vetus Testamentum* 30 (1980): 154–73.

Barr, James. "Hebrew Orthography and the Book of Job." *Journal of Semitic Studies* 30 (1985): 1–33.

Barton, George A. "The Composition of the Book of Daniel." *Journal of Biblical Literature* 17 (1898): 62–86.

Bianchi, F. "The Language of Qohelet: A Bibliographical Survey." *Zeitschrift für die alttestamentliche Wissenschaft* 105 (1993): 210–23.

Clarke, Ernest G. "Jacob's Dream at Bethel as Interpreted in the Targums and the New Testament." *Studies in Religion* 4 (1974–75): 367–77.

Cook, John A. "The Semantics of Verbal Pragmatics: Clarifying the Roles of *Wayyiqtol* and *Weqatal* in Biblical Hebrew Prose." *Journal of Semitic Studies* 49 (2004): 247–73.

Dahood, M. "The Language of Qoheleth." *Catholic Biblical Quarterly* 14 (1952): 227–32.

Emerton, J. A. "New Evidence for the Use of *Waw* Consecutive in Aramaic." *Vetus Testamentum* 44 (1994): 255–58.

———. "Further Comments on the Use of Tenses in the Aramaic Inscription from Tel Dan." *Vetus Testamentum* 47 (1997): 429–40.

Gordis, R. "The Original Language of Qohelet." *Jewish Quarterly Review* 37 (1946–47): 67–84.

———. "Was Qoheleth a Phoenician?" *Journal of Biblical Literature* 74 (1955): 103–14.

———. "Qoheleth and Qumran—A Study of Style." *Biblica* 41 (1960): 395–410.

Kaufman, Stephen A. "On Methodology in the Study of the Targums and their Chronology." *Journal for the Study of the New Testament* 23 (1985): 117–24.

Levine, Etan. "The Biography of the Aramaic Bible." *Zeitschrift für die alttestamentliche Wissenschaft* 94 (1982): 353–79.

Miller, James E. "The Redaction of Daniel." *Journal for the Study of the Old Testament* 52 (1991): 115–24.

Muilenberg, James. "A Qoheleth Scroll from Qumran." *Bulletin of the American Schools of Oriental Research* 135 (1954): 20–28.

Muraoka, Takamitsu, and M. Rogland. "The *Waw* Consecutive in Old Aramaic? A Rejoinder to Victor Sasson." *Vetus Testamentum* 48 (1998): 99–104.

Pröbstle, Martin T. "The Advantages of W. Richter's Approach for a Lexical Description of Biblical Hebrew." *Journal of Northwest Semitic Languages* 21, no. 1 (1995): 95–110.

Rechenmacher, Hans, and Christo H. J. van der Merwe. "The Contribution of Wolfgang Richter to Current Developments in the Study of Biblical Hebrew." *Journal of Semitic Studies* 50 (2005): 226–42.

Richter, Wolfgang. "Verbvalenz und Verbalsatz: Ein Beitrag zur syntaktischen Grundlegung einer atl. Literaturwissenschaft." *Journal of Northwest Semitic Languages* 4 (1975): 61–69.

Rosén, H. B. "On the Use of the Tenses in the Aramaic of Daniel." *Journal of Semitic Studies* 6 (1961): 183–203.

Rowley, H. H. "The Bilingual Problem of Daniel." *Zeitschrift für die alttestamentliche Wissenschaft* 50 (1932): 256–68.

———. "The Unity of the Book of Daniel." *Hebrew Union College Annual* 23, no. 1 (1950–51): 233–73.

Sailhamer, John H. "A Database Approach to the Analysis of Hebrew Narrative." *Maarav* 5–6 (1990): 319–35.

Sasson, Victor. "Some Observations on the Use and Original Purpose of the *Waw* Consecutive in Old Aramaic and Biblical Hebrew." *Vetus Testamentum* 47 (1997): 111–27.

———. "The *waw* Consecutive/*waw* Contrastive and the Perfect." *Zeitschrift für die alttestamentliche Wissenschaft* 113 (2001): 602–17.

Shepherd, Michael B. "The Distribution of Verbal Forms in Biblical Aramaic." *Journal of Semitic Studies* 52 (2007): 227–44 .

———. "Daniel 7:13 and the New Testament Son of Man," *Westminster Theological Journal* 68 (2006) 99–111.

Snell, Daniel C. "Why Is There Aramaic in the Bible?" *Journal for the Study of the Old Testament* 18 (1980): 32–51.

Steinhauser, Michael G. "The Targums and the New Testament." *Toronto Journal of Theology* 2 (1986): 262–78.

Talstra, E. "Text Grammar and Biblical Hebrew: The Viewpoint of Wolfgang Schneider." *Journal of Translation and Textlinguistics* 5 (1992): 269–97.

———. "Tense, Mood, Aspect and Clause Connections in Biblical Hebrew: A Textual Approach." *Journal of Northwest Semitic Languages* 23, no. 2 (1997): 81–103.

Torrey, C. C. "The Question of the Original Language of Qoheleth." *Jewish Quarterly Review* 39 (1948–49): 151–60.

Van Deventer, H. J. M. "Testing-Testing, Do We Have a Translated Text in Daniel 1 and Daniel 7?" *Journal of Northwest Semitic Languages* 31, no. 2 (2005): 91–106.

Wesselius, J. W. "Language and Style in Biblical Aramaic: Observations on the Unity of Daniel 2–7." *Vetus Testamentum* 38 (1988): 194–209.

———. “The Literary Nature of the Book of Daniel and the Linguistic Character of Its Aramaic.” *Aramaic Studies* 3 (2005): 241–83.

York, A. D. “The Dating of Targumic Literature.” *Journal for the Study of Judaism in the Persian, Hellenistic, and Roman Periods* 5 (1974): 49–62.

Zewi, Tamar. “Time in Nominal Sentences in the Semitic Languages.” *Journal of Semitic Studies* 44 (1999): 195–214.

Zimmermann, Frank. “The Aramaic Origin of Daniel 8–12.” *Journal of Biblical Literature* 57 (1938): 255–72.

———. “The Aramaic Provenance of Qohelet.” *Jewish Quarterly Review* 36 (1945–46): 17–45.

———. “The Question of Hebrew in Qohelet.” *Jewish Quarterly Review* 40 (1949–50): 79–102.

Index

E

F

G

O

P

Q

Studies in Biblical Literature

This series invites manuscripts from scholars in any area of biblical literature. Both established and innovative methodologies, covering general and particular areas in biblical study, are welcome. The series seeks to make available studies that will make a significant contribution to the ongoing biblical discourse. Scholars who have interests in gender and sociocultural hermeneutics are particularly encouraged to consider this series.

For further information about the series and for the submission of manuscripts, contact:

Peter Lang Publishing
Acquisitions Department
P.O. Box 1246
Bel Air, Maryland 21014-1246

To order other books in this series, please contact our Customer Service Department:

(800) 770-LANG (within the U.S.)
(212) 647-7706 (outside the U.S.)
(212) 647-7707 FAX

or browse online by series at:

WWW.PETERLANG.COM